OPINIONS

ON

SPECULATIVE MASONRY,

RELATIVE TO ITS

ORIGIN, NATURE, AND TENDENCY.

A COMPILATION,

EMBRACING RECENT AND IMPORTANT DOCUMENTS ON THE SUBJECT,

AND EXHIBITING THE VIEWS OF THE MOST DISTINGUISHED WRITERS RESPECTING IT.

BY JAMES C. ODIORNE.

I spake openly to the world, and in secret have I said nothing.
JESUS CHRIST.

BOSTON:
PERKINS & MARVIN, 114, WASHINGTON ST.

1830.

PREFACE.

The several documents comprised in the following work have been published at various times, and in different sections of our country. They have principally appeared in the *pamphlet* form; and wherever circulated have been read with avidity, and have exerted a powerful influence. Those which have been presented to the public only through the medium of *newspapers* have not received that general circulation and perusal which their value and importance demand, owing to the fact, that those organs of communication are for the most part subjected to masonic influence, and that but few papers are enlisted in the Anti-masonic cause.

They are here republished, with the hope that they may receive from the public that attention which they merit; and that the influence which they are calculated to exert may be felt, and be widely extended.

Collectively, they form a volume which may be of some service to those who have given to the subject on which they treat but little attention, and who have not informed themselves in relation to the principles of the Masonic Institution, as they have been developed by recent investigations.

The nature and tendency of the institution are here clearly exhibited, and its principles and practices fully illustrated and exposed. From the fact that most of the writers of the pieces herein contained have been members of the institution, and consequently acquainted with its secret principles and designs; and also from the uniformity of their testimony, we may rely on their statements as correct, and consider their representation of its character as in accordance with truth.

The increasing demands of the public for information on the subject of Masonry, and the persuasion that a work which should present at one view the opinions of the most distinguished writers respecting it, would be useful, and well adapted for distribution, were the causes which led to the publication of the present volume. The compiler indulges the hope that it may subserve the cause of truth, by diffusing light on the subject of Masonry, and by exciting a more general inquiry into the nature of its claims.

Boston, Feb. 22, 1830.

RECOMMENDATION.

THE *State Anti-masonic Committee of Massachusetts* have examined the Prospectus, and a considerable portion of the Documents proposed to be published by Mr. JAMES C. ODIORNE, in a distinct volume. The work appears to be judiciously selected, well arranged, and ably conducted. A great mass of information, of the most important kind, is brought together in a manner deserving the attention and patronage of the public.

ABNER PHELPS,
Per Order.

CONTENTS.

APPENDIX.

FREEMASONRY.

EARLY HISTORY OF FREEMASONRY.

The early history of Freemasonry, like that of Rome, is involved in obscurity. The conquerors of the world were not satisfied with the plain truth of their national origin. They taught that the "Eternal City" was founded and first ruled by the son of Mars, whose name was Romulus; who was taken to the gods in a tempest of lightning, and became Quirinus, the patron saint of the city, and one of the chief gods of Rome. This was lofty and sonorous, and unexceptionable, had it been true.

Our modern power, which seeks, with Roman ambition, to lord it over the whole habitable earth, also styles itself *eternal*, as did Rome; deduces its origin from Heaven; claims the wisest man for its lawgiver; and some mighty thing in the nature of the philosopher's stone for its secret—all which is equally credible and as well attested as that Romulus was nursed by a wolf, or Jupiter was a god that could save. And the masonic fables are told, to cover the meanness of Freemasonry's origin; for she, too, sprung from a confederacy of lawless plunderers: and it mortifies the pride of the high priests, it tops the vanity of the grand masters, and makes the puissant sovereigns of Freemasonry to tremble for the security of their thrones, to be told that their boasted order, sprung from the mire of the Rosicrusians, and spread abroad over the face of the earth upon the licentious cupidity of its speculative fathers; that it originated within the 18th century, among men capable of the most atrocious falsehoods, and base enough to sell their reputation for money, and to barter a good conscience for the delusion of a lodge room; men who sold masonic charters for an appearance of mystery, but of a truth for gold.

Stone masons, in common with ninety-one other crafts and trades in the city of London, have been in the habit for centuries, of meeting in club, for the purpose of improvement in the elements of their business and craft. Each craft has its public hall, its admission fee, its coat of arms, and its charity fund. The companies are given by name in the order of their rank, in Rees' Encyclopedia, *Art. Company;* and out of only eighteen whose form of government is particularly mentioned, sixteen are governed by a *Master, two Wardens, and a various number of other assistants.* So Freemasons' lodges are governed; and the titles, *Worshipful and Most Worshipful,* now peculiar to masonic officers, were common to gentlemen of the 16th and 17th centuries, as Esquire and Honorable are common at the present day.

The Lord Mayor of London, at his election usually makes himself *free;* i. e. becomes a member of one of the twelve principal societies, if he were not a member of one of them before: "for these twelve," says the Cyclopedia, "are not only the oldest, but the richest; many of them having had the honor of kings and princes to be their members, and the apartments of their halls being fit to entertain a monarch." But Masons are not among the first twelve: their rank is 31, hall in Basing Hall-street, charter Charles II., 1677. Some of these societies meet by prescriptive right; the oldest charter is that of the Parish Clerks, A. D. 1233, Henry III.; the Bakers, A. D. 1307, Edward II. Six were chartered in the 14th century, eighteen in the 15th century, twelve in the 16th century, forty, (and among them the Stone Masons,) in the 17th century, and some in the 18th century.

Handicraft Masonry is an ancient *trade,* and has ever received the fostering attention of distinguished princes. Both in France and in Scotland, the craft were allowed a peculiar jurisdiction over all disputes growing out of the exercise of their trade. (Lawrie's History of Masonry, p. 110, and p. 297.) This was granted in France, A. D.

1645; and in Scotland, near two hundred years earlier, to real builders.

In the rude times, when men, ignorant of chirography, impressed the seal of their parchments with the tooth in their head for their signature, it was usual for master masons to give their apprentice *a grip or sign*, by which he should make himself known to any mason as a regularly entered apprentice to the trade; and another when he had completed his apprenticeship, and passed to the rank of a journeyman or fellow-craft; and a third, when by assiduity, experience, and skill, he had become himself a master of work, took buildings to rear, hired fellow-crafts or journeymen, and received apprentices. The *word*, the *sign*, and the *grip*, in those unlettered ages, were the certificate of the craft to its regularly taught members; and in Germany were common before *Freemasonry* was imported from England. (See Prof. Robison's Proofs, p. 54.)

Masonic historians claim the men to be Freemasons against whom the statute was passed in the 25th of Edward III., and again in the reign of Henry VI., forbidding them to assemble in lodges and chapters. (See *F. M. Library, p.* 25; *Hardie's Monitor, p.* 20; *Lawrie, p.* 94; *Encyclopedia Brittanica, Art. Masons, Sec.* 62.) Now Edward III. dealt with Englishmen of that day, as George III. would have dealt with Americans in his day; as if they had been slaves. A plague had swept away a fearful portion of the English population, and the scarcity of laborers, caused all classes of mechanics to demand an increase of wages. Edward had several castles and magnificent edifices in building, and to make his money hold out, must compel the masons and mechanics to work at the old rates. He issued such an ordinance, and enforced it by his sheriffs. Under that ordinance, masons were returned from the several counties of England to work on Windsor Castle, as jurors were returned to serve in the king's courts. (See Hume's History of England, reign of Ed. III.) This was equally agreeable to the Lords of Parliament and to himself, and accordingly it was enacted A. D. 1350, that "as servants, not willing after the pestilence, to serve without taking excessive wages, had been required to serve in their accustomed places at the rate they had received in the 20th year of Edward III.; and as it is given the king to understand in this present Parliament, that the said servants have paid no regard to the said ordinance, but to their ease do withdraw from the service of great men and others, unless they have livery and wages to the double or treble of that they were wont to take in the said 20th year and before, to the great damage of the great men, &c. be ordained and established the things underwritten."

Chap. 1. Fixes the day and year wages of *farm servants.*

Chap. 2. The price of threshing all sorts of corn by the quarter.

Chap. 3. Prescribes the wages of several sorts of artificers and laborers; among whom *Carpenters* and *Masons* are particularly specified.

Chap. 4. Requires artificers to make oath that they will use their *crafts*, as they did in the 20th year of the same Edward III. (See Ruffhead's English Statutes, Vol. 1, p. 251.)

Seventy-four years after the enactment of this statute, which plainly is applicable only to handicrafts, Henry VI., in Parliament at Westminster, ordained that "no confederacies and congregations shall be made by masons in their general chapters and assemblies, whereby the good course and effects of the *statute of laborers*, (25th Ed. III.,) are violated and broken, in subversion of law; and if any be, they that cause such chapters and congregations to be assembled and holden, shall be adjudged felons." Coke's 3d Ins. p. 99.

The common pretence of Freemasons, that these statutes were levelled particularly against their mystic order, by the influence of bigoted priests, because the *secret* was not betrayed in the office of auricular confession, is too shallow, after once reading these statutes, to cover the nakedness of the falsehood, or to conceal the evident duplicity of its first publishers. But one thing these statutes conclusively show with the aid of masonic historians, viz. that in the reign of Edward III. and Henry VI., there were no Freemasons in England, but stone masons; who met in general chapters and assemblies, not to cultivate the knowledge of a wonderful mystery, but to impede the execution of the laws, and to violate the statutes of their country.

With this view faithful history fully concurs. That a society claiming the glories of Freemasonry should have existed for ages unnoticed by any writer, noble or contemptible, foolish or learned, is wholly incredible, and unworthy of belief. The Puritans and the Presbyterians, the Cabalists and the Rosicrusians, the Gypsies and the Necromancers, the Alchymists and the Jesuists, are each liberally noticed in the works of various authors during the 16th and 17th centuries; but *Freemasonry* has not so much as a name, until the 18th century. To any historical scholar, this alone is enough. We read of the *Fraternitas lathomorum*, or company of bricklayers; but it requires not a lawyer to discern, that these are the men against whom the statute of laborers was directed, in the 25th year of Edward III., and are not the men who have at this day in their lodges the language of Eden, and the mysteries of the Antediluvian world. * * *

Of the same tenor is the fact, that Papacy and Freemasonry cannot dwell together in peace; but we hear not a word of their disagreement, until the 18th century. Certainly Papacy is older than 100 years; and if Freemasonry be much above that, how did it previously escape a conflict which has never ceased since first it commenced, A. D. 1730 to '40? The canons of the church require full and free confession to the priests from all good Catholics. The oaths of Freemasonry require absolute secrecy upon the transactions of the brethren from every good mason. Now, these canons and oaths nowhere abide together without discord and a deprivation of church privileges, and they never could harmonize for one moment. Therefore, the time when they first fell out and contradicted each other, must have been near the beginning of one, or both of them. That time is determined by the Bull of the Pope, 1738, 1739. Wring and twist the brother mason may, but there is no escape; the date is correctly stated, *seventeen* hundred thirty-eight, issued by Clement XII. (See Lawrie's Hist. Mas. p. 122; Ency. Brit. Art. Masonry, last edition.)

What has been said is proof, not only that the account which Freemasonry gives of itself, is erroneous, but grossly erroneous; not only that the order was not organized by Solomon and patronized by St. John, but that it had no existence even in the days of Edward III., and of Henry VI. of England. The question becomes interesting, whence did it originate? and who first promulgated its falsehoods?

The Rosicrusian mania sprung up in Germany, A. D. 1610, nearly; and overspread Christendom. This puff of indefinable extravagance originated from the writings of John Valentine Andrea, a celebrated Theologian of Wirtemberg; (*see London Mag.* 1824, *Vol.* 9, *p.* 143,)—who amused himself with tales of spiritual wonder and mystical glory, as a literary hoax, in the style of Munchausen's wonderful adventures in his memoirs. The visionary minds of that day took his work in earnest. They claimed, in general, for the rosy cross philosophy, whatever is now particularly claimed for Freemasonry, a heavenly origin, a magic influence, a wonderful secret, and unbounded excellence. The universal medicine and the philosopher's stone, were gravely professed for the glory of its mystical laboratory; and to so great a pitch of extravagance did its vain professors run, that modern Freemasons are sober men in the comparison. This folly was greatly admired in England by some men of a strange fancy, and of great learning; and by others publicly professing the black art. Among the former, the name of Elias Ashmole, the antiquary, stands conspicuous; and among the latter, Wm. Lilly, the astrologer; and somewhere between them, is Robert Fludd.

This *Ashmole,* is greatly accounted of as a brother by masonic historians, and is the first accepted Freemason claimed by professor Robison. Ashmole says he was "*elected*" in Mason's Hall, Basing Hall-street, A. D. 1646. (*See Biog. Brit.*) This is the Hall of the London Company of Stone Masons, chartered 1677, 31 years after Ashmole's admission into its livery, and remaining to this day, as it ever has been, in the possession of the Stone Masons; a society distinct from, and independent of the modern Freemasons. And it is evident that Ashmole was only made *free* of the Mason's Company as his friend Lilly was made *free* of the Salters Company, and as the Lord Mayor is usually made *free* of some one of the

12 principal Companies of tradesmen or mechanics in the city of London; and that Ashmole was *not* initiated, passed, and raised to the Sublime degree of Master Mason, as in a modern Lodge of Freemasons. Therefore we think the record must be wrong, which makes Ashmole a Freemason of the modern type.

It is an undeniable fact that the conceited mystery of the Rosicrusians, and their vainglorious pretences to every thing good and great and magical, or *holy*, are united with the emblems and working tools of a handicraft mason, the compasses and level and square and leather apron, to form that lying wonder of the 19th century which is commonly called Freemasonry. This union did not take place in one day; nor until the false philosophy of the Rosicrusians fell into merited disgrace, and the sect ran out. Ashmole died A. D. 1692, and with him the last of the rosy cross philosophers; but the spirit of this order, after lingering a few years among men of less note, passed by a species of metempsychosis, into a new body, the company of masons, with whom it first appears in the early part of the 18th century.

When Ashmole died, 1692, Sir Christopher Wren was at the head of the English architects, holding the office of Deputy Surveyor of the king's buildings: in 1698 he was made by William III. Surveyor General of the public works; and in 1714 to 1718, for political considerations, he was removed from office by George I. All masonic historians call Sir Christopher Wren *Deputy Grand Master*, at the time when he was Deputy Surveyor, and *Grand Master of the Freemasons*, at the time when he was Surveyor General to the throne. But in doing this they make a very short rope to hang themselves; for by their own showing the first Grand Lodge was formed in 1717;* then, how could Sir Christopher Wren be Grand Master in 1698, nineteen years before there was a Grand Lodge?

During this period the Rosicrusian pretensions were seeking, like a troubled spirit, for some resting place.—The age is one of the most extravagant speculation: and moved with a strange desire of fame and money and conviviality, four companies of STONE MASONS, who were left

* See any masonic history of that year: *Preston*, *Dermott*, *Lawrie*, *et alias*.

of those that had been associated in building the proud edifices of London after the fire of 1666, met, the lodge that had worked on St. Paul's Church being at the head, and formed the Grand Lodge of London, in February, and elected their officers June 24th, A. D. 1717. With a view to fill up their ranks, and to increase their consequence, they voted to accept men of other trades and professions, as members of the society. (*Vide Preston, Smith, Lawrie, Hardie, Tannehill, et alias*, particularly the Ahiman Rezon of *Lawrence Dermott*, quoted in the 4th No. of the A. M. Review and Magazine.) Three years they struggled, accommodating the Rosicrusian pretensions to the emblems of a handicraft mason; and then, in 1720, burnt their papers for the benefit of the mystery. (See all the above writers.) They gave out that this bonfire was made "*by some too scrupulous brethren,*" who feared that the secrets of masonry would be exposed in the Book of Constitutions about to be published; but the smoke of that fire was not thick enough to envelope the origin of their mystic order in impenetrable obscurity. No doubt they hoped by burning their pretended parchments, to destroy all evidence disproving their claim to immemorial customs and imprescriptible rights, which claim was in a course of preparation for the public in the dreaded Book of Constitutions. After three years more, the volume came forth from the hands of Anderson and Desaguilliers, or Desaguliers, and blowed the first strain of masonic vainglory and unearthly mystery, which is heard from any book or printed treatise!

Anderson and Desaguilliers, a Scotchman and a Frenchman, in London, were the men who first published to the world, the high pretensions of Freemasonry; men of a low character, and of a base spirit, whose *Book of Constitutions of Masonry*, was ushered from the press, A. D. 1723, and is hardly older than our grandfathers! (*See Robison's Proofs of a Conspiracy, p.* 19, *and p.* 60; *Lawrie, p.* 92.) This Volume of mock Constitutions, is the basis of all masonic history, and its delusive statements have been servilely copied and greatly magnified, until the mystic wonder has grown beyond the size and power of the fabled monsters of antiquity.

Now the false spirit of the rosy cross philosophy was

fairly embodied with the emblems of a mechanic's society; and was brought forth by the *Book of Constitutions* in the form of Freemasonry. From the time of its birth the lying wonder began to run to and fro in the earth, wherever British commerce could convey it; and charters for holding masonic lodges were everywhere sold at a cash price, and an annual stipend, by the Grand Lodge of London. To that Grand Lodge the inhabitants of most parts of continental Europe, of the East and West Indies, of Africa and of America, paid an annual tribute for the right to confer the three degrees of Morgan's Freemasonry! The date, and Grand Master who issued the warrant, are carefully recorded, in *Preston*, *Smith*, *Tannehill*, and others, for holding lodges in all quarters of the earth. A. D. 1729, Freemasonry was first introduced into the East-Indies; 1730 the Grand Lodge of Ireland was formed; 1731 a patent was sent from England to erect a lodge at the Hague; 1733 Freemasonry established itself in North America at Boston; 1736 at Cape Coast in Africa, and at Geneva in Europe; in Scotland the same year the first Grand Master was elected: and so the tripled-headed monster, ENTERED APPRENTICE, FELLOW CRAFT, and MASTER, went deceitfully round the earth while it was yet in its *teens*.

* * * * * * * * * * * *

That masonry is as old as Babel, we do not refuse to believe; it is Freemasonry, otherwise called *Speculative Masonry*, of which we treat, and of which we affirm that its era is A. D. 1717; no man need mistake our meaning. Neither do we pretend that the order was then made up of new principles, or of a newly created race of men; but certain men and certain principles, previously existing, were then for the first time formally united and embodied into that mystic order called Freemasonry; and a system was formed, which did not exist before even by name, which system we know by the name of Speculative Masonry. We do not even suppose that all the materials of this coat of many colors came out of one fleece, or was spun and wove by the same king Solomon. The aprons and trowels and temple were taken from the masons; the divine origin, mystic virtues and wonderful secrets of the order came from the Rosicrusians; the magic and fortunetelling from the Necromancers; the morals from the Jesuits; and the horrid oaths of the order, from its own bowels. But the time that all these were first publicly stitched together to form Speculative Masonry, was when the only four companies of Operative Masons in the south of England, met at the Appletree tavern in London, Feb. 1717, and constituted themselves "the Grand Lodge" of England *pro tempore* in due form. *Vide Preston p.* 166. ANTHONY SAYER, *Grand Master.*

The proof that it had no earlier existence is perfectly conclusive. Speculative Masonry, or Freemasonry, is a matter of great notoriety. Any question in a future age, of its existence in the 18th or 19th centuries, could be answered satisfactorily by pointing to splendid Masonic Halls, to quarto volumes of constitutions, and octavo histories, to medals and monuments and deeds of parchment, as well as deeds of wickedness. The literature of this age abounds with it. Those who read the account of laying the corner stone of the Bunker-hill Monument, will point to that pillar of national glory, as a proof that Freemasonry existed A. D. 1825; and, if that is not enough, the foundation may be removed, and there a medal be found with inscriptions of vanity, which in this republic can only belong to Most Worshipful Freemasonry: unless an indignant people should justly tear the disgraceful plate from its proud resting place.

In vain we search for any proof of this sort existing earlier than the 18th century. We find constitutions of Jesuits, Rosicrusians, and Alchymists. We find histories of political parties, religious sects, and Bucaneers. We find text books of Cabala, necromancy, astrology, magic, fortunetelling, and various proofs of witchcraft; but not a particle of evidence to show the existence of Freemasonry, or Speculative Masonry. It is not mentioned or alluded to; it is not painted on canvass, or stamped on paper, or indented on plate. That its universal language must have been spoken; that its mystic characters were certainly understood, and its omnific word even then possessed some share of omnipotence, no one who believes in Freemasonry, can for a moment doubt. But all the proof is found in pages and documents, in fraternities and monuments of the 18th and 19th centuries; and this in such abundance, as quite to supply the failure of *five hundred* years preceding; although it admits of a doubt, whether there is enough to supply the deficiency of the other five thousand years from the year of light. Fifty centuries are a long period for the active labors of a great mystery spread over the face of the whole world, to pass entirely unobserved: and there is no accounting for it, only as a great mystery, and such, Freemasonry may undoubtedly be; for men do not well understand it, when it is fully revealed.

We have read the volumes of Hume and Smollet and Bisset with care. They give a connected history of England from the earliest dates to the 19th century, and no mention is made of Freemasonry to our recollection. Then we have run over Mosheim, who gives a faithful history of the church, century by century, from the year of our Lord, to the 18th century, and Freemasonry entirely escapes either his notice or our memory. * *

We lay them away, and turn to honest Scotland. Robertson tells its story in the most exquisite manner; he spreads upon his page every fact of importance, and Walter Scott fills the world with the poetry of its history. But where is the mention of Freemasonry, or Speculative Masonry, or the men of the cabletow? In the lights and shadows, in the tales and legends, in the songs and histories of Scotland, as well as of England, where is the mention of Freemasonry prior to the 18th century? We know of none. * * *

It is too much after this to search Gibbon, Gillies, Ferguson, and Rollin for Freemasonry; if we did, it would be of no use; they take no notice of it. * *

Neither poet nor moralist, politician nor controversialist, historian, biographer, antiquary, or novelist of continental Europe, previous to the 18th century, can be named, who mentions such a thing of oaths and degrees, as modern speculative masonry; or who so much as writes the name 'Freemasonry,' or any of its present modifications, in any language of Europe. We do not pretend to have read all, but we understand enough to challenge the most learned professor of masonic lore, the very sublime, elect, and perfect masons, to show any author with a title page older than one hundred and six years, who mentions or alludes to the mystery in any part of the earth; or to produce any medal, or manuscript, or monument, or well authenticated copy of any inscription upon any medal or monument, naming, or having allusion to *Speculative* Masonry, or Freemasonry, of a date earlier than the beginning of the 18th century, in any country on the face of the earth.—*Anti Masonic Review.*

THE PRETENSIONS OF FREEMASONRY TO AN ORIGIN IN THE DAYS OF SOLOMON.

Extract from Letters of Rev. Henry Jones.

At a time like the present, when the institution of Freemasonry is undergoing the faithful scrutiny of the public, it seems to be of very great importance, that the question, so frequently asked, "*What is the origin of the Institution?*" should receive the answer which it demands, in order that an impartial and correct judgment may be more readily formed. If it originated with the people of God; and was patronized as a good and useful institution by many of the most eminent characters whose names are recorded in holy writ; at a time too, when they were enjoying the special guidance and approbation of the Most High; a favorable judgment must be rendered of it, at least while in its native purity, though now so degenerated and perverted:—But if, on the other hand, this institution originated with men of corrupt principles, who have falsely founded it, on pretended important facts, which never existed; then of course, considering also, its present deformed character, it must be condemned by the public, as a base and wicked fabrication, an insult upon community, and only worthy to be utterly expunged from all ranks of society. Each of these suppositions, for the origin of the institution, is considered correct, by the opposite parties who feel interested in the subject, and are exhibited by them, respectively, as proof of its merits, or demerits.

It is my design on this occasion to show, that *its own claims to an origin at the building of the temple of Solo-*

mon, among wise and holy men, are unfounded, and that consequently, *it must have had its origin since that time, among false and wicked men, so that those wise and holy men had no part nor lot in the matter.*

It is well known to all the fraternity who have become somewhat familiar with the lectures of the first three degrees, that they do teach us, that Speculative, or Freemasonry, originated at the building of Solomon's temple, and that a large share of the mysteries of the institution are established on certain events, which are said to have transpired at that time and place. I shall not consider it necessary to repeat over those parts of the lectures to which I allude; but for the benefit of some who may still be unacquainted with the subject, I would concisely bring into view some of the pretensions of masonry, as to its having its origin at the building of the temple with Solomon and others, which I am to endeavor to show, as being false.

Passing by much in the first and second degrees, which teaches the same, I shall confine my remarks to the third degree; and would observe, First, that the lecture of this "sublime" degree, teaches us that Freemasonry was founded at the building of the temple, by these important circumstances, which it professes to record, *viz.* that there were employed in building it, three Grand Masters; Solomon king of Israel, Hiram king of Tyre, and Hiram "Abiff," as he is designated in masonry, but in the scripture, Hiram the son of a widow, &c. who alone constituted the Master's lodge at that time, and who alone possessed the Master's secrets or word, holding their secret meetings in the sanctum sanctorum, or holy of holies of the temple. They are represented also, in this degree, as having agreed together, never to give the Master's word to any other person, unless they all three were together in doing it; so that, when Hiram "Abiff" is represented in this degree, as being slain, before any of the craftsmen had received this secret word of the Masters', it could not afterwards be given, for want of the three Grand Masters together, and was, in consequence of this, for many years lost, having another word substituted in its stead.

Having brought forward these things as the pretended

matters of fact, on which the institution of Freemasonry professes to be founded; I would observe, that they bring with themselves no proof that they are matters of fact in reality, unless we are bound to consider them so proved by the bare assertion of an individual, who says that he was secretly told so, by a second person in the preceding generation, who in like manner, received his information from a third, and so on through fifty or an hundred generations, to go back to the days of Solomon: But no tribunal has ever been authorised to allow the least credit to a witness like this, on any important question between opposite parties.

Although it is often difficult to prove a negative in such a case as this; I am prepared to prove, unless I greatly mistake, that these masonic pretensions to the origin of the institution at the building of the temple, are false; by showing from scripture history, that Hiram King of Tyre and Hiram "Abiff" never were associated with Solomon as Grand Master in the building of the temple, so that they three, never constituted a Master's lodge there, assembling in the sanctum sanctorum for their secret meetings. Every one must know, who is acquainted with this history, 1 Kings, 2 Chron., that Solomon was Master alone, over all the work of the building, that he was especially endowed with wisdom from above to qualify him to form so great a work, and that the Lord furnished him with particular directions, through the agency of David his father,* which was equal to a pattern of the building, and more than this, Hiram king of Tyre, as it seems from scripture and reason, never left his kingdom to go and dwell at Jerusalem, while the temple was building, as he only bartered with Solomon in a friendly manner, by furnishing timber for the temple, and sending his servants to cut and prepare it, &c. for which Solomon made satisfaction in wheat, barley, wine and oil; with twenty cities. It is evident, also, beyond dispute, that Hiram "Abiff" was not a Grand Master with Solomon in building the temple, and with him constituting a Master's lodge, meeting privately in the sanctum sanctorum, as the third degree represents; because

* 1 Chron. xxviii. 11, 12, 19.

he was employed only as a very skilful workman in metals, and because, he labored *not* on, or about the temple, but exclusively in casting the furniture, &c. for the temple, under the direction of Solomon, "*In the plain of Jordan—in the clay ground between Succoth and Zarthan,*" *or* "*Zeredathah.*"*

Again, the instructions of the third, or "sublime" degree, give us to understand that Freemasonry originated with wise and good men, under the patronage of God, at the building of the temple, by its establishing the principal part of the mysteries of that degree on the pretended murder of Hiram "Abiff," with the various circumstances in its connexion, while he was in the temple, before it was finished, at a time too, when he was daily employed in planning work for the craft, and overseeing them on the building. All who have taken the third degree, or have examined Morgan's book, may know, that there is a long secret dialogue or tragedy, to be acted out, by the members of the lodge whenever the degree is conferred, in imitation of the whole process, and all the circumstances, of the pretended murder of this Hiram, and that the candidate who takes the degree, must always represent Hiram, and experience a mock murder, two burials, &c.: But of Hiram's being thus murdered in the temple, before its completion, masonry gives us no better evidence than what has been noticed in case of the other pretended facts, on which, not the least dependence can be placed, even if there were nothing to disprove it.

If such a horrible assassination as this is represented to be, of so important a character as Hiram was, had taken place under those circumstances, it is unaccountably strange, that the sacred writer, in recording the remarkable events connected with that great work, should pass over so important an event as this, in utter silence; and strange too, that Josephus, who has given such a particular account of the building, workmen and circumstances of the temple, in his 8th Book, 2d and 3d Chapters, should not intimate a word of any such important transaction.

Although both Josephus and the scripture are entirely

* 1 Kings, vii. 46; and 2 Chron. iv. 17.

silent about any such murder of Hiram in the temple, before its completion; the scripture on the other side of the question, is not silent, but it speaks out, and gives us to understand that he was *not* thus there murdered.

The first proof to be mentioned from scripture of this fact, is what has already been noticed, viz., that he never wrought as an overseer on the building of the temple, as I think we must conclude, from the consideration, of his being employed by Solomon only as a cunning workman, in casting the metallic vessels, furniture, &c. of the temple, "*in the plain of Jordan*," at a place, not less than thirty or forty miles from Jerusalem, where the temple was built, as it appears by consulting sacred geography on the subject.

Another scripture testimony which is positive, against the pretended fact of Hiram's being murdered in the temple before its completion, and before he had finished the work which had been assigned him, is that he was *living* when the temple was completed, and that he lived to *finish* all the work, which had lain upon his hands, for the use of the temple. The first passage which declares this, is 1 Kings, 7th Chap. 40th verse, *And Hiram made the lavers and the shovels and the basons; so Hiram* MADE AN END *of doing all the work that he made for king Solomon for the house of the Lord.*"

Then, lest this plain text should be perverted, the same Chap. enumerates all the wonderful castings of Hiram, and in the last verse, which is in the same connexion, with Hiram's making an end of all *his* work for king Solomon, it is said, "*So was* ENDED *all the work, that* KING SOLOMON *made for the house of the Lord.*" Then according to the sacred writer, the very next thing was, the dedication of the temple by Solomon, as it is particularized in the next Chapter.

To set the fact of Hiram's being alive, at the finishing of the temple, still further beyond all doubt, the same testimony of it, is recorded again, in 2 Chron. 4th Chap. 11th verse, "*And Huram* [or Hiram] *made the pots, and the shovels, and the basons. And Huram* FINISHED *the work that he was to make for king Solomon, for the house of God:*" So it is said again, in the same connexion of the subject, in the first verse of the next Chap. "*Thus all the work that Solomon made for the house of the Lord was* FINISHED," &c. immediately upon which, as the history informs us, the people of Israel were assembled for the dedication of the building.

Having shown now, as I would hope, to the satisfaction of all who rely upon scripture testimony, and the exercise of reason, for evidence; that Solomon was *alone*, under God, a 'Grand Master,' or the builder of the temple; that Hiram king of Tyre, never *left his kingdom* to go and dwell at Jerusalem, to be a Grand Master in the building, forming a Master's lodge, &c; that Hiram "Abiff," was *not* a Grand Master at Jerusalem with Solomon in erecting the temple, and that he was *never slain* there before the finishing of his appropriate work, having lived to *make an end* of it, and see the temple completed; What are we to think of the institution of Freemasonry? the lectures of which tell us, that Hiram king of Tyre, and Hiram "Abiff," *were* Grand Masters with Solomon in building the temple; that they three constituted a Master's lodge assembling in the sanctum sanctorum, &c. and that Hiram "Abiff," *was slain* in the temple before its completion, while busily employed in the great work. And what shall we think of it too, when it professes in its lectures to have its *origin* in connexion with these reputed events, and to be *founded* upon them, while nearly the whole substance of the mysteries of the third degree, is a dialogue, in imitation of Hiram's assassination, &c.? Considering that the first three degrees of Freemasonry which were established, must be the corner stone, or foundation, on which all the latter degrees are built, would it be unreasonable for me now to ask; On what then does the whole superstructure of Freemasonry rest but a base fabrication of wicked men, who in some dark and apostate age of the world, have risen up, united into a secret society, and darkly handed down their inventions, to flatter us to believe that their institution is good as having originated among wise and good men; and being ignorant of the manner in which their false pretensions would be exposed; have told us, that it was established on certain specified facts and events, which, by looking at them carefully, and comparing them with our Bible, we find, never had existence? Was there ever an imposture of such magnitude as this, so generally palmed

2*

upon mankind? And yet, here is the origin of the foundation of Speculative Freemasonry; and here is a portrait of the character of its founders and first principles.

THE ABUSE AND PERVERSION OF THE MASONIC INSTITUTION.

Extract from Rev. M. Thacher's Address before Montgomery Lodge.

The original design* of this institution appears to have been, to cherish the social virtues, enforce the principles of moral rectitude and equity between man and man, and to extend the hand of relief to indigence and distress. Viewed in this light, and so far as it is calculated to answer these designs, it *may*, and *ought*, to be considered no more nor less than a *moral* and charitable institution. So far as any society is combined to promote general interest, merely, it should be regarded merely as an object of *utility;* so far as it enforces moral virtue, or upright external conduct, it may be considered as a *moral* society; and so far as it extends relief to others, it may be considered as an institution of *charity*. We will take, for example, a society for the promotion of useful knowledge

* It is here taken for *granted*, that this *was* the primary intention of the masonic society; because this is what masons have always avowed. Query. Would any class of men have instituted a *secret* society, to act *merely* as a moral and charitable institution? But, suppose the original design of the masonic institution was *merely* what masons have *avowed;* another important question arises, Is it *possible* for a *secret* society to exist, without becoming corrupt, and being turned into an engine of wickedness? Our Saviour declared to the Jewish high priest, "*I spake openly to the world;—and in secret have I said nothing.*" What would now be thought of the *church*, if she should close and "*tyle*" her doors, impose obligations in secret, and place a perpetual seal upon the lips of her members? Would it any longer be *believed* that her *sole object* is to promote the religion of the gospel? Now if the *church*, which is the purest body on earth, *could not* and *would not* be trusted, as a *secret society*, who can blame conscientious and judicious men, for drawing the conclusion, that *any secret society*, of whatever description, is altogether unnecessary, and cannot exist, without becoming an object of *suspicion*, if not an engine of wickedness.

in the Mechanic Arts. So far as this society tends to facilitate the theory and practice of mechanism, it may be valued for its *utility*. If its members enter into an agreement to shun certain known vices, and to practise certain known virtues, it may be considered as a *moral* society. If they go farther, and engage to appropriate a certain portion of their funds for the relief of indigent widows and orphans, it may then be regarded both as a *moral* and a *charitable* institution.

Considering Freemasonry, therefore, in its original design, as a *moral*, as well as charitable institution, one of the first abuses, of which we are called to take notice, is, THE ADMISSION AND RETENTION OF UNPRINCIPLED MEMBERS.* It is absurd to the last degree, not to say ridiculous, to think of advancing the cause of morality by immoral men. To any man who professes to take the Bible for his guide, to make himself an example to others, and to enforce the first principles of moral virtue, and who still appears to have no regard to his own moral conduct, we may, with propriety, address the language of the great apostle of the Gentiles:—"Thou, therefore, who teachest another, teachest thou not thyself? Thou that preachest a man should not steal, dost thou steal? Thou that sayest a man should not commit adultery, dost thou commit adultery? Thou that abhorrest idols, dost thou commit sacrilege? Thou that makest thy boast of the law, through breaking the law, dishonorest thou God?" There cannot be a greater perversion of any moral institution, than to admit and retain those members, who counteract by their example what they profess to maintain by precept.

* Freemasons often say, "There are bad men in the *Church*, as well as in our institution." This is true; but the cases are not parallel. All persons, whether in the church or out, have opportunity to *know* on what *principles* members are received; and that these principles do *not justify* the admission and retention of bad men. But this *cannot* be known with respect to any *secret* society. Those, who do not belong to the masonic institution, have no opportunity to judge from *principle*, but merely from the declarations of its members; and nothing but such declarations *can* afford them any evidence, that the *secret principles* of Freemasonry do not justify the admission and retention of just such men. The fact, therefore, that there are bad men in the church of Christ, while it militates nothing against the principles of the Christian religion, *does* and *must*, in regard to masonry, militate against the principles of the institution.

It cannot be denied however, nor ought it to be concealed, if it could be, that the masonic fraternity have knowingly admitted, and willingly harbored in their community, *just such members*. Such an abuse as this, has, in many places, rendered the institution an anomaly and a caricature. There is no part of masonry more public, than that masons *profess* to take the BIBLE as their guide in moral conduct. This they have openly avowed, and *reiterated*, time out of mind. What a burlesque, then, must it be upon every principle of moral virtue, to see men, and even those who stand high on the rolls of our Lodges, Chapters, and Encampments, conducting like libertines! When one of the primary precepts of DIVINE TRUTH requires us to deal *justly*, love *mercy*, and walk *humbly* with our God; what an incongruity for those, who profess to be guided by this "great light," to set at defiance every principle of honor, honesty, and compassion, and act as if there were no God to call them to account! When the Bible enjoins that "golden rule," that summary of the law and the prophets, "All things whatsoever ye would that men should do to you, do ye even so to them;" how inconsistent for those, who profess to receive its precepts as the rule of their faith and practice, to discover that sordid selfishness, in their intercourse with their fellow men, which characterizes not a few of the masonic fraternity! But these are facts, which candor cannot conceal, and which it would be impious to deny. How many, who have voluntarily bound themselves to the "mystic order," and who are owned and acknowledged as "free and accepted masons," are daily sending up oaths and curses "into the ears of the Lord of Sabaoth," in direct violation of that peremptory command, "*Swear not at all!*" How many there are, also, of the same class of men, who are among the first in profanation of holy time, in direct defiance of that perpetual precept of the divine law, "*Remember the Sabbath day to keep it holy!*" It would, likewise, be the grossest self-adulation to evade, and the grossest imposition upon others to dispute, the affecting truth, that the Holy Bible has sometimes been borne in public by the hand already palsied with intemperance, and its sacred truths pronounced by the tongue already stiffened with the poisoned chalice. If masons are disposed to shut their eyes upon such an abuse of a *professed* moral institution, it is not strange that others should be disposed to write upon the walls, and pillars, and furniture of their "temple,"—"MENE, MENE, TEKEL, UPHARSIN."

Another abuse of Freemasonry, which grows directly out of the evil to which we have just attended, is, A PERVERSION OF THE INSTITUTION FROM ITS PRIMITIVE DESIGN. When corrupt men are admitted and retained in any society, especially in such numbers as to gain the ascendency, it is strange indeed if the original object of such community is pursued for any length of time, and still more strange if the institution is not rendered an engine of wickedness. What object can it be for *immoral men* to promote morality? Or who can depend upon those, who are given to licentiousness, to relieve the distresses of the widow and orphan? They who pamper their own lusts, and are determined to pursue a course of sensual gratification, will generally make every thing bend, so far as possible, to facilitate the execution of their own selfish designs. This will account for many lodges, in different parts of our country, becoming nurseries of conviviality, and even of intemperance; instead of asylums for the poor, the needy, and the afflicted. It has been said, with sarcastic severity, but with too much truth, that "Freemasons boast of their moral and *charitable* institution; but they expend more in pageantry and feasting, at one of their anniversary celebrations, than in all their acts of munificence during the year." Now it is easy to see, that any thing like this, is a perversion of the original design of the masonic association. We have seen that this design was, to foster the principles of moral virtue, and afford relief to the indigent. Every thing, therefore, which tends to counteract this grand and primary object, must necessarily tend to sap the whole foundation. It must, too, be the grossest violation of every principle of the masonic institution, to make it an instrument of political intrigue, or of sectarian influence. It is impossible that this should be done, without removing the "ancient landmarks," and disregarding the strongest obligation of every member of the society. But, that such an unhallowed influence as this, has, from time to time, been exerted, in various branches of the masonic community, its history fully demonstrates; and, although many such charges against the institution in our own country I must think are altogether without foundation; yet we ought not, by any means, to consider ourselves beyond the reach of corruption. The example of the Illuminees, who crept into the lodges of Europe, and converted masonry into an engine, which overturned the religion and government of a whole nation, should surely prove a most solemn admonition to all the members of the fraternity in this infant Republic. A republican government, of all others, affords the fairest opportunity for demagogues and men of corrupt minds, to execute their base designs. It would not be strange, therefore, if such men, who had connected themselves with the masonic institution, should make every possible attempt, by intrigue and deep laid plots, to rob this people of their dearest rights, which our fathers purchased with their blood.

In pursuing the chain of evils, by which the masonic institution has been made a subject of abuse, it is not out of place to take notice of FALSE PRETENSIONS. It is notorious to every judicious and candid member of the institution, that Freemasonry has often been made to rear false beacons, and to hold out false colors. Many have seemed to suppose, because they are not allowed to tell what masonry *is*, so far as its "*mysteries*" *are concerned* that they are authorized, and even *obliged*, to represent it as being *what it is not*. In order to gratify the curious, and raise their highest expectations, they have represented the peculiarities of the institution to be something, which would strike the peculiar fancies of individuals, or gratify their ruling passions: and so have induced persons to become members from mercenary motives, which has often been the occasion of the greatest degree of disappointment and disgust. Some for example, conversing with an avaricious man, have led him to believe that masonry affords peculiar facilities for the acquisition of wealth. In conversing with an ambitious man, they have represented the institution as pointing out a very safe and easy road to honor and promotion. Men of studious habits have been led to believe, by similar false representations, that it was one grand and principal object of masonry, to lay open the profoundest mysteries of science and the arts, in the most direct, easy and lucid manner. In like manner have been treated men of different professions. The attorney has been presented with the highest encouragement of aid in the mazes of the law; and the divine* has been told that masonry throws light upon different incidents recorded in the Bible, and teaches to explain different passages of scripture, which, otherwise, must forever remain in obscurity. Now, to pursue such a course as this, with those who are ignorant of the mysteries of masonry, is not only to act a dishonest part, but must be productive of the most serious and lasting evils. It is easy to see, that when any person is initiated to the order with high expectation of some peculiar advantage, which has been held out to him by *false* and delusive representations, he must not only be disappointed, but disgusted. If so, his disappointment and disgust may not only lead him to overlook any real merit in the institution, though of a very different kind from what he expected, but will probably drive him to abandon the institution altogether. It ought ever, therefore, to be a maxim with all masons, whenever they say any thing respecting their institution, to " speak the words of truth and soberness." If they cannot converse with others, without making false impressions, and false representations, let them keep silence. It may be presumed, that there is not one mason in ten, if there is one in a hundred, who has not been in some degree disappointed and disgusted in consequence of false expectations, raised by the disingenuous allurements of imprudent members.

In connexion with the last mentioned abuse of the masonic institution, we may add, BOASTING OF ITS GREAT

* The writer here speaks from *experience*. He was repeatedly told, *perhaps* sincerely, that the masonic society was not only a scientific institution, but that there were many incidents and passages revealed in the Bible, which could be explained only by masonic light. This representation he has since found to be altogether *false*. Masonry, indeed, alludes to *scripture*; but I have nowhere found, after the most diligent research, that scripture alludes to *masonry*; unless (which is very probable) the sacred writers allude to it *prophetically*, in describing the scenes of the latter days.

ANTIQUITY AND PRETENDED PATRONS.* It seems to be a natural and rather curious trait in the human character, to value some things merely because they are *old*, and others merely because they are *new*. It is always impolitic, however, to claim, for any institution, greater antiquity, than can be fairly made to appear by conclusive evidence, in view of the public. To prize any thing, either because of its real or pretended antiquity, when others are able to see neither internal nor external evidence of the fact, is rather to turn the subject into ridicule, and detract from its real merit, than to sanction its utility by proper means, and give demonstration of its excellence. When masons, therefore, have boasted that their institution is as old as the creation, and that all the renowned men of antiquity have been its patrons, they have betrayed a want of confidence in what *ought* to constitute its real worth, and which cannot in anywise depend upon its being either old or young. It matters not to me, whether the institution was founded by Solomon, or by John the Baptist, or, what is more probable, by certain mechanics in the sixteenth century; I consider the main question to be, Whether the institution is good or bad; and whether it has maintained or departed from its original design? I can, however, with what little know-

* "Enthusiastic friends of our institution have done it much injury, and covered it with much ridicule, by stretching its origin beyond the bounds of credibility. Some have given it an antediluvian origin, while others have even represented it as coeval with creation; some have traced it to the Egyptian priests, and others have discovered its vestiges in the mystical societies of Greece and Rome. The erection of Solomon's temple, the retreats of the Druids, and the crusades to the holy land, have been at different times specified as the sources of its existence. The order, harmony, and wonders of creation, the principles of mathematical science, and the productions of architectural skill, have been confounded with Freemasonry. Whenever a great philosopher has enlightened the ancient world, he has been resolved by a species of moral metempsychosis, or intellectual chemistry, into a Freemason; and in all the secret institutions of antiquity, the footsteps of Lodges have been traced by the eye of credulity. Archimides, Pythagoras, Euclid, and Vetruvius, were in all probability not Freemasons; and the love of order, the cultivation of science, the embellishments of taste, and the sublime and beautiful works of art, have certainly existed in ancient, as they now do in modern times, without the agency of Freemasonry."—*Extract from the Masonic Address of Dewitt Clinton, delivered Sept.* 29, 1825.

ledge I have been able to acquire on the subject, see no propriety in celebrating the birth of any ancient patron, whether *real* or *supposed;* and, for my own part, I frankly confess, that I have never yet seen one spark of substantial evidence, that either Solomon, or John the Baptist, or John the Evangelist, was a Freemason. I make this declaration as an *honest man;* and not, by any means, to cast reflections upon those, whose judgment may differ from mine. I am persuaded also, that the annual celebration of John Baptist's nativity has, for years past, been productive of serious evils, by an example of conviviality, not to say intemperance, and an inducement to extravagance, parade and idleness; vices which, more than almost any thing else, have tended to blast the reputation of the order, as a moral and charitable institution. But, supposing masonry can boast of great antiquity, and of renowned patrons; what then? This simple fact can render it, in its present state, and at the present day, neither the better nor the worse. An institution cannot, in reality, be any the more valuable for being old, nor any the less valuable for being new. I cannot consider Louis XVI. any the better for being able to "boast of a long line of dead ancestors," who had reigned before him, and his claiming the prerogative to wear the crown by "the right of blood;" nor Napoleon Bonaparte any the worse, for having placed himself at the head of an intended dynasty. If *antiquity* is necessary to prove the value of an institution; then the government under which we live, should be undervalued and cried down, merely because it was founded in the close of the eighteenth century; while we sing the praises of the British monarchy, because it has existed for a thousand years. It is laboring in vain, therefore, and spending strength for nought, to attempt demonstrating the merits of Freemasonry, by proclaiming its antiquity, and celebrating the nativity of a supposed ancient patron. It is true, the pageantry of that day may excite the curiosity of idle brains, and give them an itch to become acquainted with the "mysteries" of the order; but members, who become such from idle curiosity, can afford neither honor nor profit to a charitable and moral institution.

The greatest abuse of Freemasonry, which deserves

notice on this occasion, is, the inclination of some TO MOULD IT INTO A SYSTEM OF RELIGION. All that can be said of masonry, and all that *ought* to be said of it, in its best and primitive state, is, that it was designed for a *moral* and *charitable* institution. Thus far it may go, and no farther. To run it into a system of religion, is an outrage upon the gospel of Christ. A man may as well be a Mahomedan, or a heathen, as adopt any thing for a system of religion, which does not recognize the atonement of Christ. This is the foundation of the Christian's faith, the Christian's hope, and the Christian's salvation. For, "there is none other name under heaven given among men, whereby we can be saved, but by Jesus Christ." Freemasons may be assured, therefore, that they cannot do their institution a greater injury, nor more effectually disgust and wound the feelings of a Christian community, than to frame it into a *system of religion.* There is not a *Christian* on earth but must reject and abandon masonry, so far as it sets itself up as a system of religion, upon which its votaries may be induced to build their hopes of forgiveness and acceptance with God. For, there is not a Christian on earth, but must build his hopes of salvation entirely upon the atonement of the blessed Redeemer. It would be just as consistent to erect the constitution of an agricultural society into a system of religion, as to erect the institution of masonry into a system of religion. I should consider it just as proper to give this sentiment, "*Religion* and *agriculture*:—what God hath joined together, let not man put asunder;" as to give the sentiment which was given at a recent anniversary, "*Religion* and *masonry*:—what God hath joined together, let not man put asunder."*

Here then lies the true secret of that opposition to Freemasonry, which is expressed by some of our most serious and conscientious men in society. They have considered masons as erecting a system of religion, in distinction from, and in opposition to, the religion of the gospel. It must be confessed, also, that they have had their reasons for so thinking. They have heard the re-

* Given by Rev. George Taft, Rector of St. Paul's Church, Pawtucket, R. I.—ED.

peated declaration, "Every true mason is a Christian; and every Christian is a mason at heart." They have heard it said, in substance, that 'religion is masonry, and that masonry is religion.' They have seen, in Charts and Monitors, prayers and other forms of religious service, in which neither the name, nor the atonement of Christ, is recognized. They have heard the burial service, as now used, which virtually pronounces the deceased in heaven, let his moral character have been what it might. They have seen "the sprig of evergreen," an emblem of the immortality of the soul, cast into the grave by the professed Deist, and even by those who profess to believe that man dies like the beast. They have seen the Bible carried in solemn procession, by the same persons; and, considering their avowed principles and general conduct, have drawn the very natural inference, "*This is solemn mockery*." Now it must be admitted, that, when serious and thinking men judge of masonry by what they see in these authorized and sanctioned publications, and by the conduct of many masons, who are known to be hostile to the religion of Christ and his apostles, it is not strange that they should fear a general combination to mould the masonic institution into a religious system, opposed to the first principles of the oracles of God. That this *has* been the design of some leading masons, who have stood high as members of the fraternity, I have not the least reason to doubt. It may be presumed, however, that this is not the design of the majority of the "craft," and that they have received the forms, to which I have alluded, without due consideration. But, so far as any have intended, that masonry shall answer as a substitute for religion, it ought to be considered as the grossest abuse and perversion of its original design; and should, in every laudable way, be reprobated by those who have pledged themselves to preserve "the ancient land-marks of the order."

CIVIL, SOCIAL, AND POLITICAL INFLUENCE OF MASONRY.

Extract from Charles P. Sumner's Letter to the Suffolk Committee.

MASONIC engagements, whether they are called oaths, obligations or promises, ought never to be made. They are not sanctioned by law, and are not obligatory. They make it a masonic crime to divulge that which the good of the community requires should not be concealed. The manner in which they are administered, and the matter of them, can hardly fail to excite disrespect for the institution, in the mind of the person initiated; but their effect is neutralized by some charge, or address, which is immediately made by the master, inculcating charity, benevolence and candor towards the whole family of mankind, and a cheerful obedience to the laws and magistrates of the country in which we live. Masonic obligations have no dignity when compared with precepts like these.

It has been said that Washington in his early life was a mason; but he never went further than the third degree: I believe that in his time, higher degrees were not conferred. It is not possible, by reading any book, to know what were the precise terms of Washington's masonic obligations: but any body may know that he never agreed to kill or be killed for all the masonry in the world. It is easy to divine the motives which probably induced *him* to become a mason. The Old Charge used in his day, when speaking of Civil Magistracy says, "a mason is a peaceable subject to the civil rulers, wherever he resides or works; and is never to be concerned in plots, and conspiracies against the peace and welfare of the nation; nor behave himself undutifully to inferior magistrates." * * * "If a brother should be a rebel against the States, he is not to be countenanced in his rebellion, however he may be pitied as an unhappy man." * * * The books abound with precepts of loyalty and benevolence. It was sentiments like these which induced Washington to become a mason; and a respect for these sentiments would have induced him to withdraw his esteem for the association, had he lived until the autumn of 1826, and heard of that outrage which evinces that masonry, probably in some of its high and recently invented degrees, can inspire some of its votaries with the grossest misconception of their duty to the magistracy and laws of their country :—I say in some of its *high* degrees, for I am convinced that neither of the three lower degrees irresistibly require that the receiver of them should become the perpetrator of a crime upon himself or upon any one else. I say this from impressions received between twenty and thirty years ago.

It is probable that Morgan has been murdered. If there is any thing in masonic ties that could have induced masons to do this, they ought to disregard such ties as a lion would disregard a net of cobweb. It will be disgraceful to the institution, if its members do not all do their utmost to bring all the abductors of Morgan to *legal light* and legal punishment. In no better method can they manifest the loyalty and benevolence which they *yet* continue to declare to be their characteristics.

In our government "the whole people covenants with each citizen and each citizen with the whole people that all shall be governed by certain laws for the common good." Whoever violates those laws cannot be a good citizen—and can he be a good mason?

A masonic obligation, if it requires any breach of the law, is what no man has a right to impose, *even on a willing receiver.* It is not binding on any one who may be so indiscreet as to take it. It cannot come to good. As it is imposed in some lodges it is illegal and wicked; and in lodges, where it is the least reprehensible, it goes to swell the amount of those idle words which we must one day regret.

The influence of masonry is not favorable to domestic happiness. It impairs a man's fondness for the pleasures, which, if he does his duty, he may justly expect to find *at home.* I once had occasion to see a man after ten o'clock in the evening. I called at his house; upon knocking at the door, I heard the words—*walk in*, uttered by a faint voice. I entered the room which served its tenants for a parlor and a kitchen. It was enlightened by a glimmering lamp. His wife was sitting in a rocking chair drawn to the hearth, on which was a small fire scarcely visible. One child was in her arms, and another in a cradle, within her reach, which she occasionally rocked. I asked her if I might at that late hour be permitted to see her husband. She replied, with a pale and melancholy look, " Sir, my husband has yet not returned from the Lodge." She then in a sitting posture, bent forward over her child, and with a shawl that hung loosely over her shoulders she absorbed a starting tear. At that very moment her husband was probably in the Lodge joining his voice in the words of a favorite masonic song—

" We are true and sincere
" And just to the fair."

I withdrew from this mason's house with pity for his young wife and infant children, and with lessened respect for an institution which could thus withhold a husband and a father from the first of social duties.

Masonry alienates the minds of some men from the common pursuits of life, and inclines its votaries to things, immoderate, incredible, and out of their reach. It styles itself but another name for Charity, but it is not modest like Charity; it vaunteth itself and is puffed up. In the subordinate lodges it delights itself in those songs which are denominated masonic, the burden of which is, that masons are the greatest and the best of men, companions of princes wherever they go; that they built all the superb temples and palaces in the world; that they are eminently benevolent, and the special favorites of the fair. It flaunts in the robes and titles that might become the high stations of piety or power in the Court of an eastern prince.

In a country, like ours, where all men stand upon a *level*, and where the fields of usefulness and honor are open to all, it cannot be consistent with the *wisdom* of a well regulated mind to cultivate those flowers that yield no fruit; or to decorate one's self with the ornaments that serve to make the wearer of them no more respectable than he would be in the plain garments suited to his daily calling.

If a mason would qualify himself to become a master of a lodge, he must load his memory with a mass of matter for which the understanding has but small affinity.

If young men would quit those scenes of almost profitless amusement and attend with equal assiduity the lectures on operative masonry and architecture; on chemistry, astronomy, botany, anatomy, mineralogy, agriculture or mechanics, which might at a small expense be heard in every city, and in some villages; they would find more satisfaction to their own inquisitive minds and lose none of that respectable standing in the community which they now enjoy. If some young lawyers would give that portion of their time to legal and historical studies, which some few of them throw away in investigating the self-asserted antiquity and universality of Freemasonry, they would find themselves in higher request in their profession, masters of the Civil Law, the Admiralty Law, and Law of Nations; and possibly their chance would be fair as diplomatists, to represent their country in the presence of Kings.

Masonry is said to be a sort of accomplishment suitable for a traveller; but a knowledge of the language of the country he visits, and of the business he goes to transact, will set him above the necessity of any aid or pleasure to be derived from masonic knowledge or masonic acquaintances; and as to those who are content to remain in their own country, if a man will mind his own affairs, and abstain from those habits of *moderate drinking*, at which the genius of masonry takes no offence, he will seldom need any of the pecuniary aid that the funds of masonry can bestow.

I have never considered masonry as having any distinct political influence in this Commonwealth. There are some who seem to think differently; and it is with grief that I have seen in print any insinuation that the administration of justice is under masonic influence. I am convinced that this is unmerited here. My observation does not permit me to believe that such influence has extended to any department of government. Let masonry be gently divested of its borrowed plumes, but not loaded with that which it does not deserve to bear.

Every man who is a mason will be frank enough to confess it, and until the question is proposed to him it cannot be right that he should be charged with masonry by those who consider it a cause of reproach. Such a charge made against any public functionary, may do harm to the Commonwealth rather than to masonry.

I have recently seen a paragraph which is said to have been printed in an oration delivered by Mr. Brainard, a distinguished mason, at New London in Connecticut, on the 24th June, 1825. It is in these words:—

"What is masonry now? it is powerful: it comprises men of rank, wealth, office, and talent, in power and out of power, and that in almost every place where power is of any importance; and it comprises among other classes of the community, to the lowest, in large numbers, active men united together and capable of being directed by the efforts of others, so as to have the force of concert throughout the civilized world. They are distributed too with the means of knowing one another, and the means of keeping secret, and the means of co-operating in the desk, in the legislative hall, on the bench, in every gathering of business, in every party of pleasure, in every enterprize of government, in every domestic circle, in peace and in war, among enemies and friends, in one place as well as another. So powerful indeed is it at this time, that it fears nothing from violence either public or private; for it has every means to learn it in season, to counteract, defeat, and punish it."

Having seen masonry only in its three incipient steps, and but little or nothing of it for many years past, I am not able to attribute to it any such mighty sagacity and power as the author of that oration so boldly arrogates for it. Every one however will judge of this, as his own knowledge and good sense shall dictate. If he has given a true description of masonry, it ought to be dreaded as a pestilence that walketh in darkness. We have no Police vigilant and strong enough to cope with it. It can, if it pleases, throw a flood of light upon the last miserable scene of Morgan's life. If any part of this mystery of iniquity is to remain undeveloped, it must be because masonic obligations, have an influence more powerful than those of justice. If what Mr. Brainard has said be not true, he has done wrong to the cause he advocates, and must in the opinion of its friends deserve some punishment, perhaps almost as severe as that which awaits a man in England who is an utterer of *false news*, or *false and pretended prophecies*, calculated to give unfounded alarm to the people.*

The abduction of Morgan, which followed soon after the publication of that remarkable paragraph, has excited perhaps a just belief that the existence of masonry is incompatible with the personal security of those who reveal its mysteries. However well or ill founded this belief may be, I hope no cause for it will long exist; but that the subordinate Lodges will upon due consideration, surrender their charters to the Grand Lodge, and close this great concern, which some pretend has been going on, (quietly till now,) ever since the days of Adam. Masonry will thus subside and come to a peaceful and honorable death. In no better way can masons display the respect and benevolence which they feel for their uninitiated brethren of the human family, than by voluntarily walking with them on the common level of citizenship.

MASONRY PRODUCTIVE OF NO PERMANENT MORAL GOOD.

Extracted from writings of Rev. John G. Stearns.†

If masonry be what it professes, its direct tendency must be to nourish the piety of the heart and the graces of the divine Spirit. Does it have such a tendency? Are those Christians who devote themselves to masonry, and have made the greatest advances, and even searched all its mysteries, any more wise, godly, and useful, than many others who have no knowledge of masonry? I will leave facts to speak for themselves, and my readers to judge for themselves, and I presume they will agree, that

* 4 Vol. Blackstone's Commentaries, p. 149.

† Mr. Stearns's Volume, entitled "An Inquiry into the Nature and Tendency of Speculative Freemasonry," is one of the ablest productions which has appeared on the subject. Its service to the cause of Anti-masonry, has probably been greater than that of any work of the kind. Five editions have already been published.—Ed.

such Christians often appear to possess the least of the humble spirit of the Saviour.

If it be the tendency of masonry to gratify and comfort the pious heart, and promote its spiritual growth, why do so many godly members of the fraternity forsake it and proclaim its leanness? The reason Mr. Bradley gives is, other important callings occupy their attention and render it inconsistent for them to attend the meetings of the lodges. This may be true in some cases, but not in all; nor does it answer the objection he has anticipated. The objection is, " Why do many good men who once attended the lodges, now neglect them?" Many good men do forsake the lodges, not, however, because of other pressing calls, but because masonry does not satisfy them. There are many devout, praying, living Christians, ornaments to the cause, and lights in the world, who have utterly abandoned the pursuits of masonry, and on their death beds, have refused its funeral honors. Mr. B.* must have known this. Why has he passed it in silence?

If masonry possesses those excellences which masonic writers ascribe to it, why do not those men, when they forsake masonic lodges, forsake the church, the bible, and the cause of Christ? Why do they forsake masonry for Christianity? If they forsook Christianity too, the thing could be reconciled. But that they should still manifest a more devout attachment to it, and an increasing relish for its requirements, while they lose their relish for masonry—and view it as wanting the one thing needful—as possessing nothing which nourishes the piety of the heart, and as inconsistent with the Christian profession; are things altogether unaccountable on any other ground, than that masonry is not of God, nor what it pretends to be. This objection can never be raised against Christianity. It never has been said, and never can be said, in truth, that good men utterly forsake it for something else, and remain good men, and even better than they were before.

The man who forsakes Christianity, forsakes God, his duty, and the path to heaven, or any thing else which

* Mr. B., since the publication of his work, has renounced masonry.—Ed.

rendered them more useful in the world. For men to forsake masonry because they are disgusted with it, and find something more excellent in the Bible, is very different from what it is to forsake it because they are crowded with other important callings. The latter may sometimes be the case, the former is often the case; and is an open avowal of the emptiness of masonry, and of its utter insufficiency to satisfy a pious mind.

What support does masonry afford the people of God? They are favored with divine support, but whence is it derived? "I will pray the Father," said Jesus, "and he shall give you another comforter, that he may abide with you for ever, even the Spirit of truth." This Spirit is the only source of consolation to the afflicted people of God. Take this away and there is nothing to sustain them in the trials of life. Will any person say that this Spirit, the comforter of saints, belongs to masonry? What a poor system of religion is that which has in it no Holy Spirit! What is there here to encourage and support the children of the Saviour, as they pass through great tribulation to the kingdom?

Masonry may afford momentary consolation to a pharisee, or hypocrite, who builds his hope on his own righteousness; but the man who rests his hopes on the merits of Christ crucified, thirsts for something to sustain his heart, far superior to a comfortless system, in which there is no Holy Ghost. If there be something in masonry which God has designed as a peculiar support for his people, masons will be found guilty for locking it up as a secret. Why may not all classes, and both sexes, be admitted to it on God's terms, "without money and without price?" The fact is, there is nothing in masonry which a suffering or a dying man needs; he may endure afflictions, live to the glory of his Maker, and die in complete triumph, without the aid, and without the hopes of masonry.

When a man is called to die, it is the most awful, the most important period of his existence! Then he needs consolation; then he needs something to sustain his sinking spirit, and to scatter light on his dark path. What will become of a poor deluded creature, when called to die with no better hope than that which is inspired by a religion in which there is no sanctifying Spirit of God, and which expunges from it the very name of "our Lord Jesus Christ?" On what rock will he then stand? The splendid edifice he has long labored to rear, will fall upon his own head, and bury him beneath its ruins. I would say to such an one, unless you possess a righteousness far superior to that which is derived from masonry, you must be damned. You must be justified by the righteousness of "our Lord Jesus Christ," or perish in your sins. "Kiss the Son lest he be angry, and ye perish from the way when his wrath is kindled but a little. Blessed are all they who put their trust in him."

According to masonic writers, if masonry were universally known, it would destroy the institution. "Were the privileges of masonry to be indiscriminately bestowed, the design of the institution would be subverted." "Were these secrets communicated, they would be of no material service to mankind; their appropriate use is to distinguish our brethren of every nation, and kindred, and language." Are there no other secrets in masonry, than those particular *signs*, by which masons distinguish each other? What are the degrees and ceremonies in each? They are as profoundly secret to the world as those signs are. If these were communicated to the world, the institution would be subverted, and mankind would receive no benefit from them.

What does Mr. Town say of the degrees, especially of the sixth? "With these views the sixth degree is conferred, where the riches of divine grace are opened in boundless prospect." The manner in which the riches of divine grace are thus unfolded, is a secret to all but masons, as much as any particular *sign* is. Would it be of no particular service to mankind, were they permitted to draw near and behold the riches of divine grace opened before them in boundless prospect? Is this of any service to masons? Why not of equal service to others?

According to Mr. Bradley, the secrets of masonry are designed to prevent their bestowing charity on any but masons. "The importance of secrecy with us is such, that we may not be deceived in the dispensing of our charities, that we may not be betrayed in the tenderness of our benevolence, or that others usurp the portion which is prepared for those of our family." If a poor sufferer makes application to masons, tells them he is a mason and entitled to their charity, had he no token to give by which they should recognize him, they might be deceived and betrayed, and bestow their charity on one for whom it was not designed. This shows that masonry is a system of supreme selfishness, and its pretended benevolence the bare love of party.

FREEMASONRY A SYSTEM FRAUGHT WITH DECEPTION AND DETRIMENTAL TO HUMAN HAPPINESS.

Extract from Letters of Rev. Joshua Bradley, a Seceding Mason.

This will appear, without any veil to cover its enormity of crime, if you will condescend to examine critically the constitution, by-laws, amendments, resolutions, and transactions of the fraternity, since it was established in America. Let antecedent ages roll, burdened with all kinds of traditions, idolatry and superstition, from which speculative masonic writers and the devotees of the craft have picked here and there an atom, which being melted in their flaming imaginations, and brought forth among stonecutters; they have clothed it, and denominated this mere creature of fancy, Speculative Freemasonry. Under this name, many of the fraternity in Europe have conjured up more than 50 degrees, and conferred titles upon certain members, taken from all the crowned heads amidst the vast kingdom that have flourished around the globe since Japheth dwelt in the tents of Shem. Restless as the ocean and proud as Lucifer, they have multiplied degrees and flattered their brethren to obtain them. When they had taken three degrees they were greeted as having obtained great information in masonry, and were told that "the ancient landmarks of the order were intrusted to their care." They are now called ***Master Masons***. When individuals have passed the Arch, and obtained the knowledge of a certain mysterious hug, and have been intrusted how to open and close a chapter, they are pronounced wise, virtuous and highly favored among mortals. A few words of the charge given to a companion, will confirm my assertion and show the imposition of masonry, for it abounds in every degree:

"Worthy companion, you are now exalted to the sublime and honorable degree, of a Royal Arch mason. Having attained this degree, you have arrived at the summit and perfection of ancient masonry."

Is this true? Why then are the higher degrees called *ancient?* Why is the 14th degree called *Perfection?* I beseech you candidly to examine into the nature and existence of all their multiplied forms of deception, their obscure interpretations, charters, diplomas, dues, continuance of membership, dresses and implements, &c. &c., and seriously inquire what all these labors, consumption of time and property, have benefited millions who have been connected with the order in all its mutations and progress amid civilized nations? A few well organized churches of Christ have done more in instructing the ignorant, in comforting the sick, in feeding the hungry, in clothing the naked, and proclaiming glad tidings to mankind, than the whole hosts of masons have done around the globe, since the commencement of their existence.

Masonry in every country has been changing its positions, constitutions, obligations and lectures, and muffling itself in fine robes, smiling and courting certain virtuous characters to form an affinity with it, that others might think favorably of it, and in this way aid in opening wider its jaws to the innocent, and proclaim abroad that the great, the learned and the good were members of this "ancient and honorable fraternity of Free and Accepted Masons." Here permit me to say, without fear of contradiction, that those great and good men, of whom masons are continually boasting, never concerned themselves about its financial affairs and intriguing management. Those great men occasionally visited a Grand Lodge or a Grand Chapter, heard an oration on masonry, and then retired and left the transactions of the fraternity to others.—Why is this? Because these gentlemen have other avocations, more honorable to themselves and more important to their fellow men, than to spend their time or intermeddle any longer with the belittling system of masonry. These gentlemen in their younger years may have been masters of lodges, or high priests of chapters; but they are no more fascinated with the low, foolish and degraded work of bringing about of candidates, &c. &c. As many may be offended at my renouncing masonry, and my plainness in stating my conviction of its fallacy, I beg leave to say, that the whole system, so far as I can trace it back, is deceptive and its members who frequent lodges and chapters become discordant and contentious—for they find nothing in masonry to render them happy, and they see many things wrong and find many individuals with whom they cannot hold fellowship, or even walk in procession at the solemnities of a funeral.

At present I will only glance at the fraternity in America. Enough has taken place in our own country, if suitably laid before the public, that would make all men gaze with astonishment, who were not twice dead and buried beneath the lumber of traditions, gathered from the antediluvians and a thousand wayward transgressors of God's holy law.

The first Grand Lodge in America was formed in Boston in July, 1733, and received its charter from England. A war among these brothers in Boston and in England soon commenced, and a second Grand Lodge was formed in Boston in December, 1769, and received its charters from Scotland. Here contention reigned, and calumny blowed loud her trumpet through every street. In September, 1781, a Grand Lodge was formed in the city of New-York, having received its warrant from the Duke of Athol. Only six years after the date of their warrant, the masters and wardens of the several lodges met; having been duly notified, closed their lodge *sine die*, and then formed a Grand Lodge, independent of the Duke of Athol, and paid him no more tribute. Here all their former obligations were considered void and new ones formed to support the laws and the regulations of the Grand Lodge of the state of New-York. From those days till the present, animosities, fraud, evil speaking, conventions called, divisions made, and every kind of malevolence and even the murder of Morgan justified, and desperadoes supported from masonic funds to unite and publish defamation against the rulers of our nation and the ministers of Jesus, whose characters are fair among the churches, and their preaching attended by the influences of the Holy Spirit to the salvation of souls. Now, my brethren, if you do not believe me, read for yourselves. Find, if you can, one single chapter or verse in the sacred scriptures, where speculative masonry is mentioned, or supported. All those passages which have been published in their books, and their having the Bible open in their lodges, is a piece of deception, and was invented to obtain influence among the more serious parts of community, that not only the men of the world, but members of churches might be taken by the craft; the fountains of justice defiled, the temple of the living God filled with confusion, the pillars of government torn away, and " the whole wheel of nature set in a blaze."

Every mason who has taken ten degrees or more, can either recollect, or can turn to obligations published in part belonging to those degrees, and can easily discern, that those obligations have been formed by different men, at different times; and by men extremely ignorant of the obligations taken in the lower degrees and are wicked beyond the power of language to describe. In these obligations one destroys the other, and therefore it is very clear to me, that no set of men in any age, or country in one assembly at the same time ever formed these preposterous and ever varying obligations. And I know, and so do many in the fraternity, that these obligations are very much abridged in some States, and augmented in others, even in our own country. In New-England, where masonry has been in some degree systematized, a general accordance prevails in administering the obligations; but pass those States, and a scene of confusion, contradiction and discordant modes of work in lodges and chapters abound from the lakes of Canada to the gulf of Mexico. Yet all the candidates are told, through this vast range of country, that no more is imposed upon them, through all the humiliating conditions in which they are placed, than was imposed upon our ancient and honorable brethren who were made masons before us. Here deception reigns, and the candidate is taught to believe what he afterwards finds by travelling, or conversing with masons from other States and countries, a falsehood. If these assertions be not credited, let a Master Mason converse with a French Mason, or visit one of their lodges and see them work; or a Royal Arch Mason visit any city in Pennsylvania, Kentucky, Tennessee or Missouri, and hear the obligations and see their mode of work. I could here show the vast difference that exists, but I shall not at this time write on this point; though I do not value those obligations that I have taken of any efficacy to me, or that I ought to obey them; for I am fully convinced that all masonic authorities are without any reasonable foundation.

In my first, or this communication, I have not sought to argue upon the absurdity of secret societies; for this has been ably enough done by Anti-masons in many papers, and especially by the Elucidator of Utica, to convince any individual who is anxious to obtain satisfaction upon this subject. My design has been to state fairly, my connexions and conclusions about masonry. Far be it from me, to wish to kindle up any indignant feelings against an individual member of any Lodge, Chapter, Encampment or any body called Masonic; but to let the public know my present views of those systems; "for they are many," and invented at different periods, and for various purposes, and so blinded that it is not a very easy task to seize all their ramifications and hold them up to wither under the sunbeams of truth. Neither do I mean to cast any reflections upon those who conferred degrees upon me, nor charge myself with sins unpardonable, in being instrumental in deceiving many; for I was captivated with the same fascinating delusion, that those were who brought me to their altars, &c. &c. If I were now to ballot for candidates, and aid in conferring degrees, as I formerly did, my criminality would be great. In those labors I firmly believe I shall never engage. And can you, my brethren, who enjoy the humble and soul nourishing influences of the Spirit of Christ? Can those lifeless ceremonies and repetitions which we used in lodges and chapters afford you any real consolation? Are you still tenaciously fond of masonry, after all that has transpired, that has been said and written upon this subject? What can you expect to accomplish by continuing your membership? The alarm is given, investigation has commenced, and more than five millions have been roused from lethargy, who will not be persuaded to lie down and sleep, while about two thousand masonic halls enclose secret assemblies, (at least one per month,) who dare not utter their transactions to their most intimate companions and friends who belong not to the fraternity? Can you enjoy religion, and feel the sanctifying influences of grace, while you are daily contending for the existence of an institution that has received its death blow, and must inevitably expire? Perhaps you fear the consequences, and are unwilling to encounter the calumnies and falsehoods that masonic presses pour out in torrents upon all who dare leave the order? This you may expect, for none have escaped who were influential among them. Had I not been willing to have my name cast out as evil and to have all kinds of falsehoods published against me, and even expose myself to frowns, jests, and as much contemptuous treatment as these giants in infidelity can raise against me through all the ranks of their beardless militia, I would have held my peace.

But, my brethren, what have we professed and what are our obligations to God, his church, and the world of mankind? Is this vain world a friend to grace? We must pass through evil report and good report. It is through great tribulation that we enter the kingdom of heaven. Shall the righteous cower and forsake the cause of God in an evil day? Is it not said in the book of God, that they "look up and are as bold as a lion"? "Say ye to the righteous, that it shall be well with him." Read the 8th chapter of Romans, and then ask yourselves if you can fear the frowns, threats, and contempt of mortals? *A lying spirit is abroad, and speaks through all masonic presses*, and this spirit inflames all who hate the truth, and will make them wax worse and worse, till sudden destruction shall overwhelm these workers of iniquity, to the astonishment of every beholder. Then masonry will rise no more to trouble Zion, and spread delusion and death amid civilized nations.

THE TENDENCY OF FREEMASONRY TO INFIDELITY.

Extract from Thacher's Letters to a brother in the Church.

You inquire "what evidence I have, that masonry leads directly to infidelity?" and, if "it is pretended that masonry and the system of illuminism are mutually coupled together?" If you had said *systems* of illuminism, I think you would have given a more just representation of the subject. Illuminism, I conceive to be *one;* but its *systems* are *many.* Illuminism is a popular name for Infidel Philosophy, comprising all its doctrines, and shades of doctrine, from Deism, to Atheism and complete skepticism. The *systems* of this philosophy are exceedingly various, and so artfully either contrived or *adopted*, as to "deceive, if it were possible, the very elect." I speak of systems belonging to illuminism, as either contrived or *adopted;* because this infidel philosophy has indeed *contrived* some, and *adopted* others, already fitted for its reception. Of some of these systems you have given the names; as, the "Society of Carbonari" in Germany, the "United Irishmen," and the "Ribbon-men," in Ireland, &c. You justly observe, that "distinctions like these are of little consequence, where one grand object is in view." Yet, I think, you have fallen into a mistake, and confounded the *systems* of illuminism with illuminism itself. Illuminism, I grant, is the same, in every place, and in every country; whether it is called "Philosophy," "Reason," "Liberty and Equality," or "Infidelity." Its *systems*, however, are not only as various, but as *distinct* as its *names;* and exactly adapted to answer its own purposes, though suited to the different temperaments, manners and habits of different nations. By systems, I here mean, those different combinations and societies, organized and governed in very different ways, *professing* to promote entirely different objects; but whose grand and ultimate design *has always centred in infidelity.* Now, I ask, What system was adopted by the illuminees of France, in order to "crush the Wretch," and to accomplish their designs against religion and government? To trace all their plans, and develope all their schemes of wickedness, would require more time, talents and learning, than can be commanded by me, or perhaps by *you*. The following, however, are among some of the measures which they adopted: To hold secret correspondence, to circulate infidel tracts, control and corrupt the press, and to superintend the instruction of children and youth. Some of their bolder steps, were, to publish their Encyclopedia, seize upon the Royal Academy, and bring it entirely under their corrupting influence; and to instil the poison of infidelity into every primary and public seminary of learning. In addition to these measures, they sought, and even obtained, the keys of the public treasury; carried their intrigue into the court and council of the king, and contrived to fill the most important offices with their own adepts. Now, it could not be expected, that *such men*, capable of devising and pursuing *such measures*, would suffer such an institution as the masonic to escape either their notice or their influence. Accordingly we are assured, by Professor Robison,* the Abbe Barruel, and others, upon the best authority, that the three degrees of masonry were no sooner transplanted from England to France, than the institution was seized upon both by the Jesuits and the Illuminees. The first soon relinquished their hold, and then endeavored to crush the institution; the others held on, and moulded it into just such a shape as would best answer their designs. They contrived additional degrees; such as have since been adopted, and are now in use in the United States. They introduced new, and additional ornaments, in dress and jewelry, to please the *fancy*, and to excite the curiosity of "the profane." In short, they found, in Freemasonry, the very *engine*, which they had long desired; and it proved just such a system, as answered their highest and most sanguine expectations. It is true, they eventually formed distinct, and what have been called, "Illuminated Lodges;" but they still kept their hold upon the mother institution.

---

* John Robison, LL. D. Professor of Natural Philosophy in Edinburg University; member of the American Philosophical Society; and of the Royal Society at Manchester; and foreign member of the Imperial academy of Sciences at St. Petersburg.—Ed.

Here then, it appears, that the illuminees* did not "*personate*" Freemasonry, but *adopted* it, as a system already fitted to their hand, which they could mould and use at pleasure, to carry into execution their schemes of infidelity. This view of the subject corresponds precisely with Professor Robison's account of the institution, and the manner in which it was moulded and adapted to the designs of French infidelity. The Professor shows, satisfactorily, that Freemasonry originated in England ; that it existed there, only in the three first degrees ; and that it was not considered of any serious importance, but merely as a kind of diversion for young men, affording them opportunity to pass away a leisure hour, or to indulge themselves in occasional convivial intercourse.—That I have not mistaken the views of Dr. Robison, on this subject, I think will clearly appear in the following extracts :—" In my early life," says this learned and sagacious Professor, " I had taken some part in the occupations (shall I call them) of Freemasonry ; and having chiefly frequented the lodges on the continent, I had learned many doctrines, and seen many ceremonials, which had no place in *the simple Freemasonry which obtains in this country.*" [England.] " I had also remarked, that the whole was much more the object of reflection and thought than I could remember it to have been among my acquaintances at home. There I had seen a mason lodge *considered merely as a pretext for passing an hour or two in a sort of decent conviviality*, not altogether void of some rational occupation." [Introduction to Proofs of Conspiracy, p. 7.]

" I was importuned by persons of the first rank to pursue my masonic career through many degrees unknown in this country. But all the splendor and elegance I saw, could not conceal a frivolity in every part. *It appeared a baseless fabric.*" [Ibid, p. 8.]

Speaking of the attention with which he was treated, at a certain festival, where "the simple system" of English Freemasonry prevailed, he says, " I do not suppose

* The Illuminees, as individuals, were very numerous, long before the " ORDER OF ILLUMINATI," properly so called, had an existence.

that the Parisian Freemasonry of *forty-five degrees* could give me more entertainment." [Ibid, p. 10.]

Of the origin of this system of Freemasonry, the Professor remarks, " Some curiosity, however, remained, and some wish to trace this *plastic mystery* to the pit from which the clay had been dug, which had been moulded into so many shapes, 'some to honor, and some to dishonor.' " [Ibid, p. 10.]

"I was frequently sent back into England, *from whence all agreed that Freemasonry had been imported into Germany.* I was frequently led into France and into Italy. There, and more remarkably in France, I found that the lodges had been the haunts of many projectors and fanatics, both in science, in religion, and in politics, who had availed themselves of the secrecy and the freedom of speech maintained in these meetings, to broach their particular whims, or suspicious doctrines, which, if published to the world in the usual manner, would have exposed the authors to ridicule or to censure." [Ibid, pp. 11, 12.]

" In their hands, Freemasonry became a thing totally unlike to the system (if it may get such a name) *imported from England;* and some lodges had become schools of irreligion and licentiousness." [Ibid.]

" It [Freemasonry] seems indeed peculiarly suited to the talents and taste of that vain and ardent people [the French.] *Baseless* and *frivolous*, it admits of every form that Gallic refinement can invent, to recommend it to the young, the gay, the luxurious; that part of society which alone deserves their care, because in one way or another it leads all other classes of society." [Ibid, p. 13.]

" It has accordingly happened, that *the homely Freemasonry imported from England* has been *totally changed* in every country of Europe, either by the imposing ascendency of French brethren, who are to be found every where, ready to instruct the world; or by the importation of the doctrines, and ceremonies, and ornaments of the Parisian lodges. Even England, *the birth-place of masonry*, has experienced the French innovations; and all the repeated injunctions, admonitions, and reproofs of the old lodges, cannot prevent those in different parts of the kingdom from admitting the French novelties, full of tinsel and glitter, and high sounding titles." [Ibid.]

"The French innovations in Freemasonry were quickly followed in all parts of Europe, by the admission of similar discussions, although in direct opposition to a standing rule, and declaration made to every newly received Brother, 'that nothing touching the religion or government shall ever be spoken of in the lodge.' But the lodges in other countries followed the example of France, and have frequently become the rendezvous of innovators in religion and politics, and other disturbers of the public peace. In short, I have found that the covert of a masonic lodge had been employed in every country, for venting and propagating sentiments in religion and politics, that could not have circulated in public without exposing the author to great danger. I found that this impunity had gradually encouraged men of licentious principles to become more bold, and to teach doctrines subversive of all our notions of morality—of all our confidence in the moral government of the universe—of all our hopes of improvement in a future state of existence—and of all satisfaction and contentment with our present life, so long as we live in a state of subordination. I have been able to trace these attempts, made, *through a course of fifty years*, under the specious pretext of enlightening the world by the torch of philosophy, and of dispelling the clouds of civil and religious superstition, which keep the nations of Europe in darkness and slavery. I have observed these doctrines gradually diffusing and *mixing with all the different systems of Freemasonry;* till, at last, AN ASSOCIATION HAS BEEN FORMED* for the express purpose of ROOTING OUT ALL THE RELIGIOUS ESTABLISHMENTS, AND OVERTURNING ALL THE EXISTING GOVERNMENTS OF EUROPE." [Ibid, p. 14.]

"In short," says Professor Robison, "we may assert, with confidence, that the mason lodges in France were the hot-beds, where the seeds were sown, and tenderly reared, of all the pernicious doctrines which soon after choaked every moral and religious cultivation, and have made the Society worse than a waste, have made it a noisome marsh of human corruption, filled with every rank and poisonous weed." [Proofs of Conspiracy, p. 45.]

In allusion to Freemasonry having originated in Eng-

* "The ORDER OF ILLUMINATI."

land, and the manner in which it was received in other countries, he says, "Thus did the fraternity conduct themselves, and thus were they considered by the public, *when it was carried over from England to the continent;* and here it is to be particularly remarked, *that all our Brethren abroad profess to have received the Mystery of Freemasonry from Britain.* [Ibid, p. 26.]

Having spoken of the additional Degrees, contrived and attached by the French, to the three first, which originated in England, the Professor continues—"These facts and observations fully account for the zeal with which all this patch-work addition to the simple Freemasonry of England was prosecuted in France. It surprises us, Britons, who are accustomed to consider the whole as a matter of amusement for young men, who are glad of any pretext for indulging in conviviality." [Ibid, p. 37.]

Of the German lodges, he says, "All of them received their institution from England, and had patents from a mother lodge in London. All seem to have got the mystery through the same channel, the banished friends of the Stuart family."—"Freemasonry was then of the simplest form, *consisting of the three degrees of Apprentice, Fellow-craft, and Master.*" [Ibid, p. 54.]

Again, he says, that the French, who undertook to improve the Germans, declared "that the home-spun Freemasonry, which had been imported from England, was fit only for the unpolished minds of the British; but that in France it had grown into an elegant system, fit for the profession of gentlemen." [Ibid, p. 58.] The Germans, however, not being altogether so credulous as the French desired, stood in doubt of such innovations, and thought "that the safest thing for them was an appeal to the birth-place of masonry. They sent to London for instructions. There they learned, that nothing was acknowledged for genuine unsophisticated masonry *but three degrees;* and that the mother lodge of London alone could, by her instructions, prevent the most dangerous schisms and innovations." [Ibid, p. 59.]

In view of these copious extracts from Professor Robison, it is easy to see, that Great Britain was, indeed, "*the birth-place of Freemasonry;*" that it existed there *only in the three first degrees;* that it has been moulded into various shapes and systems; that it was exactly fitted for an engine of infidel philosophy, particularly as new modelled and ornamented by the French; and that it was used for the very purpose of fostering infidelity, for at least "*fifty years*" before the "Order of Illuminati" had an existence, and literally became the harbinger of this atheistical and revolutionizing association. It seems, therefore, that instead of this new system being disowned, and denied fellowship by the masons, and the lodges being "closed, as if to exclude the dangerous innovater;" the system of Freemasonry became the real mother of Illuminism, and the "Order of Illuminati" was the legitimate child of the Freemason's lodge. It does seem "that the mason lodges *were the hot-beds, where the seeds were sown and tenderly reared of all the pernicious doctrines which soon after choaked every moral or religious cultivation, and have made the society worse than a waste, have made it a noisome marsh of human corruption, filled with every rank and poisonous weed.*"

Such, is *some* of the evidence, that Freemasonry has led directly to infidelity in Europe; and I purpose now to show, that it has an equally dangerous tendency in this country.

We cannot suppose, that so large and fair a portion of the earth as America, should be entirely free from the machinations of infidelity; nor have we any reason to believe, that such an extensive and opulent society as the masonic fraternity have arisen to be in this country, would be overlooked by the eagle eyes of the Illuminati. There is no society on earth, in which infidelity can remain more effectually concealed, and more effectually carry on its secret operations. It is *convenient* for illuminism to have its own societies, *whose avowed object*, every one knows, is, to propagate *its own doctrines*. But, it is still *more convenient* to employ societies, *professedly* devoted to *other objects;* because, in these, it can more easily "conceal the hand that gives the blow." That societies of the first kind, which I have mentioned, exist in this country, there can be no reasonable doubt. The society of "United Irishmen," was formed in the United States, years ago. Beside this, there have existed lodges, in several sections of the country, which originated from the

5

"Grand Orient of Paris." We may doubtless add, "The Society of Odd Fellows."

Now, if French infidelity has gained such a footing, and been of so long standing, in this country; what evidence can we have, that our lodges, chapters and encampments are free from its influence? There are certainly *very many* leading masons, of high standing, in this country, who are Deists; and I have personally known several, who were not ashamed to avow their atheism. Besides, it is beyond all dispute, that *many* of the higher degrees of masonry, as practised in this country, were imported directly from France. Masons will not admit that these degrees were manufactured in this country; and they certainly did not originate in England. In 1730, there were but *three degrees* of masonry known, either in England or in America. In 1799, the British Parliament passed an act,* prohibiting any more than *three degrees* being given in that kingdom. English gentlemen, who took any higher degrees than the three first, received them on the continent. When, therefore, we consider, that the masonic institution, in this country, embraces from three to forty, forty five, or forty eight degrees, (some say more,) and that the most of these degrees were imported from infidel France; we cannot *reasonably* doubt for a moment, that illuminism exists, to a very great extent, in this institution, even in the United States. Accordingly, this fact was testified, on the best authority, years ago. "A letter from a man of the first respectability in New England, written in 1798, says, 'Illuminism exists in this country. And the impious mockery of the sacramental supper, as described by Mr. Robison, has been acted here.' The writer proceeds to state, that his informant, a respectable mason, and a principal officer of that brotherhood, declares, that among the higher orders of masons in this country, this piece of illuminism (the mockery of the holy supper) is at times practised." [See Smith on the Prophecies, 2d ed. p. 176.]

Since making the above extract, I have received a letter from the author of that celebrated dissertation, which, being a little more circumstantial, and giving cer-

* George III. 1799.

tain authorities which I do not find in the work, I here insert in full.

HANOVER, MASS. JUNE 29, 1829.

Rev. and Dear Sir,

Your letter is before me; and I return an answer by transmitting to you the following extracts from the second edition of my Dissertation on the Prophecies, published 15 years ago. "President Dwight, in 1798, wrote thus, 'Illuminism exists in this country; and the impious mockery of the sacrament, described by Robison, has been acted here.' Again: 'Under these circumstances, (says Dr. Dwight,) were founded the societies of Illuminism.* They of course spread with a rapidity which nothing but fact could have induced any sober mind to believe. Before the year 1786, they were established, in great numbers, through Germany, Sweden, Russia, Poland, Austria, Holland, France, Switzerland, Italy, England, Scotland, *and America*.—In all these places was taught the *grand sweeping principle of corruption*, that the goodness of the end sanctifies the means!' Dr. Dwight said, he received his information from a principal officer of the American masons.—A mason of high standing at the south, in a letter to Dr. Dwight, dated March 23, 1800, says, 'the lodge in Portsmouth, (Va.) to which you allude, called the French lodge, was considered, by me, as under the modern term of masonry (Illuminism.)' In another letter from the same to President Dwight, he says, 'That you had good reason to suspect the de-

---

* Mr. Smith quotes from a Fast Discourse of Dr. Dwight's, delivered in Yale College. The passage is as follows:

"The serpentine system of this order (Illuminism) Weishaupt perfectly understood. The great design of the Jesuits had always been to engross the power and influence of Europe, and to regulate all its important affairs. The system of measures, which they had adopted for this end, was superior to every preceding scheme of human policy. To this design Weishaupt, who was more absolutely an Atheist than Voltaire, and as cordially wished for the ruin of Christianity, superadded a general intention of destroying the moral character of man. The system of policy, adopted by the Jesuits, was, therefore, exactly fitted to his purpose: for the design, with this superaddition, was exactly the same.

"With these advantageous preparations, he boldly undertook this work of destruction; and laid the axe at the root of all moral principle, and the sense of all moral obligation, by establishing a few fundamental doctrines, which were amply sufficient for this purpose. These were, that God is nothing; that government is a curse, and authority an usurpation; that civil society is the only apostacy of man; that the possession of property is robbery; that chastity and natural affection are mere prejudices; and that adultery, assassination, poisoning, and other crimes of a similar nature are lawful, and even virtuous. A large branch of the *Masonic Societies* in Germany and France had already adopted the same objects, as the great and controlling ones of all their personal and united labors. Here secrecy furnished the most advantageous opportunities for the formation of every design, and the most advantageous contrivance for its successful execution. Here the spirit of hostility against religion and government was kindled, and blown up into a flame. Here, in a word, all that vice could wish, and profligacy attempt, was proposed, matured, and set forward for execution. Under these circumstances, were founded the societies of Illuminism."

signs of the French lodge, at Portsmouth, I have no reason, nor ever had, to doubt. Their work was to effect the plans of France in our country.'——A member of that lodge boasted that he belonged to a lodge in Europe, in which the French revolution was planned.——A gentleman of the first respectability informed me, (with leave to publish it, if I pleased,) that while he was *Grand Master* of all the lodges of the State, in which he lived, a bundle of papers from the Eastern Continent came, by a natural mistake, into his hands, in which were masonic language, and emblems, altogether above his comprehension. This was before he had heard of the existence of Illuminism. The packet by some means went out of his hands. After he heard of Illuminism, he said he was prepared to believe it, and that it was established in this country!'—In a printed oration, delivered before the grand royal arch chapter of New York, Feb. 2, A. L. 5801, by Rev. John Ernst, Grand Chaplain, are the following words:—'The deep designs of masons called the Illuminati, who have almost inundated Europe, and are *fast gaining ground in America*, have clearly demonstrated the abuse which untiled mason lodges have met with, and how they, when not guarded, can be revolutionized and moulded at pleasure!' An acquaintance of mine, a man of name, who with his wife were professors of religion, both informed me, that their son had occasion to reside some years in ———, the capital of a middle State. When he returned, they found, to their great grief, that he had become a *gross infidel.* He assured them, 'he had learned this wisdom in a society there, instituted from France, with a view to propagate the sentiments he had imbibed:—That such societies abounded in our land:—That soon gospel ministers would not be supported; and if they existed, the finger of scorn would be pointed at them:—That *the Christian religion was all an imposition, and would soon be abolished!*' A letter was intercepted from a lodge of Illuminees in Virginia, to another in New York, in which were emblems of carnage and death, and things unknown to the lower grades of masonry in our States.—The lodge Wisdom, in Portsmouth, (Va.) was the 2260th descendant from the Grand Orient of Paris. This great number were scattered in twelve different nations, of which America was one. Girtonner, in his Memoirs of the French Revolution, says, 'The active members of the Propagandists (propagators of French masonry) were, in 1791, fifty thousand, with funds then of six millions of dollars. These men were sent over the civilized world. And it was a maxim in their code, that 'it was better to defer attempts *fifty years,* than to fail of success by too great precipitancy!' Robespierre, in his contention with the Brissotine faction, declared, that revolutionary designs were the object of the diplomatic mission of Genet to this country. Genet's haste and impertinences to effect this design soon, by the wisdom of Washington, occasioned his recall. In an intercepted letter of his successor in this country, this object of French Illuminees, in this nation, was ascertained;—and that the insurrection in the west of Pennsylvania, (to suppress which cost our nation one million of dollars, and the raising of an army of 15,000 men, with Washington at their head,) was the fruit of the secret machinations of these French Illuminees! Washington himself was denounced by this horrid agency, and was declared to be an enemy to his country. And the people were called upon, when he left his presidential office, to keep a jubilee on the occasion. Washington, in a letter to a friend, spake of this abuse as being in '*such indecent terms as could scarcely be applied to a Nero, or to a notorious defaulter !*' In another letter he says, 'That the self-created societies that have spread themselves over this nation, have been laboring incessantly to sow the seeds of distrust, jealousy, and discontent, hoping thereby to effect some revolution in the government, is not unknown to you. That they have been the fomenters of the western insurrection, admits of no doubt.' He again says, 'It is doubtful still, whether that *party*, which has been a *curse* to this country, may not be able to continue their delusions!' No wonder, then, that this Father of his nation should, in his farewell address, warn his country to beware of all secret societies! Even Bonaparte boasted, 'We well know our strength in America; and let us do what we will, we can turn all the odium of it on those who favor not our designs.'"

These few extracts I transmit. You may make what use of them you please. I have long since given them to the public.

I am, dear sir, affectionately yours,

ETHAN SMITH.

Now, dear brother, in view of these facts, it is more than evident to my mind, that French Illuminism has been incorporated with American Freemasonry. It does appear, from unquestionable authority, that, as long ago as 1798, "the impious mockery of the sacramental supper had been acted here," in the "*higher degrees of Freemasonry.*" This fact accords precisely with Webb's account of the "Ineffable Degrees,"* in one of which the "Most Perfect" is represented as saying to the novitiate, "*Eat of this bread with me, and drink of the same cup.*" We have substantial evidence also, even from respectable masons, that *many* of the lower lodges had been moulded to suit the designs of French infidelity, nearly thirty years ago; and that this corruption was, at that time, "fast gaining ground in this country."

Can we, then, foster Freemasonry, even in the three lower degrees, without, either directly or indirectly, aiding the cause of infidelity? Even admitting, that the three lower degrees are as pure as you seem to imagine; still, they are the portal to the labyrinth of Illuminism. This is an avenue, which must be shut, or our country is undone. The lower degrees are, and have been, con-

* Freemason's Monitor, 1816. p. 276.

strued into every thing, and any thing, which was calculated to promote the designs of infidels; and these designing men have repeatedly "laughed in their sleeve," in view of the farcical ceremonies of the third degree, as cunningly devised, and directly calculated to bring the scriptures into disrepute, and cast contempt upon the death and resurrection of Jesus Christ. Even on the supposition, therefore, that *you* and *I* may not have considered these pernicious doctrines as "taught in the lodge-room;" yet the work is so constructed, that others may, and *do*, construe it into whatever they please. I must confess also, that though I did, for a time, argue with myself, as you do, on this subject; and although I endeavored to persuade myself into the settled conviction, that this was pure morality; yet, after all, when I witnessed the various ceremonies of the several degrees, my conscience has secretly whispered, 'this is no place for a Christian, and especially for a Christian minister.' These secret whispers, and a scrutinizing observation of the effect, which those ceremonies have upon the fraternity, have led me more critically to examine the subject; which examination has led me to the present result. Reflecting upon the snare, from which I have escaped, I would not be placed back, where I was six months ago, for all the honors and treasures of earth. I have, dear brother, repeatedly seen the smile of mirth playing in the countenance of many a mason, during even, what are called, the most sublime and solemn parts of the work. In reflecting upon past years, also, and the several revivals of religion, which I have had opportunity to witness, I can now recollect but *very few*, comparatively, who have become hopefully pious, *after* joining the masonic institution. I understand that the same observation has been made by a clergyman,* who has doubtless had more experience in revivals of religion, than any man now living in our own country. Among professors of religion, too, I think the observation will hold good, that the lodge-going brethren are not *generally* among the most engaged and active members of the church. I do not say this, by any means, to make invidious comparisons; and I am willing

* Rev. Mr. Nettleton.

to admit that there *are* exceptions. But I have never known a church member, who gave decisive evidence of piety, who would not spontaneously abandon the lodge, during a revival of religion. Neither have I ever known a professor of religion, however apparently engaged before, but what, in one way or another, gave decisive evidence of religious declension, immediately after joining the masonic institution. I can also recollect of several instances, in which young men had appeared very seriously concerned for the soul and the things of eternity; but who, on being initiated into the mysteries of masonry, immediately banished all serious impressions, and, from that day forward, appeared perfectly careless and secure. I am also constrained to think, that no professor of religion ever found himself improved in moral feeling, in consequence of attending a communication of the lodge; or that he scarcely ever went away, in consequence, with one *profitable* serious reflection, unless with this, that he had worse than thrown away his precious time, and would better stay away in future. Permit me, also, to ask you, dear brother, (and I wish to do it most tenderly and affectionately,) if you have felt in your heart, generally, that glow of religious warmth, *since*, as *before* you became a member of the masonic institution? Have you been as much disposed to attend religious meetings *since*, as before; or to take a part in those religious meetings, as you frequently did, four or five years ago? Permit me again to ask, if you feel like going from your closet to the lodge, or from the lodge to your closet? Or, if you do, is it with that freedom and holy fervor, which you believe you have felt in years past? These are plain and significant questions; and I doubt not you will answer them to yourself, in the fear of God, and with a reference to the judgment day.

You add, "I am told that Royal Arch masonry has much to do with a Saviour, while he is only darkly prefigured in the three first." Here, I am sure, you are laboring under a sad mistake. I wish to know wherein the Saviour is even darkly prefigured, in any part of the three first degrees. Is it in the mock representation of death and the resurrection? It must be here, if any where; but, for my own part, I should as soon and as seriously think of looking for the Saviour in one of Shakespear's tragedies. It cannot be. This ceremony is so contrived, that it may be construed to please the Christian, Jew, Deist, Mahomedan, and Pagan idolater.—Would these last think of looking for the Saviour here? I have been informed, that a Jew was, for a considerable time, Grand Master of the Grand Lodge of Rhode Island. This same Jew, if I mistake not, was actively engaged in forming the General Grand Chapter of the United States. Now, would this Jew, do you imagine, consider Royal Arch masonry as having much to do with the Saviour; or that Jesus of Nazareth was even "darkly prefigured" in the third degree? But, supposing your idea to be correct; what is the need of having the Saviour "darkly prefigured," when "the true light" respecting him, has now shone for more than eighteen hundred years? Is there any need of going into the lodge-room to *observe* what God, in his word and providence, has made so plain? I deny, however, that Royal Arch masonry has *any thing* to do with the Saviour, except to degrade and rob him of his glory; and this would please the Jew, as well as the Deist. In the Mark Master's degree, those passages of scripture,* which, in the Bible are applied exclusively to Christ, as the chief corner stone of his church, masons apply exclusively to a *literal stone*, which in this degree, is "rejected by the builders" and thrown away among "the rubbish;" but in the Most Excellent Master's degree, is found again, and becomes the key of the arch, or "*the head of the corner.*" Now what does this mean? Is it to exalt or to degrade, the Son of God? Who shall tell us—the Jew, or the Deist? Let the

---

* The passages of scripture here cited, are the following:—Ps. cxviii. 22. The stone which the builders refused, is become the head-stone of the corner.

Matth. xxi. 42.—Did ye never read in the scriptures, The stone which the builders rejected, is become the head of the corner?

Mark xii. 10.—And have ye not read this scripture, The stone which the builders rejected, is become the head of the corner?

Luke xx. 17.—What is this, then, that is written, The stone which the builders rejected, is become the head of the corner?

Acts iv. 11.—This is the stone which was set at nought of you builders, which is become the head of the corner.—[See Webb's Monitor, 1816, p. 78.]

Christian speak, and his soul must recoil within him! He will say, if he says the truth, "This is, indeed, my God and my Saviour, degraded to a *literal stone*, mocked, and cast away, despised and rejected of men!!" "O my soul, come thou no more within their secrets; unto their assembly, mine honor, be not thou united!" In the Royal Arch degree, the name of the Saviour is not mentioned; but the titles and attributes of the great and terrible GOD, are used with the most shocking familiarity; and JEHOVAH is literally *personified*, while the passage relating to the "*burning bush*" is cited in full.* In the "Order of High Priest," which properly belongs to Royal Arch masonry, Christ is again robbed of his honor; and passages which apply to him, and to no other being in the universe, are addressed to a mortal worm of the dust. What is said of Melchisedec, in the New Testament, as representing the eternal Priesthood of the Saviour, mason's address to the High Priest of a Royal Arch Chapter!† This degree was doubtless contrived by Weishaupt, a most subtle adept, and was intended and calculated to deceive, "if it were possible, the very elect." Of this, however, I shall say more hereafter.—In like manner, are the agonies of Christ in the garden turned into mockery, in the order of Knights Templars. Here, the "*bitter cup*"‡ is prepared for the candidate to drink, when he receives his obligation. Here is represented "the place of a skull," literally indeed, because the skull is the cup from which the novitiate receives his libation. In allusion to the bitter cup, the scene of Christ's agony in the garden is *rehearsed*,§ (does not your soul recoil?) particularly that passage, in which he repeatedly and earnestly prays, "O my Father, if it be possible, let *this* cup pass from me."—"Father, if *this cup* may not pass from me, except I drink it, thy will be done."!!! In allusion to the skull, it is read,§ "And when they were come unto a place called Golgotha, that is to say, *a place of a* SKULL, *they gave him vinegar to drink*, MINGLED WITH GALL: and when he had tasted thereof, he would

* Freemason's Monitor, 1816, p. 136.
† Freemason's Monitor, p. 153.
‡ Town's Speculative Freemasonry.
§ See Webb's Monitor, 1816, p. 232.

not drink."!!! Now, is it difficult here to see the haggard features of Illuminism? Professor Robison, who had every facility to learn, declares,* that this degree was formed in an illuminated lodge at Lyons, which, at that time, "stood at the head of French Freemasonry." It seems also, from other authentic accounts, which I have seen of the history of this order, that those who contrived it, to render the deception complete, seized, as a kind of model, the chivalry of the dark ages, and pretended to trace the degree back, as Webb does, to the eleventh century.† We may, then, consider it as established beyond a reasonable doubt, that the "Order of Knights Templars" is the legitimate offspring of French illuminism.

ON THE OATHS AND OBLIGATIONS OF MASONRY.

An abridgment of Rev. Mr. Jones's Letters.

It is my intention in the present letter, to notice some things in the OATHS or OBLIGATIONS of masonry, which are *objectionable*, and, in my opinion, *destroying their binding nature*, as to *perpetual secrecy*. Before I proceed, however, it may be suitable to remark, it is my purpose not to introduce any thing as belonging to these obligations, except what was actually taught me as such while a regular member of the institution. If any individual shall question my *ability* to present the *very form* so far as I may need to do it, I would observe, for the satisfaction of such, that I should hold myself in readiness, if required, to submit the question to disinterested judges, and to abide their decision. It was not my intention, and I should not have thought it expedient now to *publish* any part of these Oaths, in the precise *words* in which they were taught to me, were it not for the fact,

* Proofs of Conspiracy, p. 44.

† See Webb's "Observations on the Orders of Knights Templars, and Knights of Malta."—Freemason's Monitor, 1816, p. 220.

which has very much surprised me of late; that many of the fraternity, as I am credibly informed, are positively denying the substantial correctness of them, as they stand in Morgan's Illustrations, thereby, as it must be considered, implicating me with the gross charge of falsehood.

The first thing to be noticed as objectionable in these obligations, is the extraordinary *mock solemnity*, *profanity*, *&c.* of their *introduction*, viz.: "*I, A. B. of my own free will and accord, in presence of Almighty God, and this Right Worshipful Lodge, erected to God and dedicated to the Order of the holy St. John; do hereby, and hereon, most solemnly and sincerely promise and swear.*" All three of the first obligations, have precisely this introduction, according to my earliest instructions; and what, let me ask, is there in them, or in the other parts of masonry, which can demand, or justify this pretended, solemn formality? As I know of no necessity for this, nor any thing which can be reasonably urged in its justification, I have no hesitation in declaring my opinion fully, that it is an absolute violation of the third Commandment, in twice taking the name of the Lord in vain; and what an unqualified violation it is, also, of the injunction of holy writ, to "*swear not at all.*" And what can it be, but a most daring insult, in the face of the Most High, for a body of men, who, with but very few if any exceptions, generally, are not those, who fear God and work righteousness, to set themselves up, as it were, by his side, clothed with such extraordinary, self-created, self-exalted titles; and what is it but an impious mockery of God, to declare such lodges, in his awful presence, *Erected to God, and dedicated to the order of the holy St. John?*" Sure, if these lodges, generally, have been erected to any god, and are acknowledged by him, as such, it must have been to some other than the God of heâven. I wish to be understood, as speaking exclusively of the *wickedness* of these *oaths*, in distinction from the character of those who may be still unconsciously giving their sanction to such wickedness.

Another clause which I shall notice at this time, is the same in substance in both the second and third degrees as follows: "*I furthermore promise and swear, that I will answer and obey, all due signs and summons, given, sent, handed, or thrown to me, by the hand of a true and lawful brother fellow craft, (or master mason,) or from the body of a legally constituted lodge of fellow crafts, (or master masons,) so far as in me lies, if within the length of my cable tow."* It is certainly difficult to find a *happy* construction of this clause, and I very much doubt, whether it has been understood by masons themselves, generally. Were it not for its peculiar phraseology, it might be understood to mean, that a person who takes this obligation upon him, is to answer all *signs*, made to him personally, by a brother of the same degree, by making corresponding masonic signs in return, so as to inspire a masonic confidence in each other; and further that such a person should obey all *summons or citations* from the lodge to attend its meetings; but as no distinction is made here, between the prerogative of a lodge and a private brother, to *make* such signs or summonses; it seems, that each one is bound to yield implicit obedience, in case of the signs and summons of an *individual brother;* as well as in case of the calls of the lodge, in all cases without qualification, when possible, unless he should be called on to travel further than the length of his cable tow; the length of which imaginary line, I believe, is not uniformly considered alike among masons; though it has been called three, four or five miles. It seems impossible to understand these "signs and summons," as signs of *distress* and calls for charitable *assistance*, because a *whole lodge*, as in this case could not be supposed to call on an *individual member* for such assistance. If we may be allowed to construe this clause of giving, answering, and obeying "signs and summons," as would seem most rational and easy from its expression; it binds a mason to be ready, on the shortest notice, to leave his business and go, at the sign of a lodge, private brother, to assist in doing any thing which they might declare necessary to be done, for the welfare and safety of the masonic institution, or its members, as such, should evil be cloaked in the design.

This suggestion, which is the only rational interpretation of the clause which I am able to obtain, I acknowledge, might not have entered my mind, had it not been, that there was such a full, and complete illustration of it, in the circumstances attending the kidnapping and unquestionable murder of Morgan, by the Freemasons two years ago, and in the masonic outrages which were committed with a view to destroy the disclosures of his, which are now before the world in the three first degrees of masonry.—Though the fraternity generally, may be yet far from adopting this opinion, I do consider myself fully authorized in the belief, that the original spirit and design of this clause, was to warrant such proceedings as those in the Morgan affair, when the life and honor of the institution should seem to be thus in jeopardy.

The next clause which claims attention, is as follows, in the oath of the third degree: "*I furthermore promise and swear, that I will keep a brother's secrets, and all others committed to me as such,* MURDER AND TREASON ONLY EXCEPTED, *and those at my own discretion,*" election, or choice. Before proceeding to state my particular objections to this clause, I would just remark, that I have no doubt, that, as it was taught me, it contains an important mistake, as it seems to level down the privileges of masons with those of other men, in reference to the safety of their secrets with their brethren, and it is presumed that these words, "*and all others,*" in the clause were added by some conscientious masonic lecturer, who, at the time, thought it a necessary and happy amendment, though usually, it is most probable, they have not been admitted into the clause.

One objection to this clause is, that, if there were any validity in such oath, it obliges masons in some particular cases to become accomplices with a brother in his gross violations of the laws of God and man, by concealing his guilt, and thus screening him from the demands of public justice. If a mason of the third degree shall be guilty of counterfeiting, theft, forgery, or highway robbery, for which he shall be about to be brought to justice, if he can find a brother mason, who has taken this obligation, and is able to afford him protection, provided he can be intrusted with all the secret circumstances in the case; then, according to his oath, he is perfectly safe, to go and relate to him the whole matter concerning his crime, to be kept as his secrets, at all events, since they are not the secrets of his *murder* nor *treason*, which he is here not bound to keep, except when he may prefer keeping them also.

Another objection to this clause, is, that it must sometimes expose those who take it, to the necessity of swearing falsely, without any possible way of escape. For instance, in such a case as has already been supposed, where one party is entirely innocent of the secret crime; or, in such a case as that of the Morgan affair, where several may have been combined in the same dark and evil designs, all of which was previously committed to each other, as the secrets of a master mason: Now, if a part of these shall be detected, or shall recant from any further share in such iniquity, and shall be duly summoned as witnesses, and sworn to tell the whole truth in the case, against the others, they cannot proceed to do it, without violating their masonic obligation; then to be silent, or keep sacred such an oath, there is no possible alternative, but to violate their judicial oath, and thus betray their country; and those who have read the testimony under oath, of masonic witnesses, who had been engaged in the conspiracy against Morgan, have seen the dilemma of masons, thus situated, and where there seemed to be the most unequivocal presumption, that they considered it a less evil to violate their judicial, rather than their masonic oath, when one only could be kept sacred.

But will some reply to these objections, that there is no such meaning in the clause, and it was never expected, from it, that a brother would be bound to keep wickedness a secret, when the public good requires it to be exposed? Then, what means this particular exception of only two crimes, and these not excepted unless it be the choice of the persons thus bound? Were it not for this particular exception of MURDER AND TREASON, only, it might have been rational, according to the common usage of language, to draw this inference from it that the secrets of masons should be most sacredly kept, in all lawful cases, only; but as the clause now stands, it is impossible to draw from it so favorable an inference, without a gross perversion of language. Will it be said, again, that the interpretation of this oath is always given to the candidate before he receives it, so far as the assurance that it contains nothing which is repugnant to his duty, either to his country or his God, and therefore, it cannot mean to bind any one to keep secret, the crimes of wicked masons? It is not pretended, but all well meaning masons have so received and considered it: but, let it be remembered, that the oath, itself, and the mistaken interpretation of it by the master of the lodge, are no more necessarily connected together, than the Bible is, with the false interpretations which are many times given it.

Again, it might be said, that the Bible itself, in the principles of masonry, is said to be the "rule and guide" of the faith and practice of every mason, therefore, all the other parts of masonic principles, must be interpreted according to the principles of that sacred volume. This is certainly plausible, were we to admit the antiquity and divine origin of the institution, which have been confidently and boastingly pretended by many. But let it be remembered, that masonry was never founded on the word of God; since it is so abundantly evident that, in a gospel land, the Bible has rather been profanely taken and placed upon masonry, as a cloak of hypocrisy, which alone could sustain the institution, in such a land as this; while the Koran, only, in a Mahometan land, could answer the same purpose. Thus it may be seen, that the Bible, and the oaths of masonry, have no connexion with each other, and the latter are not, necessarily, explained by the former. What impartial observer then, cannot see the wickedness of such a clause, in the masonic oaths, however innocently they may be explained, and however innocent the intention of masons most generally, as I cheerfully grant, in their unsuspectingly taking upon themselves, so wicked an obligation.

The next clause which remains to be examined in the obligations of masonry belongs to that of the third degree, and though it binds a master mason to be *chaste* in his outward conduct, in *some* cases which are there specified, it seems, by an irresistible inference, to allow *unchastity* in all other cases, *not* particularly specified. I shall be excused from repeating this clause in the language in which I learnt it, though I would say, there is scarcely the least difference in the phraseology of it, from the manner in which Morgan has expressed it in his disclosures. The substance of this clause is simply this; it binds those who take it, *to keep the seventh commandment inviolate,* so far as may relate to the female department of a *brother master mason's family;* provided however, they shall *know,* at the time, that such females do belong to such a family; or sustain such a relation, to a master mason.

It is true, that the clause does not *enjoin* a violation of the seventh commandment in other cases not specified, but certainly it contains the *allowance* of it, or else there is no meaning in the obligated *restriction* of chastity to a few specified cases. What else can we infer from this *limiting* of a master mason's chastity, to a few particular cases, but that his masonic obligation is designed to leave him the fullest liberty to trample on the seventh commandment in any *other* case, which it might be desirable? And even if he shall set at nought this commandment, in any of the cases where he is required to *keep* it in the obligation, when he is not aware, that his unchastity or lewdness is thus connected with a master mason's family, his obligation in that respect is not to be considered violated. It may give us a more clear and definite view of what is enjoined, and what is allowed in the clause here examined, if we bring forward some of the other commandments, under the same restrictions and indulgences as parallel cases. How would obligations like the following appear, if imposed upon members of the fraternity—that they will not take the name of the Lord in vain, in presence of any of a *brother* master mason's family, "knowing them to be such," or will not murder one of *them,* nor steal from *them,* nor bear false witness against *them,* &c., "knowing them to be such?" What masons of moral principles, let me ask, could endure with obligations like these, which contain the allowance of a violation of the several commandments named? And yet, they are precisely like the one which I have been reprobating, as still held in the fellowship of the lodges.

Another objection to the masonic obligations, is, that they are frequently given to bind men to the performance of things, of which, at the time, they are left in profound ignorance. It has been no uncommon thing with the unskilful master of the lodge, not being able to repeat the whole of the oath, when called to administer it to the candidate, to make up his deficiency with a concluding and all comprehending clause, prepared for such an emergency, to this amount; that if any part of such oath has been omitted in the administration, the candidate must swear that he will hold himself bound by it, as soon as he may be informed what it is. Thus, if nine tenths of it are omitted, he must swear to be bound by the whole, as soon as he may hear it. Can such a manner of administering and receiving oaths be justified? Is it not literally, if I might use the phrase, a swearing at random? If such be not a profane trifling with the solemnity of oaths, it seems difficult to conceive, what would be called profanity.

The next and last part of the obligations, which I think of noticing at present, is the *penalties* which are attached to their violation. Though I recollect that the penalty of the oath of the Royal Arch degree, is such as to forfeit life, by having the upper part of the skull struck off, I shall confine myself to those of the first three degrees, because these are most familiar to me, and sufficient for my purpose. The first penalty is, having the "*throat cut from ear to ear*," the "*tongue torn out by the roots*," &c. The second, having the "*left breast torn open*," the "*heart taken from thence and thrown over*," the "*left shoulder, to become a prey to the beasts of the field, or the vultures of the air*;" and the third, I will write out in full, as it was taught me, viz. "*All this, I most solemnly and sincerely promise and swear, with a fixed and steady resolution to keep and perform the same, without any equivocation, mental reservation, or self evasion of mind in me whatever; binding myself under the no less penalty, than having my body severed in twain, my bowels torn from thence, and burnt to ashes, those ashes scattered to the four winds of heaven; my body severed in quarters, those quarters placed on the four cardinal points of the compass, with my head in the centre, never again to be reunited until the general resurrection or the judgment.*"

Passing by the gross and heathenish abominations which are so abundant here: I shall attend in this discussion, to but one particular point, which is this: *these penalties are at variance with the sixth commandment of the decalogue, "Thou shalt not kill."* None will presume to say, that either of those penalties could be inflicted, without its producing instant death. So the candidate is made to pledge to the lodge, or institution of Freemasonry, as a surety, that he will safely keep its secrets, *not* his money, nor his sacred honor; but his very *life;* as though that was his own property, and he had an undisputed right to give it into the hands of assassins when he pleased. This would be no less than suicide, or a positive violation of the sixth commandment. Certainly, a man has no more right to forfeit his *own* life, as a penalty for the violation of his oath, than that of his wife, child or friend. Then is it not great wickedness to do it, in violation of a plain command of God, as it is done in each of the penalties which have been mentioned?

Should it be said, that in these penalties, it is only meant that the candidate should express his strong determination not to suffer the secrets of masonry to be *extorted* from him, even should ruffians put him to death in any form whatever, it might be answered that the expression of these penalties, *disproves* such an explanation; for the penalty of death, we see, is not attached to that clause of keeping the secrets *only*, but to *every* clause, thus, "*All* this, I most solemnly," &c. "binding myself under the no less penalty," &c. so that it cannot mean, that the penalty is only to be suffered from ruffians, when the secrets would otherwise be extorted.

Although these penalties have so long been explained as not allowing the craft to execute them, thereby murdering the mason who may knowingly and purposely violate the obligation; and though it has been so common for masons to believe, that no such wickedness was intended, or thought of, in the origin of these penalties, it must certainly be doing violence to our language, so to understand them, from the words in which they are expressed. It has been said, that masonry knows of "no penalties worse than expulsion." Then let me ask, why are these horrid *things*, in every obligation, *called* penalties? Are they to be understood as a mere, solemn, unmeaning exclamation, showing the strong determination of the candidate to keep the obligation, like the profane and thoughtless character, who sometimes says, he will *die*, if his assertion be not true, or if he shall not fulfil his word? Considering that the candidate at the time of taking this oath and penalty upon him, is on his knees;

and also he is caused to say, "in the presence of Almighty God, and that" "Right Worshipful Lodge," it will not be supposed, that the language of these penalties was meant to be trifled with in such a manner.—If these awful penalties *have* any meaning, what can they mean less than death; to be inflicted on the candidate, in case of a violation of his oath, in the very shape there represented? Certainly, nothing less than this, for so it is expressly declared, "Under the *no less* penalty than having my body severed in twain," &c. And who then are the persons authorized to inflict those penalties but masons, themselves, who are the only persons aggrieved or injured by such violations? And if these penalties are not to be so understood, what must we think of the recent declaration of masons in a multitude of instances; that if Morgan *was* murdered by the fraternity, as it is generally allowed that he was, he was treated just as he should have been; and if still living, he *ought* to be disposed of in such a manner? And further, if these penalties were never intended to authorize the craft to inflict any punishment on offenders worse than expulsion; how is it to be explained to us, that a great number of masons should be engaged in the outrages against Morgan and Miller, and though several of them have since been convicted of their crime in the affair, and punished by the civil authority, and others have absconded to evade such punishment, while masonry, or all the lodges connected with those masons, stand mute, or look upon those enormities with approbation?

If these penalties do *not* forfeit the life into the hands of the fraternity, and of course, masonry has no laws, which authorize kidnapping and murder of its offenders, why were not *all* those masons who were engaged in the conspiracy and mob of forcibly seizing and carrying off a free citizen to be murdered, as none can consistently deny, expelled from the lodges to which they respectively belonged? Instead of this, not one of them, it appears, has violated the laws of masonry in that matter, so far as to procure his expulsion. Does not this declare, in language too plain to be misunderstood, that such is *not* unmasonic conduct? Does it not seem to say to us, that an offender like Morgan, according to the laws of masonry, has *forfeited* his person and *life*, to be at the disposal of the brotherhood, so that such individuals have only acted in behalf of the fraternity, and of course, are not to be called to account for so doing? And does not this prove, that masonry, so far *does* consider these penalties to mean precisely what they express? And that they forfeit life, in violation of the sixth commandment? To show more particularly that these oaths are not binding, will be my next object.

This is a point which I have endeavored to keep prominently in view from the beginning, and if not deceived, all the arguments which have been adduced, are calculated, more or less, to establish the position: But now, I have arrived at a place in the discussion, where it seems to come in course, to take up this point by itself, and bring forward arguments, with particular design to show that *these oaths are, in no sense binding upon masons;* although it is admitted that there are some things in them, which according to the gospel all men are under obligation to observe and do; still, no one is to be considered under any greater obligation for the same by reason of these masonic oaths.

First, I would say, that these oaths are not binding, and masonry ought not to be kept a secret, because of the wickedness which is inculcated in its principles, and because of their dangerous and destructive tendency with regard to human happiness. My *premises* here will doubtless be sharply contested by some; but I appeal to the candid and disinterested, who have carefully perused my former numbers, to decide, whether I have not already brought forward facts and arguments, abundantly sufficient to establish my position on a basis which cannot be removed. Then taking it for granted that masonry is an engine of evil, and calculated to diminish the sum of human happiness for time and eternity, and of course greatly to displease and dishonor God, what can be plainer than this, that every mason is at liberty to disclaim all further allegiance to these oaths and this institution? And is it not his duty, at such a time as the present, to investigate the subject faithfully and impartially, if he has not done it before, and as soon as he may obtain a just and clear view of the principles of this institution, to come out and separate himself from her abominations, and bear testimony against them, to counteract, if possible, the unhappy influence of his sanctioning and upholding them heretofore? Still, some may be ready to say, though they are convinced of the evils of masonry, they see no way to break away from them, and condemn them before the world, without becoming guilty of perjury. As it might be expected, under existing circumstances, there will be some to contend, that these oaths are so sacred that no man can possibly disengage himself from them, without the grossest perjury, as though they were in fact, paramount to his obligation to his country and his God; yet why should the conscientious any longer be guided by this sentiment? Surely, the pretended antiquity of masonry, nor the number and respectability of those who tenaciously adhere to it, nor their unwillingness to have its merits or demerits tried at the bar of public opinion, can be any reason why human happiness should be diminished and God dishonored, for the sake of keeping sacred such wicked and abominable oaths. No reflecting person can imagine, that Herod, in murdering a distinguished man of God, was more approved in the sight of Heaven for the deed, though it was done to keep sacred his rash oath, than had he repented of his heedless profanity, and set the good man at liberty.

It is believed to be universally agreed among the thinking part of community, that all other similar obligations to that of Herod, found in the scripture and elsewhere, should not be considered binding, until we come to those of the masonic institution, where many are ready to make exceptions. It will probably be said by some, that the oaths of masonry are in no degree, parallel to the oath of Herod; to which I would reply, by again appealing to the candid and disinterested, to decide, if I have not sufficiently shown, that they are parallel; by showing that they are rashly taken before their contents are known, and that like Herod's oath, they require men, in some particulars, to do evil.

Some may be ready to inquire and say: but why may we not *silently withdraw* our connexion from the institution, without coming out in hostile array against it, by bearing testimony to the world against its internal abominations, since there is at present, so much in the influence of the institution, which renders such a course, most terribly forbidding? I answer, because in this way, you would continue to show favor to the institution, and in a great degree, would still be a partaker of its abominations. You could not discover our country to be in danger from any unsuspected source, though your own person and property might be considered safe, without giving the alarm, and using your influence for the safety of others.

Another argument which shows that these oaths are not to be considered sacred and binding, is, that *they are unlawfully administered and taken, both as they relate to laws human and divine.* Although oaths, as a general thing, are most solemnly prohibited by the word of God, it is believed, that there are some exceptions made, where they are to be considered necessary and lawful; but the lawfulness or expediency of such a common multiplicity of them, as we have sometimes witnessed in civil affairs, is to me more than doubtful. And I am confident, that the scripture, in its solemn prohibitions, makes no provision for the oaths of masonry, and more especially so, since the proof is so abundant, that they are needed and used there merely as a canopy of impenetrable darkness to the secret abominations of that institution. By what authority then, shall the master of a lodge, in that capacity only, presume to administer these oaths? and how can an individual receive them from him, without a violation of the divine command?

Shall it be said, that such oaths have so long been locked up in secrecy, and out of the way of the world, that they have not come in contact with the civil authority, and of course, are not to be judged, nor condemned by human laws? It is true that they have long been shrouded in thick darkness, as to a view of the world; yet no darkness could hide them from the view of Him who searches the hearts and tries the reins of the children of men; and now the lock is broken, they may come in contact with human laws, and their being so long hidden from the world, instead of making them more tolerable, only shows them to be so much the more among the unfruitful works of darkness, for which the people of God are commanded to have no fellowship. Men may promise, and make oath to their promise, to perform some lawful things, and their *promise*, if lawfully made, would lay them under a corresponding obligation to fulfil; but an unlawful oath, annexed to it, would add to it no further obligation; and certainly so far as they may promise with an oath to do things contrary to the will of God, as in case of the masonic obligations, instead of keeping and fulfilling them, they seem to be called upon by divine authority, to withdraw from them and disown them. Seeing then, that these oaths are not administered or received lawfully, but in direct violation of the divine law, I ask, where is the sanction of God upon them, which alone can give them the lawful validity of an oath? Certainly such sanction is not to be found, but the contrary is clear. These unlawful oaths then, do not, nor cannot, impose the least obligation upon those who may take them.

It is now further to be shown, that the oaths of masonry are not to be considered binding upon its members, because *the condition on which they are taken is not ascertained to be found in truth.* So far as I have been able to learn, in all lodges, it has been the undeviating practice of the Master, or presiding officer, when about to administer these oaths, in behalf of the institution, to inform the candidate who is required to take them, in substance as follows: that they "contain nothing contrary to his allegiance to his country, or to his God." And sure, it is now too late for any to say, who have attended candidly to this discussion, that such oaths are free from every thing which is contrary to the religion of the Bible, when it has been shown so abundantly, that they do contain much that is of an evil character, and at variance with the duties required in the gospel. Then how does it appear according to the previous *agreement* between the administrator and the receiver, that such oath is binding. The agreement made between the two parties at the time, is like this: while the master or officer acting for the institution, requires the candidate to take the oath, only with this condition, his submitting, and taking it under that condition, is no less than saying though not spoken with words, that he will take it, and be bound by it, provided the statement of the condition is true, but not otherwise. Then so soon as he shall discover the contents of such oath, to be contrary to the condition to repeat it after the master, why is he not just as much at liberty to be disentangled from it as before.

We may be told, that such objections, if ever made, should be made at the time; or before repeating the oath from the lips of the master; and that, if on hearing the oath it should be objectionable to the candidate, he need not have taken it. But let all fairly understand this matter, and that the candidate has no reasonable opportunity to examine the oath before taken, for he is not permitted to know one syllable of its contents, nor, that there is any oath to be taken, on joining the institution, if possible to keep him ignorant of it; until he is caused to kneel at "the altar, neither naked nor clothed, barefoot nor shod, hood-winked, with a cable tow," or rope, "about" his "neck," and told that he is "now about to take the solemn oaths or obligation of an Entered Apprentice," &c. and then he can know nothing of it any faster, than a few words of it are said over for him to repeat after the Master, sentence after sentence, or half sentence, or word at a time, until it is finished, like the stupid school boy, who knows not one word of his lesson, but repeats it as he is commanded, word for word, at the lips of the teacher. How little then, could be learnt, or understood, of a long oath taken in this manner, amid so much, at such a season, that is calculated to distract the thoughts. If ever it is to be fairly examined and tried by the scale of moral rectitude, it must be done after it is taken, when a person may see and examine it, as other things are tried, to be approved or condemned. How unreasonable then, that he should be required to judge of it, and condemn it at such a critical and unexpected moment, or be forever debarred the privilege afterwards. Besides considering the incapacity of the candidate of judging of the moral character of such oaths, at the time of taking them, his condition is such as every one may see, as will not allow of his usurping authority, to judge, and condemn them, even if his mind could be then sufficiently enlightened. Before the first step is taken towards the institution, he must promise upon his honor, before a number of the fraternity, that he will conform to all their customs and requirements in taking the degree, as all others have done, on becoming masons. Then he hears and learns many things, of the secret forms of initiation, before he comes to the oath, when circumstanced as I have mentioned, and knowing that there is no possible way of escape, if he should protest against the oath, or any part of it, and refuse to take it, he cannot feel, while taking it, as though he was acting for himself, but that he has blindly and voluntarily placed himself in a condition where he must inevitably comply with the usages of the lodges, and though he should, at the time, before finishing the oath, perceive that there was more matter proposed to him in it, which appeared wrong to be taken, how can he do otherwise, having gone so far, than finish it, hoping to make the best of it afterwards. Thus, when he shall have an opportunity to examine it for himself separate from the specious interpretations which are given it, by those who have themselves taken it upon trust, and finds it contains things contrary to the condition on which he took it, what can be plainer, than that he is not bound by it, according to the previous agreement? If I make a promise to a stranger, that I will grant his request, before he makes it known to me, provided, that it is both lawful and reasonable, shall I be holden to fulfil such a promise, and grant the request, though when declared, I find it both unlawful and unreasonable?

Though it appears, that none, having commenced the taking of these oaths in this their blind and helpless condition, make their escape without having the whole of them imposed upon them, it is confidently believed, that no men of moral principles would have been caught there, could they have known positively, before making up their minds to unite with the fraternity, that in going forward, they must take upon themselves oaths of precisely such a moral character as those of masonry.

The last reason which I now think of assigning to show that the masonic oaths are without validity, is, that *the word of God absolutely condemns them, and requires them to be repented of, and put away.* Separate from the general prohibitions concerning the taking of oaths in the scriptures, some of which have already been briefly noticed, I shall now produce a passage, which if I mistake not, seems given to settle this question beyond any further dispute, in the minds of all who shall carefully and truly compare it with the oaths of masonry. The passage is in Leviticus, 5th chap. 4th and 5th verses. "*If a soul swear, pronouncing with his lips, to do evil, or to do good, whatever it be, that a man shall pronounce with an oath and it be* HID *from him, when he knoweth of it, then shall he be guilty in one of these. And it shall be, when he shall be guilty in one of these things, that he shall confess, that he hath sinned in that thing.*" Surely nothing could have been written on the subject of oaths, more appropriate to the oaths of masonry than this passage of scripture; and nothing could more expressly condemn them, and declare their invalidity. And truly it seems as though the passage could not be applied to any other kind of oaths which are at present in use among men; and it is believed, that the masonic, are the only oaths which are taken, the contents of which are "*hid from*" the receiver, and the only oaths, to my knowledge, except such as are openly and grossly profane, which a man takes, "*pronouncing with his lips,*" as mentioned in this passage. Many men among us have been called, to take hundreds of solemn oaths, but not one of them was pronounced at the time by the receiver, with his lips, except in masonry. Where else then could this passage be applied, but to the oaths of this institution? It certainly seems to set the matter beyond all reasonable dispute between masons and anti-masons, as it goes farther than any thing, for which the latter have ever contended, since it does not condemn the oath that is unwittingly taken, merely because of the *evil* which it may contain, but condemns it because it is *so taken;* whether it be evil or good; "*whatever it be that a man shall pronounce with an oath,*" in that manner. Is not the requisition in this scripture so plain that a child might understand it, that when an individual has thus sworn "*to do evil or to do good,*" when it was thus "*hid from him,*" as in the masonic oaths, he ought to withdraw from them, as soon as he may know what he has done, and "*confess that he hath sinned in that thing!*" At present, I can see but one way by which they will be likely to endeavor to evade the conclusion which is so clear from this passage; which is: it may be said that the passage stands connected with Jewish ceremonies, which are now done away, and of course, that this passage must now be as much out of date as those ceremonies. But the thoughtful and candid will not be thus easily convinced, that the moral law of God, or his law respecting the wickedness of oaths, has been changed or done away with the ceremonies of the Jewish Church.

ON THE VALIDITY OF MASONIC OATHS.

Extract from an Address delivered at Lyons, N. Y. by Miron Holley, Esq.

FREEMASONRY administers oaths—are these oaths binding? Assuredly not. They are promissory. A promissory oath is the calling upon God to take notice of what is promised, and of invoking his vengeance, by the promiser upon himself, if it is not performed.

Promissory oaths are not binding, where false or erroneous representations and inducements are held out to those who take them. The representation made to the brethren before admission, that "the oath will effect neither their religion nor their politics," is of this character; and so are all the inducements arising from the unfounded pretensions of Freemasonry, heretofore examined

To take an oath is a solemn and deliberate act of the mind. Understanding is essential to its obligation; on which account oaths impose no obligation upon idiots, lunatics, madmen, or young children; they not having sufficient knowledge, either of the nature of the things promised, or of the penalties of non-performance: and both of these sorts of knowledge are requisite. There can be no moral obligation, in any case, without knowledge. The obligation of obedience to God himself, is no more than co-extensive with our knowledge of his laws; and in respect to the nature of the promises and penalties, in the oaths of Freemasonry, all the persons before alluded to as being free from the obligation of oaths, for the want of understanding, have as much knowledge, as the wisest of the brethren had, before the oaths were taken.

To render a promissory oath obligatory, it is necessary, that both the authority administering it, and the performance of the promise it contains, should be lawful; reference being had in this case, not merely to the enactments of the civil government, but also to the law of a good conscience.

The right to administer oaths, if not wholly denied by religion, is one of the prerogatives of the sovereign power, a right which cannot be enjoyed concurrently, by the government and its subjects. Every man would regard it as both wrong and ridiculous for any individual to pretend to a natural right of administering oaths, in such form, with such penalties, and for such purposes as he might choose to dictate; and such pretension would not be made valid by his finding any man or number of men, who would consent to take them. Even if the form, penalties, and purposes were all good, this would be incontrovertible. The right of administering oaths, does not exist anterior to the establishment of government, nor independently of it. Wherever it exists, it is a conventional right, of that description too, which may be denominated resulting; that is, a right, springing from the necessities of government, after its organization, and founded on the utility of its exercise. It never exists, in individuals or associations of men; except when conferred upon them by government. There is no rightful government, in this country, but religion, or the laws regularly adopted under our established constitution. But neither of these has conferred upon Freemasonry the right to administer oaths. Would it not be a violation of every good man's conscience, as well as a scandalous breach of his allegiance to our government, for him to administer an oath among us, under the pretence of authority conferred upon him by the Great Mogul? It is equally so, under the pretence of authority conferred by Freemasonry—a government more foreign from ours, and more barbarous than Turkey. This is a kind of unlawfulness, which shows there is no obligation imposed upon the conscience, by masonic oaths.

It is a gross immorality to administer such oaths on other grounds, and therefore a man is not bound by them. The master of a lodge, without any shadow of authority, in the midst of the most degrading mummery, calls upon a candidate, in a state of indecent nakedness, with a bandage round his eyes, in order that he may have no more of natural, than he has of moral light, solemnly and sincerely to promise and swear, as in the presence of Him, in whose sight the angels are chargeable with folly, to do —he knows not what—under penalties the most revolting and inhuman. Is not such a scene calculated most injuriously to lessen the sanctity of all oaths? Must not the frequent repetition of it, amazingly diminish the value of that solemn form of ascertaining truth, by our constituted authorities, in relation to all our dearest rights? Recollect there are near 100,000 Freemasons in the United States, of whom many have taken more than forty degrees, in each of which an oath has been administered. Did not the Father of his country allude to these proceedings of Freemasonry, in his farewell address, when he emphatically asked, "Where is the security for property, for reputation, for life, if the sense of religious obligation desert the oaths which are the instruments of investigation in courts of justice?"

The performance of a promise to calumniate, to conceal a criminal action, or to assassinate, is always unlawful, and is therefore not binding; because the promiser in these cases, is always under a prior obligation to the contrary. From such prior obligation what shall discharge him? His promise? His own act and deed? But an obligation from which a man can discharge himself, by his own act, is no obligation at all. The guilt of such promises lies in making them, not in breaking them. Whoever makes them is already bound to break them. The masonic oaths do not require all those unlawful acts, except upon certain conditions. Where the condition exists, there the oaths are imperative. But the acts are unlawful under all possible conditions, and therefore the oaths are not obligatory.

Besides, the penalty of every masonic oath, is the forfeiture of life, to be taken in the most impious and bloody manner. No man has a right to subject himself to such a penalty. His prior obligations to God and his country forbid it. The penalty is unlawful, and therefore the oath not obligatory.

Herod's promissory oath to his daughter in-law, "that he would give her whatsoever she asked, even to the half of his kingdom," when she asked the head of John the Baptist, imposed no obligation upon Herod to give it, because it was unlawful.

Christianity interposes other objections to the lawfulness of masonic oaths. "Thou shalt not take the name of the Lord thy God in vain." "I say unto you, swear not at all." On these authorities many Christians wholly refuse to take judicial oaths. They have universally, and always, condemned all others. Whatever is against the command of Christ is sinful. All sins must be renounced even the most favorite.

An oath can never bind a man to do what is morally wrong. If it is a bond of duty, let us consider what is the authority of duty. It is the command of God or general utility; opposition to which, is the very definition of wrong. It would be both preposterous and impious, deliberately to call upon God to take notice of what was in opposition to his command. In such case, to take an oath, would actually involve the guilt of perjury.

A good man always acts under a conviction of the presence of God, and in the fullest expectation of his righteous retributions; that is, under all the sanctions of an oath.—And there could be no stronger attestation to the excellence of Doctor Johnson's moral character than that, which is involved in the declaration of one of his associates, that in common conversation, he always talked like a man under oath. What would such a man do, supposing he had taken the oaths of Freemasonry? Could he conceal what he knew to be criminal? Could he derange the business, oppose the interests, or traduce the character of a brother for any cause? He plainly could not; because, he would be under all the obligations imposed by an oath, not to dò so, prior to his taking the masonic oaths; that is, all the obligations arising from the command of God, or general utility.

In reality, the use of an oath is, to bring freshly to the mind of him, who takes it, the obligations of duty, which actually would rest upon him, without it. It does not increase those obligations in the least degree. Do not the obligations of duty, then, as with the force of an oath, require all good men to renounce Freemasonry? If, in the honest convictions of their minds, Freemasonry is wrong, in its secrecy, in its oaths, in its injunctions, or in its effects and consequences, they assuredly do.

VINDICATION OF FREEDOM FROM MASONIC OATHS.

Extract from the Anti-Masonic Review.

What sort of religion have you, thus to expose the mysteries of ancient Freemasonry, contrary to your solemn oath? A fearful question, to which we solemnly reply.

We justify ourselves in three several positions, either of them sufficient alone for our defence; and altogether rendering our defence impregnable.

In the first position, we say, that *ancient Freemasonry*, to which we have sworn fearful secresy, had never an existence. The word Freemasonry, and the thing signified by that word, is not ancient, but modern; is not three thousand years old, nor three hundred, nor the half of three hundred. We took the oath with assurances, and with the belief, too, that *ancient Freemasonry* meant an institution organized by Zerubbabel, and patronized by St. John, and by the apostles of our Lord. As such we have sworn to it allegiance; and if ever we meet with such an insitution, or any fraction of it, whether on the plains of the Scioto, or of the Genesee, whether on the Green, or the Alleghany mountains, we will hail its signs, and conceal its mysteries, so far as they may be intrusted to us, with the most praiseworthy fidelity.

But a certain institution pretending to come from under the hand of Solomon in the land of Judea, we now know to have come from worthless names in the island of Great Britain; not three thousand years ago, but in the last century. *Its* secrets and signs we do not feel bound to hail, even in a lodge room. And the oath which we honestly took in favor of king Solomon's institution, shall not, with our consent, be converted into an obligation of fidelity to any lie.

Is it not provoking beyond sufferance, that we should be ensnared in early life, to take a secret oath of fidelity to an institution patronized by the holy St. John, which proves to be not one hundred and fifty years old? And, when we would open our lips to expose the imposture, that we should be checked with the remembrance of our oath? As if, when deceived to swear fidelity to an impostor, we were bound for our oath's sake forever to maintain that impostor, or at least, to take no important step to exhibit his true character to the public.

Freemasonry comes to us sustained by the best names of the age, and setting forth with great authority, that it was the chosen friend of Enoch, and Noah, and Moses; that it received an improved form from the hands of the wisest man, and additional glory from Joshua, Zerubbabel, and Haggai. It offers to those who will pay it fealty, a rare and rich reward. In the simplicity of youth, we have yielded our necks to its yoke, and sworn to it allegiance; but, in riper years, we find these chains to be barefaced falsehood.

Now, shall the institution, which has thus insulted us with falsehood, still hold us to our solemn obligation to keep it a secret? Shall it impose on us most egregiously, and, when we would expose the imposition, thunder in our ears; "You have sworn to keep all my mysteries an entire secret!" and, thus, compel us to give the countenance of our name, and the influence of our example and character, to sustain the deceiver, and to perpetuate the falsehood? No; Freemasonry shall not hold our name, by any obligation, responsible for its contempt of truth.

Indeed, Freemasonry, *a fire is kindled in the walls of Damascus that will consume the palaces of Benhadad.*

What are the walls of Freemasonry but her oaths? And these are like an oath of a faithful subject to one whom he had reason to suppose, and did suppose, was his rightful sovereign; but who, in the event, proved to be a barefaced impostor; which oath is not binding at all. And should such an impostor use Freemasonry's argument, and say, "your oath was to me; you took it voluntarily, and you are bound forever to be faithful to my interests and commands." What think you his sworn subjects would reply? They would hang him between heaven and earth, as unworthy of either.

This, then, is our first position: that an oath to be

faithful to ancient Freemasonry is precisely like the oath of a subject to an impostor prince, and is binding neither in the sight of God nor man.

> " Whose tongue soe'er speaks false,
> Not truly speaks; who speaks not truly, lies."

Persuaded by the great names of the good men belonging to the institution, that Freemasonry was the truth and no lie; that it had a rightful claim to our attention as the handy work of the wise Solomon; that it deserved our reverence, as the glory of the first temple, and the joy of Christian martyrs, and saints; we swore allegiance to it, as to a rightful sovereign; we submitted to its teachings, as to the teachings of men who had been employed by divine inspiration in penning the holy oracles of truth. But now assured that a more gross imposition was never practised on a Christian people, we scorn Freemasonry and its oaths; and, in the name of the just One, we burst them asunder, as Samson burst the green withs and hempen cords of the treacherous Delilah.

Our second position is like the first, viz. that an oath like a promise, obtained by false pretences, is void from the beginning. Freemasonry pretends to the sanctity of the patriarchs and prophets and apostles; it pretends to confer a most illustrious and important secret, able to make wise; it pretends to be founded on divine revelation, and to ennoble its faithful adepts with titles of Sir Knight, Thrice Illustrious, and Most Worshipful; and to decorate its followers with trappings, like a steed accoutred for a military review. It pretends to much more, and in return for its honors, and its benefits, Freemasonry asks twenty dollars, and some oaths. The money is irrecoverable, and may well enough be the forfeit of our folly. But oaths obtained on pretences entirely false, which oaths serve only to enable the impostor to practise his frauds upon other men, and other generations, are not registered in Heaven's high chancery, are not obligatory upon the servant of the Most High.

It has been a question with moralists, whether oaths, or promises, extorted by violence, or fear, are binding; but we are not aware, that any writer has maintained, that men are morally obliged to perform an oath, or a promise procured by fraud. Men are sometimes *compelled* to perform such promises; but it is invariably done with conviction of *legal* necessity prevailing against moral right.

Suppose a spirited gentleman in gorgeous attire, goes about proclaiming, that for a liberal fee he will confer the gift of second sight. One pays, and another and another. The public eagerly inquire, "How does he do it?"

"That is a secret he made us solemnly swear not to tell."

In the ardor of youth, we would learn something, if not have second sight; and apply to the gentleman with our fee advanced. He blinds us most satisfactorily, solemnly prays and administers the oath, of absolute and profound secrecy, by the great God who will not hold him guiltless that taketh his name in vain; then coolly removes the bandage from our eyes, and congratulates us upon the receipt of second sight! Now, is that oath binding upon the deceived youth? Shall he patiently submit to this insult upon his understanding, lest he break his oath? Shall he see the same trick playing, and to be played, upon hundreds of others, and upon generations to come, and be restrained from warning them by a regard to his oath?

We say no. The fine gentleman had no right to demand the oath. The error was in submitting to take it, profaning the name of the Holy One to cover an imposture; and no sooner do we become certain, that the oath is used to cover deceit, than it becomes our duty to regard the glory of God in the breach, and not in the observance of that oath.

Now this is our second position, That Freemasonry is the splendid gentleman, who secures his fee beforehand, and administers his oath to the hood-winked candidate; and then, confers the promised gift by removing the hood from his eyes! The novice is taught to enter the lodge in pursuit of light. Behold how it is conferred upon him. Kneeling hoodwinked before the altar immediately following the administration of the oath, the master of the lodge asks him:

Mas. "Brother, what do you most desire?"

Novice. "Light." (By help of a prompter.)

Mas. "Brethren, stretch forth your hands, and assist

in bringing this new made brother from darkness to light." (*Members form a circle around the novice with their hands and right foot raised.*)

Mas. "And God said: let there be light, and there was light." *At the same instant every brother claps his hands, and stamps his foot, and the bandage is slipped from the novice's eyes;* this brings him to light.

Thus the sacred scripture is abused, to hallow the barefaced deceit of Freemasonry.

The glory of God is advanced, not by the observance but by the breach of the oath, which covers this deceit; and the sin of profanity lies in taking God's name to sanction the deed of imposture: and it cannot lie in the exposure of that imposture.

"O, let thy vow
First made to Heaven, first be to Heaven performed;
That is, to be the champion of the church!
What since thou sworest, is sworn against thyself,
And may not be performed by thyself.—
It is religion that doth make vows kept,
But thou hast sworn against religion;
Therefore, thy latter vows, against thy first,
Is in thyself, rebellion to thyself."*

We confess we have been the dupes of this imposture, to take the yoke of its obligations upon our necks; the good Lord help us to break that yoke, "like an earthen pitcher, that is broken in pieces; so that there shall not be found in the bursting of it, a shred to take fire from the hearth, or to take water out of the pool;" to rend it so that no man may be able to gather up the fragments, or to cement the broken pieces.

Our third position is diverse from the two former, and yet equally sufficient for our defence in making all necessary use of the oaths and mysteries of Freemasonry, to enable the candid reader to acquire a just estimate of the worth and character of that institution. The oath is prefaced with words to this effect: "The obligation you are about to take is not to interfere with your duty to God, or to your country."

Now, we say it not lightly, but with a solemn view to the day when the secrets of all hearts shall be revealed,

---

* King John, Act 3d, Scene 1st.

that any construction of our masonic obligations, which prevents us from using publicly the mysteries of Freemasonry, *so far as is necessary to show the false and depraved nature of the institution*, and its injurious tendency to infidelity and crime, does interfere with our duty both to God and our country; and, therefore, in animum jusjurandum imponentis, *by the express understanding of him who administered the oath*, we were made free in the night of our initiation, from any such construction of its words, as might ever interfere with our civil or religious duties.

Our duty to promote the glory of God, and the welfare of our country, bids us declare, that Freemasonry is an impostor; a fraud upon its members, and upon the community; and, if in the further discharge of this duty, we bring any part of the mysteries of the institution to support our declaration, we are not prevented by our oath; for that is never to interfere with the sacred discharge of our civil and religious duty.

These, brethren, are our three positions, either of which is alone sufficient to justify our public use of such parts of the mysteries of Freemasonry as are necessary to expose the dangerous nature of the institution, and which positions altogether are impregnable. We see no fault in the reasoning, no mystery, or sophistry, or chicanery, in the argument by which either of our positions is maintained: and either of them alone being sound, no brother having our matured views of the history and character of Freemasonry, is under the least obligation to the impostor, or to withhold one jot of the fraud from the abused public. * * * * * *

If in this renunciation of Freemasonry there seem any implication of the honor of the fraternity, it is not intended. They are imposed upon, or we are. They verily believe Freemasonry to be venerable for its antiquity, &c. &c. But when they become satisfied, that we have all been made the dupes of a shameless imposture, they, too, will feel resentment and indignation for this abuse. We think they, too, will forsake, or renounce it with contempt, and with thankfulness that they are at length made free from its ruthless obligations, and from its impious oaths

In this vindication of our freedom from the oaths of

Freemasonry, we appeal neither to Paley nor Burlemaque, to Vattel nor Puffendorf, but to the conscience of Christians, who fear God; to the hearts of freemen, who love their country; and to the common sense of men, who have understanding. We might lose the reader's attention in an argument drawn from the books of civilians and moralists, books he may never have read. We prefer to draw our argument from the common sense of mankind, that we may carry with us the convictions of every heart, and stand in the conscience of every just man, disenthralled from our obligations to Freemasonry, as we are from that obligation to an impostor, which would interfere with bringing him to a righteous condemnation; from that oath to a swindler, which would prevent our warning the public against his practices; from that penalty to a traitor conspiring against the liberties of our citizens, which would frighten us from sounding alarm, and from proclaiming the danger to our countrymen.

"Is this Freemasonry! It cannot be."

We say, this is our vindication for the use of some things with which we make free, and our reply upon the adversary, who will attempt in his defence to plead what any impostor would plead under like circumstances, viz. "these men are solemnly sworn to *me;* they despise their *oath;* their *word* is not to be taken."

And, now, the judgment of wise men confirming our own, and unanimously assenting to the soundness of the argument, and to the righteousness of our conclusions, we are ready to treat the oaths of Freemasonry, as a man has a right, both by human and divine law, to treat the marriage oath in case of adultery. No man would hesitate instantly to repudiate a wife, whose life was stained with transgressions against purity. Because he took solemn vows of fidelity to her before the throne of God, believing her to be pure and chaste, is he held to his marriage vow, after he knows that she is an adulteress? It is not possible. Freemasonry we wedded as the truth of God; we repudiate it as the falsehood of the devil.

———" Thou mayest hold a serpent by the tongue,
A caged lion by the mortal paw,
A fasting tiger safer by the tooth,
Than keep in peace the hand which thou dost hold."

We were taught to believe Freemasonry has virgin purity; but we find it is corrupt: we were taught to believe thas it was founded and patronized at least three thousand years ago, by men acknowledged to be of God in the holy scriptures; but we find it was founded in the era of the South Sea Company, by men whose names are no warrant for truth or righteousness: we were taught to believe that Freemasonry is the handmaid of religion; but we find that it is very far from aiding the doctrines of the cross of Christ; and, in an extensive and thorough, a protracted and patient examination of the subject, we have found Freemasonry, by its own showing, carefully collated from its approved writers, and books of constitutions, to be the synagogue of Satan.

We have sworn to it in the belief which was taught us; we abjure it in the convictions which careful investigation has produced. We gave it the pledge of our right hand, believing it to be a blessing from the Lord, fraught with heavenly mercies; we withdraw that pledge, upon finding Freemasonry to be the work of the father of lies, fraught with hidden mischief. We received it as sanctioned by the best of names, both ancient and modern, patriarchs and prophets, statesmen and divines; we renounce it as the angel of light, so cunningly attired that he deceives even the elect.

As our forefathers broke the yoke of foreign bondage, so we break the yoke of internal tyranny; as they performed their duty to God, to their posterity, and to their country, by renouncing their allegiance to George III. and to the British constitution; so we, in the fear of God, in the service of our country, and posterity, and with a view to a day of final retribution, renounce and make void our allegiance to Freemasonry.

ON THE PRINCIPLES AND PRACTICE OF THE MASONIC INSTITUTION.

Extract of a letter addressed to the Committee of the Worcester County Convention by Pliny Merrick, Esq.

WHY it has been, that so many men of distinguished attainments, should, in different generations, have devoted their time and lent their reputation in support of speculative Freemasonry, I cannot now comprehend. The sense of shame that they voluntarily submitted to the practices of masonic ceremonials, after they had been found to be "trifles light as air," may have prevailed with some; others may perhaps have been unwilling to destroy those anticipations, resulting from the mutual pledges of fraternal assistance which is one of the great characteristics of the craft, of personal advantage in the prosecution of their schemes of business or projects of ambition. Some may have felt themselves restrained by respect for the venerated individuals whom they have known to have given the sanction of their membership to the institution; others, influenced by a long line of examples, may have tacitly yielded without a struggle to its vaunted pretensions to great antiquity, and to a lofty character for science, benevolence and morality. It is probable that a still greater class has entertained a vague and undefined, but gloomy and shuddering belief, that the obligations of Freemasonry are binding upon the conscience—that its penalties have power over the body, and its oaths over the soul; and have felt as if it would be sacrilege, and known that it would be dangerous, to break the seal of its profound and cherished mysteries. Whatever may have been the cause, the fact is unquestionable, that multitudes have been subdued to a heavy and lamentable thraldom. A wide and almost universal despotism has prevailed; and while its dominion has constantly kept in view those appalling imprecations which every mason has invoked upon his own disregard of the "mystic tie," it is not strange that a corresponding feeling should have been infused into many minds, that punishment for its violation would be sure, and its infliction meritorious—The better lights of our own times have vastly weakened, and to a great extent overcome, those debasing feelings. But there are still those who do not hesitate to denounce a separation from Freemasonry as a crime; and even since our late convention in Worcester, it has been said, that it will not do for a seceder from that Institution to *brave the indignation* of the two thousand active men, now its members in the County of Worcester.

It has been the custom of the fraternity to speak of the venerable age of their Institution; and to boast that through the long lapse of ages, it has sustained its character, its identity, and its principles, without change or modification. Recent investigations have denied and disproved its claims to antiquity; but without discussing the question of its age, it may be remarked, that those claims, if they could be substantiated, would afford no proof of its fitness or of its adaptation to the present times. Whatever is the work of man is susceptible of improvement. The march of mind, like that of time, is onward; and it would be as wise in the present generation to give up the steam engine and the mariner's compass, by which the elements are conquered and oceans traversed in safety, for the shore-bound oar boats of the ancients, as to adopt with thoughtless and debasing credulity their formal and cumbrous institutions.

It is, however, altogether unnecessary to speak of the age, or the origin, of Speculative Freemasonry.—For whatever purpose it was contrived, or at whatever period its cumbrous formalities were imposed on the world, it ought to be enough to insure its rejection, that it possesses neither precept nor principles, peculiar to itself, which are now either necessary or useful.—Whatever is valuable in any of the abstract truths which it has contrived to incorporate with its system, and with which it has hitherto too successfully concealed the clumsy machinery of its mysteries, is equally well known and much better taught, without the pale of the institution. Of itself, strictly speaking, it possesses neither the means of affording gratification, or of imparting knowledge.

Of its sources of agreeable entertainment, it is perhaps almost too trifling to speak. It possesses indeed small power in this particular. Of the hours which are spent when, in its own technical language, the craft are called from labor to refreshment, there is nothing peculiarly inviting, unless it may be supposed, that the uncommon dulness of the preceding work may have created an unusual zest for the excitements of the flagon. Social intercourse surely cannot be the more agreeable, because the ligature of companionship is an oath of fidelity, instead of that cordial sympathy which springs from common pursuits, and kindred feelings, and refined sensibilities. The pageantry, which throws its attractive drapery around the proceedings of a lodge, is as idle, as it is fictitious; and its lofty pretensions tó grandeur, its gaudy display of rank and titles, ought to afford but little satisfaction to the plain simplicity of a republican people. Quite as little entitled to regard is there in the actual occupations of the fraternity in their secret sessions. The unvaried and unmeaning forms of opening and closing the lodge are cold and heartless. Its initiations mingle the ridiculous with the painful. A half dressed novitiate is led round with mock solemnity, to exhibit his grotesque appearance to those who have gone before him, sometimes the object of their speculation, but oftener the sport of levity; and a weak and vain and boisterous gratification is often extracted from the awkward surprise and miserable disappointment, which are I believe uniformly exhibited by the blindfolded candidate, when he is brought to light, and discovers the matchless vanity of the bubble, to which so much formidable preparation and pomp of ceremony has introduced him.

But Freemasonry assumes higher claims; it arrogates to itself extraordinary wisdom; and affirms that it is of itself a science, and that its secret and inviolable signs have become an universal language. No proposition can be more utterly without foundation. The members of the fraternity, who travel in our own country only, find it difficult to make themselves intelligible to their brethren in its different parts on account of the variations in the forms and ceremonies which different lodges have adopted. And it is worthy of remark, that itinerant lecturers have, at different times, been commissioned by the several grand lodges to pass through the country, to give such instructions as would enable the fraternity to observe something like uniformity in the practice of the rites, ceremonies, and secrets of an Institution, which boasts that it has been immutable for ages.

All other pretensions that this Institution is of itself a science, or that it is the depository of valuable information, are equally a mere gratuitous assumption.—Indeed if Speculative Freemasonry were to perish to-day, and all knowledge of its forms, rites, ceremonies, proceedings, and secrets, were at once obliterated from the memory of mankind, I know of no useful or desirable fact, or doctrine, or theory, which would be lost to the world. Its fables are far less valuable than the ingenious tales with which modern literature amuses the expanding minds of infancy; and as for its science, it is but a shadow and a pretence. The operative mechanic never goes to its instructions or its archives for any assistance: the mathematician would seek there in vain for a solution of the problems of geometry—the science on which it professes to be founded. The historian cannot find among its idle fictions the materials for the narrative of the manners and actions of men; and the speculations of philosophy would be vain indeed, if they embraced nothing but the knowledge contained within its barren circle. Some simple truths, of which few men in any enlightened age can be found ignorant, is the utmost reach of instruction, to be deduced from the lectures of masonry. Those lectures, with which it has been the pride of many masons to incumber the memory, give information only of such humble truths, as that the sun rules the day, and the moon governs the night; that chalk is a convenient substance with which to make marks on the wall; that ignited charcoal creates a fervent heat; and that the earth brings forth its fruits in due season—truths which, long before they are unfolded to the Entered Apprentice in the lodge, are learnt by lisping childhood from its own observation. How idle to suppose, that the royal monarch of Israel, whose chief glory was wisdom, could have invented and transmitted to posterity a system so poor and barren as this! If there were indeed sufficient evidence to prove that he did so, the veneration which has been accorded to his wisdom would dwindle into contempt, and his fame would be tarnished forever.

Freemasonry has found, and still finds, many advocates

for its cause on the ground that it is an association for the purposes of benevolence and charity. It is not, however, to be forgotten, that its charities are mostly of a narrow and selfish character; and that it pays little regard to that broad rule of Christian benevolence which finds a neighbor in every victim of sorrow and distress. There are, besides, difficulties in the very organization and construction of this institution, which must necessarily greatly curtail its means of charitable assistance. It collects certainly great funds by means of its fees for initiation; but it has great expenses too. It must have its own appropriate temples; its decorations must be georgeous, to correspond with the high sounding titles of its dignitaries. Charity vaunteth not itself; but masonry is every where puffed up. If its theory is right, its complicated organization, its schemes of grandeur, and its occasions of display, disarm it of its means; and accordingly, it has been the experience, I believe, of all our lodges, that the donations for benevolent purposes have been extremely limited. Go where we may, to the city or the village, and examine the records of the treasury, and far less will be found to have been contributed to suffering humanity from its resources, than from the humble and unpretending associations of Samaritans by its side. This is an evil necessarily resulting from the institution itself. The funds which are gathered, as it affects, for the sacred purposes of charity, it compels its members to waste in idle decorations and profitless baubles. The jewels which glitter on the bosoms of its priests, and the diadem which sparkles on the brow of its kings, are abstracted by its very organization from the treasury of the poor; but they are far from inspiring apostolic disinterestedness in the one, or of inducing royal munificence in the other. Whenever Freemasonry is thoroughly known and candidly considered, it will never be pronounced a useful, philanthropic or charitable institution.

Freemasonry claims also to be the handmaid of virtue; but it is a claim which its intrinsic merits cannot sustain. Of instructions in morality, it may be safely affirmed, that its books and lectures and secrets afford but a poor and scanty supply. Those books indeed which are published by authority of the lodges, as an exposition of its external characteristics, contain many valuable observations, though not so remarkable as ever to have attracted or deserved very high praise; and its lectures, preserved heretofore, as is supposed, by tradition, occasionally indicate a moral. But miserable indeed would be the condition of mankind, if their hopes of moral improvement, and their immortal desires of goodness, were supplied only with the light which gleams from the faint beams of Speculative Freemasonry. Mingled with its mass of unmeaning form and unprofitable ceremony, a few scattered passages selected from the scriptures, and a few good thoughts collected chiefly from other writers, are occasionally presented; but in the rubbish of its own peculiar characteristics, they are little better than the talent, which was wrapped in a napkin and hidden in the earth.

But it is no longer to be disguised or concealed, that this show of morality is but "the banner on its outward wall." It has other and decided peculiarities, which prove it is not a moral institution; and which leave it an object of doubt and dread—if not of detestation. It assumes, in the midst of society, and in the face of government, to impose oaths and obligations, which bind its members to feelings narrow, selfish, and exclusive; more than that—which bind them to that at which patriotism ought to shudder, and integrity start back abashed. When it is considered, that this institution, of its own power, assumes to administer oaths which are to be binding above all other obligations; that those oaths, administered to every man who becomes a member, are filled with the most awful and appalling penalties; that under those penalties the members are required and bound to "conform to all the by-laws, rules and regulations of the lodge," without any exception in favor of the laws of the land; "to keep the secrets of a brother inviolable;" "to espouse the cause of a companion so far as to extricate him from difficulty, whether right or wrong;" to refrain from the disclosure of his crimes whatever they may be, and to extricate him from every difficulty, though he be a 'murderer or a traitor;' and to warn him of, and defend him against every danger—when all these things are considered, it is vain, and worse than vain, to say, that Freemasonry is a moral institution. It strikes at the root of every thing that is good; it breaks up the great cause of country, and prostrates the still greater cause of virtue. It bids its members unite in the defence of flagrant crime; and to forbear from exposing to violated law, and injured humanity, the felon or the traitor, if they too are but of the fellowship of the craft. Surely its pretensions to virtue, and its self praised morality is but the song of the syren to allure; but when its victim is once bound by its heart-rending oaths, and his mind is shackled with apprehensions of its daring and awful obligations, it then carries him to deeds of darkness—shows him his brother and his companion in every act of baseness and treachery—bids him behold the assassins dagger, yet reeking in the blood of its violence, and watch the foul conspiracy of his country's desolation—and then stifles and overwhelmns his most anxious wish to speak but a word for justice—for patriotism—for humanity—with menaces of the dreadful vengeance of masonic penalties.

I speak only of the institution and its principles, and not of the members of the masonic fraternity. Wicked as such oaths are, and corrupting as they must be, it is cause of most grateful reflection to believe, that they have not frequently, in cases of flagrant criminality been observed. There has been a practical disregard of them every where within the circle of my own observation; and I have never known a culprit escape, or a felon saved, because he has given and taken the grip of a mason. But in rendering this justice to its members, I make no concession to Freemasonry. Its requirements are as positive, as its laws are arbitrary and its requirements cruel. The savage warriors of the dark ages, whose brutal violence may have been looked back to as a fit example for the formation of this institution, might have deemed it a virtue, to have followed with scrupulous exactness such requisitions as are demanded of the craft; but they only could bear such feelings in the bosom, whose minds were ignorant, and whose moral sense was never informed; or whose understandings were betrayed by phrenzy and madness. Instances of extraordinary perversion of the intellect, and of ruinous infatuation wrought by the awful imprecations of masonic oaths, have undoubtedly occurred. To this cause is to be referred the abduction and the immolation of William Morgan. That that man was torn from his family and from society, and was finally sacrificed by infuriated and desperate members of the fraternity, can no longer be made a question. The evidence is full—complete—irresistible. To nothing else can be referred that horrid slaughter, but the baleful influence of masonic obligations. Happily for us all, that deed, almost without a name, stands a rare, as it is an appalling example. But may we not justly fear, that the same cause, which has once deluded and overwhelmed so many minds, as were certainly engaged in that nefarious transaction, may again produce its effect, when the hour shall arrive that masonic vengeance shall again demand her blow?

There is probably little, if any evidence, that Freemasonry has essentially affected the political transactions, or interfered in the adjudications of the bench or the jury in the judicial tribunals, of our Commonwealth. It may, however, and it would be strange if it were otherwise, have occasionally produced effects imperceptibly. In the few years in which I have known it by experience, I have seen nothing to justify an opinion, that its baleful influence has been meddling with the politics, the religion, or the laws of the land. Others, in whose judgment I feel that it is safe to confide, have informed me that their experience in this respect does not correspond with mine; and from the nature of the obligations of the craft, it seems not improbable in itself. While the character of its obligations, and the nature of the bond which constitutes the association, render such interference probable in itself, there is direct proof, than in other countries, it has exercised a prevailing and powerful influence. Who can doubt, that during the disastrous times of the French revolution, Freemasonry was exerting its full share of power amid the sanguinary scenes which stained the whole face of Europe with blood. Later still, in the convulsions with which Italy was torn, Freemasonry lighted the torch, and the sword of the Red Cross Knight leaped from its scabbard at the command of the encampment. And we know that now, the energies of a young Republic in our own hemisphere, and on our own immediate borders, are wasted in civil discord under the banners of the craft. And nearer still, the ancient parties of the great State, on the western limits of our own Commonwealth, have been broken to atoms, by an event produced by the unhallowed conspiracy of many masons linked together by no other ties than their fraternal obligations: and there, an excitement has been produced, which they who among us adhere to the institution, and they also who know little and have thought less of it, are deploring as untimely and unnecessary. Let us not be deceived—the like causes will produce the like effects. The time may come, and perhaps is not now far distant, when the same malignant influence which has blighted other hopes, and scattered elsewhere the seeds of confusion and desolation, may be in the midst of us; corrupting the fountains of justice, and polluting the sources of political power. Can it be, that the evils which others have felt, shall speak no warning to us? or must it be, that, deaf to the cries which are pouring in on every side, and blind to the effects which have been elsewhere wrought, we are to wait until desolation at home shall arouse our vigilance and urge us to our duty?

You perceive, gentlemen, that I have spoken with great freedom of the institution of Freemasonry. I have denied the pretensions to esteem which it assumes, and denounced it as unworthy of being permitted to remain as a rock of offence among us. And you must have noticed, that it doing so, I have adverted to topics, which could have been discussed only after the secret recesses of the institution had been laid bare. That has already been fully done. It is vain—useless—false—to deny it. The publication prepared by William Morgan—the martyr whose life paid the forfeit of his broken obligations—disclosed all that could be disclosed of the secrets of the fraternity, as far as he wrote: and since his immolation, the work has been pursued by pure and able and faithful hands, until there remains little or nothing to be told. The testimony in proof of the truth of these disclosures is as full as human testimony can be; and I add in my own language to our Convention, "that my own testimony cannot alter it. They who will not believe it after a full and candid examination, would and could not believe me; neither, in my opinion, would they believe, though one should rise from the dead."—But I seek not to shrink from any responsibility in this high and solemn cause: and at whatever hazard, and in defiance of every consequence, I affirm, that having myself been admitted to the degree of a Royal Arch Mason, and to the several preceding degrees, as far as I have heretofore advanced in the degrees of masonry, the disclosure of the secrets of Freemasonry, as contained in the volume published by David Bernard, a clergyman of the Baptist denomination, entitled "LIGHT ON MASONRY," is true—that the forms, ceremonies, lectures, and oaths contained in that book are substantially as I myself received them; and as I have, again and again, seen and heard them, in the bodies of regular lodges and chapters, communicated and administered to others.

I believe that the institution of Freemasonry ought no longer to exist: lamenting, as I most sincerely do, that I have ever been connected with it, and that a voluntary assumption of its obligations has left me only the painful alternative, of submitting to its slavery, or of bursting its bonds, and thus exposing myself to the reproaches of those who still adhere to it, and of those also who believe that, if it be not as exalted and virtuous as it pretends, it is at least harmless and innocent, I can find consolation only in the hope, that I may be the humble instrument of attracting some portion of the public attention to the great cause, which I trust will prosper till the final overthrow and the utter extinction of Freemasonry shall be accomplished. I come forward in no spirit of hostility towards any of the members of the fraternity. I revere the venerable men whose names are recorded on its rolls. There are those also, in the circle of my own acquaintance, now members of this institution, towards whom I have cherished, and still cherish, no other but sentiments of respect, and feelings of affection. Whatever may be the emotions of their minds, no animosity or ill will exists in mine; and I ask only, that if our communion has ever hitherto been grateful, they will do me the justice to believe, that I now speak with a sincerity, certainly equal, and with a degree of reflection and meditation far greater, than I ever spoke to them before. Let them unite with us; and let the people be all awakened to a sense of the necessity of exertions for the removal of an evil, hitherto little suspected, but which may in the end become an engine of destruction.

It is vain and idle to expect, that an institution which has spread itself abroad into many lands, whose ramifications have reached the heart of almost every country, is to be extinguished without many efforts. They who calculate that it will fall of itself and crumble to decay, reckon not upon the interest which is enlisted in its support. It will yet withstand many shocks; but if the people are true to themselves, and to the best interests of their country, and of their posterity who are to inherit it, they will unite in the common cause, and move forward "through good report and through evil report," till the great end of the extinction of Speculative Freemasonry is fully, finally, and happily accomplished.

Since the publication of the foregoing letter, there has appeared in the "*Free Press*," an interesting correspondence, *on the nature of the Royal Arch obligation*, between the author and Mr. Oliver, a member of the Massachusetts Anti-Masonic Convention, from Lynn.

The letter having been read by Mr. Oliver, to a friend of his, who was a Royal Arch mason, objection was made only to that part of it which had reference to the Royal Arch obligation. [See page 92.] On the reading of that passage, he unhesitatingly declared the statement therein contained *a lie*, and that the author, on writing it, knew it to be so. A letter was accordingly addressed to the author, with a "view of ascertaining whether the literal meaning of the Royal Arch obligation, was capable of a construction that could justify such a declaration, or whether it was of such doubtful import as to be liable to ambiguous signification."

The following is Mr. Merrick's Reply :—

Worcester, January 8, 1830.

Dear Sir,—Your letter of the 2d inst. was duly received; and I have availed myself of the earliest time I could command to reply to its contents.

You inform me, that a "Freemason of sound judgment

and good understanding," declared to you, that that part of my letter of the 17th Dec. to the Worcester Committee, relating to the Royal Arch obligation, was "a lie;" and that if I was a Royal Arch Mason, I knew it was "a lie."

I have certainly been a Royal Arch Mason; and I as certainly know that my statement relative to the oaths taken by masons of that degree are true. In reply to your inquiry, if there be any "ambiguity" in the terms of that oath, I cannot place the subject in a better light before you, than to extract from the obligation the several parts of it, in the very words in which it is administered. The whole oath is quite long; but its several parts are distinct passages and complete sentences of themselves; and the sense of each of its clauses is in no way affected by being separated from the rest of the obligation. The extracts are as follows.

1. "*I furthermore promise and swear, that I will support the constitution of the General Grand Royal Arch Chapter of the United States of America, and also the constitution of the Grand Royal Arch Chapter of the State under which this Chapter is held, and conform to all the by-laws, rules and regulations of this, or any other Chapter of which I may hereafter become a member.*"

2. "*I furthermore promise and swear, that I will aid and assist a companion Royal Arch Mason, when engaged in any difficulty, and espouse his cause, so far as to extricate him from the same, if in my power, whether he be right or wrong.*"

3. "*I furthermore promise and swear, that a companion Royal Arch Mason's secrets, given to me in charge as such, and I knowing them to be such, shall remain as secure and inviolable in my breast as in his own, murder and treason not excepted.*"

To my mind, nothing can be more explicit, than the several clauses of the Royal Arch Mason's oath, which I have here extracted. I cannot perceive the least ambiguity; nor how they can be "capable of a construction that could possibly justify the declaration," that my statement to the Worcester Convention was "a lie."

The obligation is positive, "to conform to the by-laws, rules and regulations of the chapter;" and no mention of the laws of the land. And for aught I can see, if it shall ever so happen, that the laws of the State and the by-laws of the chapter shall conflict with each other, a Royal Arch mason is bound *by the terms* of the obligation to disregard and disobey the laws of the government, in order that he may "conform to the by-laws, rules and regulations of the chapter."

The obligation of a Royal Arch mason is in its language perfectly explicit; and the express provision, "murder and treason not excepted," evinces too clearly, to admit of misconstruction, the nature and character of those secrets, which are to remain in the bosom of him to whom they are communicated, as inviolable as they are in his own. It necessarily comprehends his crimes, whatever they may be.

The obligation to aid and assist a companion Royal Arch mason is in the broadest terms. That aid and assistance is to be afforded to a companion when he is in "ANY" difficulty; and his cause, whether "RIGHT OR WRONG," is to be espoused, so far as that he may be extricated from that difficulty. If this obligation does not, in its own terms, require that in every difficulty a Royal Arch mason shall be aided and assisted until he is effectually extricated, I confess I know of no language which could express that intention.

In fine, I see nothing in the terms of the Royal Arch mason's oath which is "of such doubtful import as to be liable to ambiguous interpretation."

To the accuracy of the extracts which I have made, as well as to the disclosures generally of the secrets of Freemasonry, my character for veracity is pledged. How far that evidence is sufficient, I leave to others to determine—not presuming myself to estimate its weight. But whether my testimony is of any avail or not, there is a mass of evidence before the public, which is full and conclusive; and I hesitate not to affirm, that if any fact was ever satisfactorily proved by human testimony, the truth of the disclosures of the oaths and obligations of Freemasonry is completely established by evidence already in possession of the public.

I cannot therefore but feel great surprise, when I learn that any man, sustaining a reputable character in the community, denies that the oaths and obligations quoted by me, in my letter of the 17th ult. from the work of Mr. Bernard, entitled "Light on Masonry," are administered in lodges and chapters of Freemasons. What those oaths are, it is possible and probable, that many, who have been initiated, never fully understood, or have wholly or partially forgotten. But how, when they are quoted, such men can deny their truth, I cannot pretend to explain, nor am I able to perceive. It may be also that, in some instances, the more obnoxious parts of these oaths may have been omitted by the presiding officer in admitting a candidate; and if so, such a person, if he has ever otherwise been instructed, may fairly and honestly make such a denial. Whether instances like these have occurred or not, I am unable to determine; I can only say, that wherever I have been, I believe that no such omissions have occurred.

Without being influenced by animosity against any member of the Fraternity, I feel at liberty to observe, that while any man continues to be attached to the institution of Freemasonry, and is influenced by the obligations of secrecy which it confessedly imposes, he is not, and cannot be, upon the subject of its oaths, a disinterested or impartial witness; for if, in a discussion upon that point upon which he voluntarily enters, he does not deny the truth of the disclosures of seceding masons, his very silence is, to some extent, an acknowledgement of their correctness. What else then, in such a situation, can *he* do, who has bound himself by obligations, which he still deems binding and sacred, "forever to conceal and never to reveal" the secrets of Freemasonry, but to hazard a positive denial that those secrets are disclosed?

There is a topic, not adverted to in your letter, and perhaps not altogether connected with it, to which I wish briefly to advert, before I close. You have undoubtedly observed, that the great stress of denial, when a denial of the truth of the oaths required of initiates into the masonic institution, as disclosed by seceding masons, is asserted, rests mainly upon the obligation alleged to be taken by Royal Arch masons. I have never yet heard any one intimate a denial of that, which has been published as the oath taken by a master mason upon his admission to the third degree. One of the clauses of that oath is in the following words, to wit :—

"I furthermore promise and swear, that a master mason's secrets, given me in charge as such, and I knowing them to be such, shall remain as secure and inviolable in my breast as in his own, when communicated to me, murder and treason only excepted, and they left to my own election."

The addition to the words "murder and treason only excepted" point out, too clearly to admit of any mistake, the nature of the secrets which a master mason is to keep inviolable. They must be his crimes as well as his other concerns of a confidential character. This seems to me to be the obvious, and necessary, and only reasonable construction. And may not this construction be held to be certain, from the very nature of the penalty—the penalty of death—which he who takes this obligation imprecates upon himself in the event of the violation of his oath?—For my own part, I see but a shade of difference, and that scarcely worthy of notice in a moral point of view, whether a mason swears with him of the *third* degree to keep all his secrets inviolable, "murder and treason *only* excepted, and those left to his own election," or with him of the *seventh*, to keep all those secrets "murder and treason *not* excepted."

I am most respectfully,

With assurances of my esteem,

Yours, &c.

PLINY MERRICK.

STEPHEN OLIVER.

OPINION OF HON. C. D. COLDEN,* UPON THE CHARACTER AND TENDENCY OF FREEMASONRY.

A reply to the letter of Col. Richard Varick, Thomas Fessenden, Esq. and Samuel St. John, Esq.; a Committee appointed at a meeting of citizens in New York, to address him on the subject.

Gentlemen,—I do not think I ought to object to communicate in this manner, the sentiments I have long held, and have frequently expressed, in relation to Freemasonry.

It is true that I have been a mason a great number of years, and that I have held very high masonic offices and honors. It is equally true that I have for a long time ceased to have any connexion with the institution, because, I have believed, and do now believe, it is productive of much more evil than good. It is also true that I have on no fit occasion hesitated to express this sentiment.

I would not do any thing inconsistent with any obligation I may have, however inconsiderately, assumed. But I know nothing of masonry to render it so horrible as it would be in my estimation, if it obliged me to be silent when I thought its influences were pernicious. It would be detestable if it did not leave me at liberty to warn others from following my example in becoming a member of an institution, of which from its very nature, I must have been ignorant until I was initiated, and of which, a just estimate can only be formed from experience.

I shall disclose none of the secrets of masonry, (if it now has any secrets,) nor shall I say any thing inconsistent with what is due to the eminent living, and illustrious dead, whose names are recorded as members of the fraternity. I have had a just pride in being associated with many of these, and now feel that I make a sacrifice in pursuing a course which may separate me from men, for whose pure motives and righteous principles, I shall never cease to entertain the most profound respect.

Discussions and expositions of the principles of masonry, of its origin, its religion, its morals, and its science, have not been considered as betraying any obligation; but on

* Mr. Colden was formerly Mayor of the city of New York, and also a member of Congress.

the contrary, have been sanctioned by the highest masonic authority. It is true that, till of late, masonry has always been a theme of panegyric; but if the advocates of the insitution are free to speak of its merits, it cannot be a violation of duty in those who hold different opinions, to express them with becoming respect and deference.

I desire that it should be understood, that the sentiments I now entertain on this subject, do not result from the alleged murder of Morgan. It is true this horrible event has induced me to think more, and more seriously, than I should otherwise have done, of the society; but I have long entertained my present opinion, *that a man who would eschew all evil, should not be a Freemason.* Perhaps I cannot give a stronger evidence that this is not an opinion recently formed than to mention that my son, by my advice, has never joined the fraternity.

I cannot mention the deplorable event to which I have referred, without exculpating, so far as any thing I can say will do it, the masonic fraternity from any participation in that outrage. For a long time I did not believe that Morgan had been put to death. But I find myself obliged to yield to the force of evidence. I yet entertain the most entire confidence that the fraternity did not participate in this crime. On the contrary, I do not doubt but that all the guilt of that transaction is confined to those infatuated men who assailed and slew him. The rest of the craft, I am entirely convinced, are as innocent of the blood of Morgan as I am. I fully believe that they hold the perpetrators in just abhorrence; they would rejoice if the guilty were discovered, and would aid in bringing the murderers to condign punishment.*

* We very much regret the mistake of Mr. Colden on this subject, for a mistake it certainly is, although easily accounted for. Mr. C. confesses frankly his dislike to the institution, and his disbelief for some time of the murder of Morgan. Had Mr. C. perused the public documents, he could immediately have had no doubt. The same cause, it seems, has produced a similar effect—that is, a mistake on the part of Mr. C. touching the institution being not implicated in the gross outrages committed. We will however no farther contradict Mr. C. nor anticipate the public opinion. We ask candid men to examine the public trials; the convictions under them; to consider the perjuries committed by masons to screen the guilty; to reflect upon the numbers indicted, suspected, and called as evidence,—

I do not believe that those who committed this crime, had any intention to take the man's life when they first assailed him. Under the influence of an enthusiasm which the forms and mysteries of masonry are so likely to excite in weak minds, they thought it would be meritorious to inflict some punishment for what they considered his delinquency. But they proceeded from step to step, until they found they had involved themselves in a responsibility that would be ruinous, if Morgan should be left to call them to account. A frantic interpretation of their masonic obligations, and their fears, assisted, probably, by corporal stimulants, led them to stain their hands with the blood of their victim.

If these conjectures be well founded, however little they will extenuate the crime of the murderers, the proof of such facts, would exonerate the great body of the craft from any participation in the guilt. But an institution, the forms, or obligations, or mysteries of which, can be so perverted, or so misunderstood, even by the weakest minds, as to induce a belief, that it may be meritorious to murder an apostate brother, no good man, on due consideration and reflection, can think deserving of his countenance and support.

If it be asked, what are the advantages of masonry? It seems to me the answer may be given in these very few words: It often, by its charity, relieves the distressed. But at what an enormous expense is this charity dispensed? When all the machinery of lodges, grand lodges, chapters, encampments, councils, visiters, &c. &c. is taken into consideration, it must be obvious, that the charitable contributions of masons are but trifles in compari-

---

all masons, and all aiming at the acquittal of the party tried,—and then say, if only a few were concerned,—or rather to say, if the institution is not fairly implicated in the guilt of Morgan's abduction and murder;—for if the crimes for which they were convicted had not been approved by the institution, how comes it that all those convicted and sentenced to imprisonment for their crimes, should not have been expelled from lodges? that on the contrary, so far from being expelled, they have been exalted in the lodges, nourished, cherished, and rewarded, and even with money, as brethren suffering in a righteous *masonic* cause, although gross violators of the laws of their country? The suggestions we make and submit them to the judgment of an impartial public, as well as to Mr. Colden himself.

son with the sums devoted to these objects. It may be doubted, whether all that has ever been applied to the charitable funds of the institution, would equal a hundredth part, perhaps I might say a thousandth part, of what has been expended by masons, for their temples and their decorations, for personal trappings, for jewelry, for funerals, for processions, for festivals and in the conviviality so inseparable from the meetings of the fraternity.

Let it be admitted, however, that the institution does relieve the poor and distressed to the greatest extent. Are the secrecy and the ceremonies of masonry necessary for the exercise of any virtue? Is it necessary that any set of men to be charitable, should do their deeds by night, in hidden places? That they should by lawful ceremonies, establish a relationship among themselves, which many of them believe imposes duties and obligations in reference to each other different from those by which they are bound to the rest of mankind? Many of the fraternity feel themselves obliged, in whatever situation they may be placed, to suffer an appeal from a brother mason to have an influence.—Offenders have persuaded themselves they could claim an exemption from punishment as masons; and even at the bar of a court of justice, a criminal has thought he secured impunity by revealing to the judge, who was about to pronounce his sentence, their masonic relationship.

If masonry separates the members of the craft from their fellow citizens; if masons are led to believe that their duty towards each other is different from what it is to the members of the community not connected with them; if a mason is bound to shield another from the general operation of the laws, or if he be subjected to any penalties beyond those denounced by the legislature; nay, if even a feeble minded man is made to believe that by becoming a Mason, he enlists in an isolated corps, the members of which may claim privileges through their brethren, and must perform duties which do not belong to other citizens, it cannot be a fit institution in our country, where no man in the discharge of his duties to the community, should act from fear, favor, or affection.

It is often alleged that masonry engenders and cherishes the social affections, by bringing men together with kindly feelings towards each other. It is not to be doubted but that a well regulated social intercourse has a beneficial influence on the disposition and character of mankind. But again, it must be asked, why is the secrecy, the parade, and the obligations of masonry necessary, if their objects be so virtuous? It is to be feared, however, that these meetings have not always a happy influence. Admitting that the utmost decorum and propriety are observed, while a lodge is open, yet the craft seldom separate without refreshment; and it oftens happens that more is taken than is necessary to repair the exhaustion of their labors, and too frequently, more than is consistent with temperance.

Attendance upon lodges sometimes leads to habits which are inimical to the prosperity and happiness of the members and their families. Every meeting of a lodge is attended by visitors, and as there are generally, even in the country, several lodges within the compass of ten or twenty miles, opportunities for these visitations frequently occur. Often the habit of making them renders a man, who would otherwise have been content with his own fireside, impatient at home, and desirous to exchange for the excitement of a masonic banquet, those enjoyments of his domestic circle with which he would have been perfectly content had it not been for the seductions of the craft.

Did I know of any other advantage than these two, charity and the cultivation of social dispositions, which any rational man at this day, imputes to masonry, I would not fail to mention it.

But it is to be objected to masonry, not only that no good comes of it, but that it is productive of positive evils. To some of these I have already adverted, and will notice others which have presented themselves very forcibly to my mind, and I may say, to my conscience.

If masonry is arrogant and impious in her pretensions, and delusive in her promises, surely she deserves to be discountenanced. If she claim to be coeval with the world, and to be of divine origin, when in truth she is but as of yesterday, and springs from the dust of the earth, what obligation can there be that should induce any man to hesitate to speak of her according to her demerits?

That operative or practical masonry was one of the earliest arts practised by mankind, is very probable. We may suppose that masons, as well as other trades, very soon formed themselves into separate societies, and adopted regulations, the better to establish and secure their interests. The employment of masons naturally brought them, as builders and architects, more than the members of any other trade, in contact with the wealthier and higher orders of society. Men, as distinguished for their science as for their rank, were placed at the head of congregations of operative masons. It then became an honor to be an associate of these bodies. Members were admitted who were not operatives. These soon changed the nature of the institution by which they had been adopted, or as their term is, accepted; and, instead of the objects of the assemblies of masons being operative masonry, they were converted to lodges of speculative masons, in which the tools and instruments of the former humble trade were retained to be transmuted into symbols of all the virtues and duties of mankind.

No man, at this day, who has taken the least pains to examine the subject, can doubt that this is the origin of Freemasonry, or that the change from operative to speculative masonry took place in very modern times. The masonic society has no more pretence to a divine origin, than the societies of stationers, butchers, bakers, carpenters, or any other trade. These, for ages, have had, like operative masons, their assemblies, in which their worshipful masters and wardens have presided; but they have been left in obscurity because their occupations did not bring them in familiar intercourse with men of wealth and power.

The first three degrees of masonry, when traced back to the actual labors of the craft, may claim some sort of antiquity; but as to all the numerous grades above these, (I think to the number of fifty,) they are of very modern invention, and are but the contrivances of ambitious or artful men to gratify their own vanity, or to obtain money from the vanity and folly of others. They have raked from the bigotry and chivalry of the dark ages of the old world, the names of certain orders, which never had any connexion with ancient masonry. These modern institutions are no more branches of the masonic system, than they are of the orders, whose titles they assume.

The pretence that masons are possessed of any peculiar knowledge, is as fallacious as their claim to a supernatural and antediluvian origin. But if they possess all that they pretend to have, of what advantage is it to themselves or to mankind? Suppose some cabalistic words have been preserved and transmitted by masons through ages, and that the fables they recite were true histories, how would it benefit themselves or their fellow men? The world must again be covered with that darkness which excluded all moral and scientific light, before such knowledge can be of any use even to the possessors.

But it is pretended that lodges are schools of the moral and physical sciences, and instruction in these is promised to those who join the fraternity. I have never heard of any attempt to impart any other moral instruction than that which could be conveyed by precepts like these: That masons must live within the compass; walk upright as the plumb; must deal on the square, and other such mystical advice. As to the sciences, the whole scope of instruction goes no further than frequently to remind the brethren than the sun rises in the east and sets in the west, and rules the day, and that the moon rules the night.

That we may be in no danger of violating the secrets of masonry, of having our judgments biassed by the antiquity it claims, or by respect for the many great and good men whose names are on the list of its votaries, let us for a moment put it out of view, and suppose that it were now proposed to establish a society, which, with awful solemnities, and dreadful denunciations, should impose secrecy on its members; that they should separate themselves from the rest of mankind, and establish an intelligence by which they could, under any circumstances, make themselves known to each other; that the duties of the members, in regard to themselves, should be incompatible with the general order of society; that when a member of the association should make himself known to another, he might look to that other for special favor, whether it was to be dispensed at the polls of an election, from the jury box, or from the bench. Suppose that the members of this association were bound to screen each other, as far as in their power, from all evil, by concealment; or by more active exertions, to relieve them from all dangers and difficulties, however they might arise from demerit. Let us suppose that all these obligations were to be imposed with awful religious ceremonies, and with sanguinary and horrible penalties, of which each member should consider himself pledged to be the executor. We may suppose this institution to have many grades, and that, at every advance, there are new ceremonies, new oaths, and new penalties, the higher differing from the lowest, only in grossness of absurdity, and impiety of imprecations. That the members of this new institution decorated themselves with the trappings of royalty, and bestowed on each other sacerdotal, aristocratic, and even royal titles. If such a society were now to be proposed, who would hesitate to say that it would be profane, and inconsistent with our religious, moral, social, and political institutions. One of the most serious objections which might be urged to such an institution, would be its frequent administration of oaths. There would be danger that even these obligations, however solemnly imposed, would become so familiar as to be little regarded; and the simple adjurations of a court of justice, administered with the least possible ceremony, would appear, when compared with the awful ceremonies of the society, to deserve but slight consideration. If the supposed oath imposed obligations which could not be fulfilled without a violation of the duties of a citizen, and indeed without crime, every honest man would shrink from the literal interpretation of it, and would find a refuge in construing it so as to reconcile it to his conscience; rejecting such parts as he did not find acceptable. Oaths, with which there must be so much tampering, could not but have a pernicious effect on society. But these effects would be still more deplorable, were the oaths to be observed according to their letter.

Masonry disclaims all interference in political matters. If, in this country, she has taken any part in the contentions of politicians, it has only been of late. While I was connected with the society, I had every reason to believe that she observed the forbearance she avows. But it must be obvious, that the whole machinery of the institution is peculiarly adapted to political intrigue; and though, in our country, its influence may not have been perceived by any party, yet we see that in a sister Republic, so far from its being considered the duty of the fraternity to keep apart from politics, the parties whose dissensions distract the Commonwealth, are arranged under different masonic denominations. Scotch masons, and York masons, in that country, no less designate masons of different sects, than they do partisans of different politics. If lodges may be converted into secret political clubs, they ought to be feared in a free country.

It has often occurred to me as a little extraordinary, that in this republican country of ours, where we claim to be such pure democrats, there should be manifested in those who become masons, such a passion for finery, pageantry, dignities, and titles. One who affects to despise the blue or red ribband, the star and garter of an English lord, or the coronet of a foreign prince, clothes himself with the utmost complacency, in all the colors of the rainbow, and decorates himself with as many jewels and medals, as are worn by an Indian chief. He expects from the fellows of his community, to be addressed by the titles of Worshipful, Most Worshipful, Excellent, Most Excellent, Illustrious, and Most Illustrious, with as much certainty as the greatest despot in the world requires from his slaves a recognition of the rank he assumes. We see from the masonic notices daily published in our papers, that Knight, Prince, and even King, are familiar titles, by which those to whom they belong are always addressed by their brethren in their assemblies. "To his Most Illustrious Highness, Prince of the Royal Secret of the thirty-third degree," is a title which emblazons the name of many a good republican in this community. Foreigners must think we are not less fond of the show, and trappings, and titles of aristocracy and royalty, than any other people, when they see that we are so eager to adopt them, in the only way tolerated by our political constitutions.

It is true there is something of equality in this, inasmuch as every man, of every grade, and every complexion, may be invested with all the finery, and the magnificent titles of the order. All others, however, are rivalled by the splendor of the Black Lodges of this city, headed by their Respectable and Worshipful Masters.

I have known many persons whose brains have been turned by their elevation from humble occupations to royal titles and imaginary thrones. Indeed, I have never known a very great mason, who was not a very great fool. I beg to be understood. I do not mean by very great masons, those who have stood highest in the estimation of the craft, and who have attained the highest masonic honors. I do not forget that the names of Washington, Clinton, Warren, La Fayette, Franklin, Robert R. Livingston, Jackson, and Marshall, are justly the boast of the fraternity; nor is it possible that I should ever forget that I have seen many venerated clergymen, sanctifying by their presence and their prayers the labors, as well as the refreshments of a lodge. But I mean by great masons, those who are proud of their pompous titles; who are fond of decorations; who persuade themselves that the affairs of the world turn upon masonry; that without it, society could hardly exist, or if it did, would be deprived of its fairest ornament, and most beneficial arrangement.

It may be asked, how it happens that I should have been so long a mason and not until this time expressed my disapprobation of the institution. It is true, it is nearly forty years since I became a member of the masonic fraternity, but I began to question its utility long ago. It must be fifteen or twenty years since I belonged to any lodge, and some eight or ten years that I have not been within the walls of a lodge room. During this time, I have not hesitated to express opinions in accordance with what I have now written.

When I was hardly twenty-one years of age, I was initiated in a lodge in New-York, which was distinguished for the respectability of its members. All of these I knew must have submitted to whatever would be required of me. My confidence, that they would not have done any thing wrong, induced me to pass through the required forms with very little—too little consideration. A like deference for the example of others, led me from step to step, with the same inconsiderateness. It was not till the buoyancy of youth had passed, that I began to see the vanity and folly, and, as I thought, the evil tendency of masonry. Morgan's fate has, I acknowledge, strengthened the unfavorable impressions I entertained previously to his murder. Since that event, I have thought the institution not only idle and useless, but this horrible catastrophe has evinced that its mysteries may engender infatuation that will stop at no crime. Since that event, I have believed it would be a relinquishment of a duty I owed to society, if I suffered my respect for those venerated men who have left the world to believe that masonry was approved by them, prevent me from expressing the convictions of my own mind of its merits. The example of the many who have stood as high in the ranks of masonry as in the estimation of the world, would have induced me to have buried my own thoughts in silence. I should have been awed by their opinions could I be sure that these patrons, of whom masonry so justly boasts, deliberately examined the merits of the institution; but when I reflect how many years of my life were passed before I gave the subject due consideration, I cannot but suppose that they, like myself, for a long time, may have been content to rest on the example of their predecessors, and that they have left their successors free to express their opinions. If these are unfavorable to masonry, no one can say that they are in opposition to what would have been the deliberate judgment of the persons whose great examples are considered of such authority.

I am happy that the letter I have had the honor to receive from you, affords me an opportunity to express, in such a manner as I presume will give them publicity, my sentiments on this subject. I have reason to believe they are in accordance with those of many good and respectable men who are masons; and who, I hope, will not by their silence, suffer their example in becoming masons to have an undue influence. I come forward the more readily at this moment, when I think no party or unworthy motive can be imputed to me; when the excitement occasioned by the murder of Morgan, has subsided into a just abhorrence of the guilty; and when the question is not whether every mason is not a bad man, but whether masonry is not a bad institution. I believe that it does no good that might not be accomplished by far better means. Its secrecy and extensive combinations are dangerous. Its titles and trappings are vain, foolish, and inconsistent with our republican institutions. Its pretensions are absurd, fallacious and impious; and its ceremonies and mysteries are profane, and lead many to believe that they impose obligations paramount to the laws. However limited the influence of my opinions might be, I should be sorry to end my life, leaving it to be believed that I had lived and died the advocate of an institution of which I entertain such views.

REMARKS ON THE CHARACTER OF FREEMASONRY.

Extract from an Address by Rev. Moses Thacher, of Wrentham, Mass. on the occasion of his seceding from the Masonic Institution.

THE subject to which I desire to call your attention, is, the standing which I have retained for some time past, in relation to the masonic institution. Although I am a minister of the gospel, set apart to take the oversight of this church and people; yet, far be it from me to feel myself above making concessions and retractions, wherein I have done wrong. That I *have done wrong* in uniting myself to the masonic society, and given just occasion of offence to some of my Christian friends, I am now fully *convinced.* I am satisfied, by a knowledge of facts, which have recently been presented to my mind, and which have placed me beyond a reasonable doubt, that the institution is very different, in nature and utility, from what I anticipated when I first became a member. I then joined upon the assurance of others of its great antiquity, of the purity of its principles, and the many advantages which it would present to me as a minister of the gospel. Notwithstanding I verily thought, that I could depend upon those assurances; I have since found, to my sorrow and disgust, that I have been deceived and disappointed. By these remarks, I do not mean to cast reflections upon those who gave me such assurances. *They* were doubtless *deceived;* and I feel much more disposed to apply to myself the denunciation, "Cursed is the man that trusteth in man;" than harshly to censure those, who were, *perhaps*, the *innocent* occasion of my folly.

With regard to the *antiquity* of the institution, I have found, by well authenticated facts, that it cannot be traced farther back than to the sixteenth century. I find that the first lodge of *Freemasons* ever instituted, was founded in *London*, and that the first, which emanated from this original stock, was as late as A. D. 1717. These facts are so authentic, that I feel myself warranted to say, beyond a reasonable doubt, that the institution is, comparatively, of recent origin. When therefore it professes to teach doctrines and facts by tradition, from before the flood, from the days of Solomon, or even from the commencement of the Christian era; it is evident that the institution is made to speak a *lie;* a lie too, which, more than almost any thing else, has been the means of infolding in the bosom of the society, the vast multitudes, who have devoted themselves to its interests.

In respect to the *principles* of the institution, it may be remarked, that this society, different from any other, holds *two classes.* The one class of principles, is, its *costume*, or dress, in which it appears before the public. These principles are, charity,* moral virtue, social intercourse, &c. all good in the abstract. The other class of principles consists in *secrecy*, secret *signs* and *obligations*, and secret *doctrines.* Upon these latter principles the whole institution is erected. This circumstance has doubtless deceived many. *It deceived me.* For a considerable time, I thought the institution was built upon those principles, which I now find to be merely *external*, designed for profession and show. The institution, instead of being built upon charity, and moral virtue, is built upon the *secret principles*, which I have mentioned; and these are principles by which genuine masons must be guided, however they may clash with other rules.

---

* It is not here admitted, that this is the charity which "seeketh not her own." All that masons, *as such*, ever bestowed, in what they call "charity," is bestowed precisely on the same principle that a mutual fire insurance company assist one of their own members in making up the loss which he has sustained by the devouring element. This is a "charity," which the sufferer has a right, in equity, to *demand*, in consideration of what he has already thrown into the common stock.

That the masonic institution has its *obligations*, no mason will deny. The great and important question, which now agitates the public mind, is, What is the nature of these obligations? Do those who take masonic obligations resign their lives to the disposal of the society; or does the society hold itself authorized to *take the life* of any individual or individuals, who may be considered as having violated its secret laws? As it respects myself, I have told masons repeatedly, that the moment I became convinced, that there was any thing in masonic obligations which either authorized or sanctioned the infliction of death, as a penalty, in case of violation, I would renounce masonry *immediately*. But I have now to confess, with pain and sorrow, that a knowledge of facts has placed it beyond a doubt in my own mind, that the masonic fraternity, as a body, do mean to hold the lives of individual members at their disposal. It does appear by numerous facts, substantiated by plenary evidence, that a free citizen of these United States has not only been kidnapped and murdered by *masons*, but that this awful transaction was contrived and executed by *masonic bodies*. It does appear, that masonic bodies, such as Lodges, Chapters, and Encampments, have secreted and facilitated the escape of the murderers; and that they did send the one, who executed the fatal deed, out of the country as soon as possible.* Were it proper, at this time, I think I could furnish sufficient evidence of what I have stated, to satisfy any candid mind. But such conduct as this, I must consider a fair comment upon the secret principles of the institution.

Besides, it appears to have been a fact, that the General Grand Chapter of the United States was in session, in the city of New York, at the time William Morgan was taken from Batavia, and that an express was despatched immediately to inform the Grand Chapter what had taken place, and what was done with the unhappy victim. From the silence of the General Grand Chapter on the subject, we must draw the natural inference, that it did, *virtually*,

* See the Affidavit of Avery Allyn, before Horace Holden, Esq. of the city of New York, March 28, 1829; also of John Mann, before Judge Tisdale, of Genesee.

to say the least, sanction the outrage. The question also may be asked, Has any Grand Lodge in the United States, or any Grand Chapter, or Grand Encampment, or the General Grand Chapter, or General Grand Encampment, ever *disavowed* that the secret principles of the institution do authorize and sanction the infliction of death as a penalty? Not to my knowledge; and it may be presumed they never have. But until these general bodies do this, it matters not what individual *masons*, or individual *lodges*, may say on the subject; because they all act in subordination. Unless the Grand Lodge of Massachusetts, for example, disavow the prerogative to inflict death as a penalty, it is vain for any individual lodge, or lodges, in the Commonwealth to disavow it; for all the lodges in the Commonwealth are in subordination to the Grand Lodge. Of what avail would it be for this town to say, that the law of this Commonwealth does not denounce the penalty of death against the murderer, unless the government of the State come out and say so too? But I have evidence, that William Morgan is not the *first*, who has fallen a victim to masonic vengeance. I have been informed by as many as three different persons, (all masons,) that a man was "put out of the way," that is, secretly murdered, a few years ago, by the Grand Lodge of a neighboring State.* In conversing also, with masons of high standing, I have never heard any of them, of a certain character, express the least regret that Morgan was put to death; but only that he was not put to death *more secretly*. A High Priest of the order, some time since, told one of my brethren in the ministry, that he had no doubt that Morgan was put to death, and that he *ought* to be put to death on *masonic principles*. With these

* The circumstances, as related to me by a mason of high standing, and who still retains such standing with the fraternity, were substantially these:—A member of the masonic institution, whom I will call A. B. and who lived in one of the back towns of R**** ******, took C. D., and made him a mason, as the masons would say, "*illegally*;" giving him such instructions that he "worked himself into a lodge." C. D. retained this illegal standing for some time, and rendered himself so familiar with the "work," that he obtained an office, I think that of junior or senior warden. By and by however, "it leaked out," that C. D. had been made a mason illegally, and by whom; when the lodge "made him

facts in view, is it possible to get rid of the impression, that the masonic institution is a *blood-stained* institution?

I am, moreover, satisfied, from what I have lately seen of the history of the institution, and the history of its degrees, that it leads on step by step into infidelity. The distinction between ancient and modern Freemasonry is altogether without foundation. *It is all modern*. It is *all* directly calculated to promote the designs of infidelity. The three first degrees, it is true, are not so exceptionable as the higher; but still *they* are exceptionable, especially as they pertain to a *modern* institution. Even in these degrees, the Master, if he proceeds according to rule, personifies, and places himself instead of, the Deity, in a kind of mock imitation of the most august scene which was ever witnessed either by men or angels; and which God permitted to be witnessed only by the latter. It is here, (and *masons* will well understand me,) the Master of the Lodge, in representation of what he is about to do himself, cites that most sublime passage of Holy Writ, "*And God said, Let there be light, and there was light.*" It is here, also, he stands, and professes to imitate the infinite and eternal God, who spake light into existence! If the institution *were of divine origin*, as masons have pretended, and this work were never performed except by those who have a becoming reverence for the Deity, it would alter the case materially. But, being a mere human contrivance, fostered too, in an age of infidelity, and managed, as it frequently is, by men, who have the highest contempt for serious things; the institution must be directly calculated, even in the three lower degrees, to harden the heart, and banish from the mind the fear of God. What then should be thought of the higher degrees, in which the infinite God is still more strikingly

over again," and he was suffered to retain his standing with the fraternity. Soon after this, A. B., who had thus violated his masonic obligations, happened to be in P*********, at the time the Grand Lodge was in session, which summoned him to appear before them. C. D. obeyed the summons, and was, by the Grand Lodge, "put out of the way," so secretly, that his friends thought he had absconded, and this was the general report.—The same mason, who related to me these circumstances, expressed his regret that the "Morgan affair" had not been conducted *as secretly*, and thereby prevented all this noise and commotion.

personified by mortal worms; where his sacred names and attributes are used as *pass-words*, and mock miracles are wrought as *signs;* as every mason knows, who has taken these degrees? Here too, is another cause of delusion; that is, the pretence, that what pertains to the Royal Arch, and its preparatory degrees, is *ancient masonry.* It is capable of the most satisfactory proof, that nothing was known of what is called "Royal Arch Masonry," even as early as 1730. It cannot be traced even to English origin. It has not been tolerated in England. In 1799, any thing higher than the three first degrees of masonry, was prohibited by law.* Upon the same stock has been graffed the Knights' degrees, which masons profess to trace to Jerusalem. But Professor Robison,† speaking of a certain lodge, situate at Lyons, in France, says, "We know that this lodge stood, as it were, at the head of French Freemasonry, and *that the fictitious order of Masonic Knights Templars was formed in this lodge, and was considered as the model of all the rest of this mimic chivalry.*" Here, then, it is evident, that the Knights' degrees originated in infidel France, at a time when infidelity generally prevailed in that nation, and when infidels had the control of almost all the lodges on the continent of Europe. This will account for their horrid oaths, and for some of their ceremonies, too shocking to be named on this occasion.‡ Connected in the same chain, are the

* See the work on Freemasonry, by "A Master Mason."

† Proofs of Conspiracy.

‡ I have it on the best authority, that a part of one obligation, administered to an Illustrious Knight, runs in the following manner:—"You further swear that should you ever know a companion violate any essential part of this obligation, you will use your most decided endeavors, by the blessing of God, to bring such person to the strictest and most condign punishment, agreeably to the rules and usages of our ancient fraternity; and this by pointing him out to the world as an unworthy and vicious vagabond, by opposing his interest, by deranging his business, by transferring his character after him wherever he may go, by exposing him to the contempt of the whole fraternity and of the world, but of our Illustrious order more especially, during his whole natural life."

In what is called the "Sealed Obligation," the novitiate "drinks wine from a human skull," and swears,—"As the sins of the whole world were laid upon the head of the Saviour, so may all the sins committed by the person whose skull this was, be heaped upon

"Ineffable Degrees," in which, among other ceremonies, there is a mock celebration of the Lord's Supper! That these degrees are in the same system of Freemasonry with the preceding, is evident, because the Freemason's Monitor prescribes the rule for this shocking service, when "the *Most Perfect* presents the candidate with bread and wine, saying, eat of this bread with me, and drink of the same cup."* Such is the shocking nature of these degrees, that it is perfectly natural to pass on, from step to step, until the Knight adept of the Eagle or Sun says to the novitiate—"Behold this monster which you must conquer—a serpent which WE detest as an idol that is adored by the idiot and vulgar under the name of RELIGION!!!"† Such also has been the artful management in some of these degrees, that certain things, most exceptionable, have been withholden from serious, conscientious men, while they have been exhibited to others of a different character; which has tended very much to deceive, and keep in ignorance, those, who would otherwise have protested, and exposed the wickedness. I have satisfactory evidence, that something was withholden from me, even in the Royal Arch Degree, which has been communicated to others.‡

---

my head, in addition to my own, should I ever knowingly or wilfully violate or transgress any obligation, that I have heretofore taken, take at this time, or shall at any future period take, in relation to any degree of masonry or order of Knighthood. So help me God."—Conversing with a minister of the gospel, of good standing, who had taken this degree, concerning the ceremony to which I here allude, he replied, "I can sincerely say, that *I* never drank wine out of a human skull; but we have our *alternatives*;" at the same time giving me to understand, that although this was the legal ceremony, yet, when it was too abhorrent to the novitiate, he was permitted to use a *substitute*, which was intended to represent the same thing. The same clergyman told me, that one of the oaths was so abhorrent, that he refused to subscribe to it, without including a *condition*, which he considered as destroying the force of the obligation.

* Freemason's Monitor, 1802, p. 263.

† See Barruel's History of Jacobinism, and Professor Robison's Proofs of a Conspiracy.

‡ A minister of the gospel informed me, not long since, that he took this degree, before he became a preacher; when an obligation was administered to him altogether as exceptionable as the one pertaining to this degree, revealed by the Le Roy Convention. This

Now, Christian brethren and friends, as I am in possession of these facts, and many more, which time would fail to mention, and convinced, as I am, that the institution of Freemasonry is Anti-Christian, is it not my duty, as a Christian and a minister of the gospel, to come out and leave it? Can *masons* blame me for coming out and leaving the institution? But, it will be said, "Why did you not come out before?" I answer; I was not in possession of these facts before, by which I might be convinced. It is not long since some of these facts first came before the public. For a very considerable time, I was so blinded, as sincerely to believe, and say, that the commotion in the western part of our country, was merely a political excitement. Others, perhaps, think so still. But, being undeceived with respect to these facts, I have very naturally been led to look at others; to examine, coolly and deliberately, the history of the institution, the history and nature of its degrees, and the nature of its secret principles. This deliberate examination has brought my mind, irresistibly, to the result, which I present before you this day.

But, "Why did you not withdraw secretly, and silently, from the institution, say nothing, either for or against it, and save the *excitement*, which must result from an open renunciation?" Answer. Such a course, I once thought, and *said*, was the most judicious. I did not think it *necessary*, that any person should come out in this *open* manner, on the supposition that it was best to leave the institution. But, I have become convinced, that I could not pursue this course *conscientiously*. Believing, as I firmly and sincerely do, that the masonic institution is Anti-Christian, I could not discharge my *duty* by withdrawing in *silence*. Now, I ask, Christian brethren and friends, on the ground that the institution is what I have stated, and its secret principles of such a nature as have been pointed out, whether you can desire me to

---

clergyman further stated, that in the obligation administered to him, the clause *was* included, "*murder and treason* NOT *excepted*." He recollected this, from the following circumstance; a Baptist brother, who was "exalted" at the same time with himself, stopped, when the High Priest came to this clause, and asked "If it was so?"

leave to *your sons* my name and influence, as a minister of the gospel, in favor of the institution? On the ground that the institution is what has been represented, do you desire, that your children may have to plead an excuse for becoming Freemasons, what thousands have done with respect to other ministers of the gospel, that "*your minister* was a Freemason?" But this must certainly be the case, were I to withdraw from the institution in *silence*. Should I do this, I must necessarily leave the weight of my name, example and influence, however light they might appear, in favor of the institution. But this I cannot do. In justice to my own conscience, in justice to the young and rising generation, and in justice to the cause of Christ, I must come out, *openly* and *honestly*, and declare my connexion with the masonic institution *dissolved*.

CORRESPONDENCE IN RELATION TO THE HISTORICAL EVIDENCE OF THE EXISTENCE OF FREEMASONRY PRIOR TO THE LAST CENTURY.

BOSTON, Nov. 11, 1829.

To the President and Professors of the Theological Seminary, Andover, Mass.

GENTLEMEN,—In order to the acquisition and diffusion of light on the subject of Freemasonry—a subject deeply affecting the welfare of our country, the citizens of Boston, at a great public meeting, appointed the undersigned a committee to promote inquiries into the nature of its claims.

In pursuance of this duty the Committee found it to be expedient, in order to arrest the attention, and satisfy the diversity of opinions on the subject, to have recourse to different sources of information, because the testimony that would influence the opinions of some, would have little or no effect upon those of others.

The views the Committee have, gentlemen, in addressing you upon this subject, are not to elicit masonic signs, pass-words, or grips—for these are all known; but their object is simply to ask your opinions upon a historical fact, believing that your familiar acquaintance with oriental literature must have furnished you with the means of a reply without much further research. The question is the following, viz;—'Is there any known history to justify the belief that Speculative or Freemasonry had existence prior to the last century?' It claims an origin coeval with time, and many believe it—some however doubt.

The expression of your sentiments upon the foregoing question, in writing, will very much oblige your respectful and obedient servants.

GEORGE ODIORNE,
JOHN D. WILLIAMS,
ABNER PHELPS,
BENJ. W. LAMB,
WILLIAM MARSTON,
HENRY GASSETT,
JONATHAN FRENCH,
THOMAS WALLEY,
DANIEL WELD,
EBENEZER WITHINGTON,
BENJ. V. FRENCH,
JOHN P. WHITWELL,
Suffolk Committee.

DR. WOODS' REPLY.

THEOLOGICAL SEMINARY, ANDOVER,
December 7th, 1829.

To the Suffolk Committee.

GENTLEMEN,—The question which you have proposed to me and my colleagues respecting the origin of Freemasonry, I shall answer very briefly. The question I understand as relating to what is *essential* to Freemasonry at the present time,—to what is *peculiar* to the *system*.

The antiquity of Freemasonry must be determined in the same way as the antiquity of any thing else. Suppose we are asked, whether there is reason to believe that *war* existed in the time of David? We answer in the affirmative, and refer immediately to the historical evidence. We have a history which has every mark of genuineness and truth, which expressly informs us that there was war in his days; and that he was actively engaged in it. And this fact agrees with the known character of David, and with the circumstances of the Israelitish nation in his days; and it is referred to in many of his Psalms, and in subsequent Jewish writings. This is proof sufficient. Rational belief rests on evidence, and this evidence we have. But suppose any man should assert that David understood the principles of Electricity as they are laid down by modern Philosophers, and that he wrote a book containing those principles: We ask him for his *proof*. Is there any thing in David's writings, or in any other ancient writings, which shows this? No. Is it probable that he understood Electricity, from the general state of philosophical science in ancient times? The probability is on the other side, especially as we are able to trace the history of Electricity to its origin in modern times.

Again, let a man assert that Solomon made a balloon, and that he frequently rode in it from Jerusalem to Tyre, and sometimes took in Hiram with him. We should put the same question: What evidence is there of this? Does any authentic history assert it; or does the supposition agree with our ideas of Solomon's character, or with the known circumstances of his times? All men will say, there is no *proof* of the thing asserted: of course it cannot be believed. The above remarks show how I suppose the question respecting the high antiquity of Freemasonry ought to be answered. If men assert that it existed in Solomon's days, and that he and Hiram, King of Tyre, were Freemasons, we inquire for proof.- Is there any historical evidence of the fact?—Where is that evidence found? Is it in any ancient book? Let the book be produced. Is it derived from tradition? Let it be shown where that tradition existed, and how it is traced back to the time of Solomon, or to any period near that. Is it derived from a *new revelation?* Let it be shown to whom the revelation was made, and what credentials he had of his being authorized to teach it to others. If there is any evidence whatever, let it be made to appear. No reasonable man will ever assert an important fact, with an expectation or desire of having it believed, without producing evidence to prove it. Now I have never seen or heard of any evidence, of any kind or degree, in support of the pretended antiquity of Freemasonry; and I suppose the same is true of all others. What then can we do, consistently with reason and common sense, but to withhold our belief.

As to *probable* evidence; it would be very proper to inquire, whether it can be reconciled to the acknowledged character of Solomon, and of the twelve Apostles to suppose, that they belonged to a society, established on the *principles* and practising the *rites* of Freemasonry. If these principles and rites are what the community at large understand them to be, and what *Freemasons themselves* understand them to be, an answer to this inquiry would be no very difficult thing.

I am, Gentlemen, with the greatest respect,

Yours, &c

LEONARD WOODS.

PROFESSOR STUART'S REPLY.

ANDOVER, DEC. 22, 1829.

To the Suffolk Committee in Boston, appointed to inquire into the nature, principles and tendency of Freemasonry.

GENTLEMEN,—In answer to your inquiries, respecting any traces of the history of Freemasonry, in ancient times, I reply, that it has not been my lot to find any thing of this nature, in any book that I have ever perused, either in any of the Asiatic or European languages. I take it to be a point conceded by all literary men, that no such traces exist, in any ancient record whatever.

The pretence that Freemasonry was known in the time of Solomon, is refuted by the internal evidence which masonic books themselves contain. For example, they tell us that Hiram Abiff, the Grand Master Mason, was killed by Jubela, Jubelo, and Jubelum. It happens, unfortunately, however, that these names are formed, (and that by no very *skilful master*,) from the Latin language, and not from the Hebrew, to which they bear not the slightest resemblance. All Hebrew names are significant and have a Hebrew shape; and it requires but a moderate share of skill, to detect gross imposture in this pretended history of Hiram Abiff.

The same is manifestly the case, in regard to a large class of names, which are given out by masonic books as very ancient; e. g. Buh, Giblimites, Toulumith, Lisha, Jaobert, Tito, Harrodim, Juha, (Animani, which the books say means, *I am that I am*,) Jubilum, Akirop, Sidach, Solo, and many others. If the meaning of masonic books be, what it seems to be, that these have come down from the days and the language of Solomon, it is gross imposture. These names would for the most part, be as good Hebrew, as *Abracadabra* is English.

If what the books state, also, about the use of such names as Jah, Jevah, Jovah, Shaddai, Adonai, be true, (names of the adorable Godhead, in the Hebrew language, and introduced it would seem, by some masons who had a smattering of the Hebrew language;) if it be true that these names are used in the connexion and manner in which the books of masons declare them to be, then it is certain that the name of God is profanely used. And what can I say of the Animani, which is pretended to mean, *I am that I am?* I confess, that I cannot help shuddering at the manner in which this is stated to be used, in books published by members of the masonic fraternity. Whether the accounts, however, from which I take this, are true, is of course more than I am able to vouch for. It is only on the supposition that they are so, that my remarks can have any bearing on the subject of masonry.

If these accounts are true, then it is time that every man in our community should know it. That any class of men among us should be encouraged to expect protection in all cases, " murder and treason not excepted," is what institutions like ours can never sanction; and the eyes of all should be opened wide in relation to this matter.

If these accounts are not true, the masons owe it to themselves, and to the world, to vindicate themselves from such charges. Especially is this the case, inasmuch as these charges are made by men of good standing, of unimpeachable integrity and veracity, and who have a *personal* acquaintance with all the secrets of masonry. For my part, I shall be exceedingly glad to see these charges refuted; as it would greatly relieve my mind in regard to many estimable men, belonging to the masonic order. But I see no way to get rid of the force of the testimony in question, until a counter-statement is made, which is worthy of credibility.

For a long time, I neither knew nor cared much about this subject. But recent attention to it, has filled me with astonishment; and as to some things contained in it, with horror. The trifling with oaths, and with the awful names of the ever blessed God, is a feature I cannot contemplate but with deep distress.

I am, Gentlemen,

Your friend and obedient servant,

MOSES STUART.

BOSTON, Nov. 4, 1829.

To the President and Professors of Harvard University.

GENTLEMEN,—At a numerous meeting of the citizens of Boston and vicinity, the undersigned were appointed a committee to inquire into the origin, nature, and principles of Freemasonry.

In performing the duties assigned them, they find the Masonic Institution to claim an origin of much greater antiquity than is supported by any well authenticated history that the undersigned have yet been able to meet with. They have discovered no book on Freemasonry written prior to 1723. Since that period to the present, the future historian will have ample materials to prove the existence of the institution. The masonic writers, which the committee have yet seen on the antiquity of Freemasonry, appear to rely on tradition. But tradition is not asked for. It would seem natural to expect, that a society, claiming for its members, the worthy, the learned, and the great, in all ages and countries, should have, at least, something more to be relied on, to prove its very existence, than vague tradition.

The disclosures which have been made, and the consequent growing excitement, that has arisen in our country on this subject, appear to justify a fearless and thorough investigation. Truth and impartiality are alone sought for. It has occurred to the undersigned, that the course most likely to give satisfaction to the public, in the present inquiry, was to present the historical question, as to the origin of Freemasonry, to the decision of high minded and honorable gentlemen of profound learning and research. Men above suspicion, and in possession of the most ancient and extensive libraries in this country.

The special object of this application is, respectfully to request an answer to the following historical question, viz.

Is there any known history, to justify the belief, that Speculative, or Freemasonry, had existence prior to the last century?

The expression of your sentiments, in writing, on the foregoing question, will be gratefully acknowledged by

Your most obedient servants,

THE COMMITTEE.

MR. QUINCY'S REPLY.

HARVARD UNIVERSITY,
CAMBRIDGE, DEC. 5, 1829.

To the Gentlemen of the Suffolk Committee.

GENTLEMEN,—I have received and laid before the Faculty of Harvard University, your letter, requesting an expression of their sentiments on the question—"Is there any known history to justify the belief, that Speculative, or Freemasonry, had existence prior to the last century."

In reply, I have the honor, by request of the Faculty, to state that they have no knowledge of any such history. On inquiry of the Librarian of the University, and on examining the catalogue of books, no such has been found. The subject is one, however, on which the members of the Faculty profess to have no precise information, it having never before been presented to them as an object of interest and inquiry.

Should any books in the College Library be found to

be important, for your purposes, in the course of your investigation, they will, without doubt, on application, be placed at the command of any person engaged under your authority in the research you have instituted.

Very respectfully, Gentlemen,

I am your obedient servant,

JOSIAH QUINCY,

President of Harvard University.

THE LAWFULNESS OF FREEMASONRY AS A *SECRET* INSTITUTION.

*Extract from "A Reply of the Genesee Consociation to the letter of the Rev. Mr. Emerson, of Weathersfield, Conn. addressed to them on the subject of their resolution relative to masonic ministers, and masonic candidates for the ministry."**

We feel prepared to take what some may consider *high* ground, that secret societies are *unlawful*. We do not mean to assert it as a fact, that we have any special statutes which prohibit them—but we mean that such an institution as yours is highly dangerous in its tendency to the best interests of society. What we have to state here may be offensive to some of your brethren, but we hope not to yourself. We say therefore that, towards masons we indulge no hostile feelings. If we give offence to any, it is from an imperious sense of duty—not from personal resentment.

We here remark again that we are unable to perceive how we can discuss this question with you and come to the point in hand, which is to vindicate the propriety of our resolution, without freely examining the nature of your institution, which now stands all unguarded by the Tyler's sword.

We do not regard your institution with any friendly

---

* Their resolution was as follows,—" *Resolved*, That the Consociation will neither license, ordain, or install, those who sustain any connexion with the institution of masonry, or who will not disapprove and renounce it; nor will we give letters of recommendation in favor of such persons to preach in any of the churches in our connexion."

feeling. We wish it prostrated to the ground, never to rise again. We are not in favor, as you are, of having its "implements," &c. laid up in the choicest of cabinets,—nor of having the least vestige of it left to her "vigorous successors,"—but we wish it to come to a complete and everlasting end. You have something to say in favor of the lawfulness of secret societies.—In page 9th, you say, that "of their intrinsic lawfulness, I have no doubt," and that "for any government to forbid them, would in my view, be rank tyranny."

1. We oppose this opinion, first, by a view of some circumstances of the case. In this country, the people, who are always the best judges of their own interest, govern—and if they are disposed to prohibit by law, the existence of secret societies, there is no tyranny in the case; for it is absurd to suppose that the people, in the free exercise of their prerogatives, will oppress themselves. Therefore should it ever become the *popular* opinion, that secret societies ought not to exist, the *omission* to prohibit them by law would be "rank tyranny," because this omission would give indulgence to the *few* without an express right, to trample on the privileges of the *many*. As the case now is, and has been, for many years in our country, the masonic institution is an "imperium in imperio." The prerogatives which it has assumed are *unchartered* It has grown up by mere *indulgence*. Society at large should never be exposed, to be *practised* upon by a few "sons of light." Masonry has been the instrument in the hands of bad men, of piratical depredations on the people. If the people have foes, it is right that they should see them and their weapons, and understand their plans—that they may have an equal chance for their lives. Masonry is such an instrument as we have, in part, described it; and there are many in whose hands it has been intrusted, who were not dull in apprehending *for what purpose* the instrument is made.

2. Another argument against the "intrinsic lawfulness" of this secret society is the great *facility* which it affords for secret transactions of an immoral character. This forms a solid objection to it which can never be passed over. These transactions which are to be kept secret under the sanction of the severest penalties, are a

temptation to the greatest enormities, and afford precisely such securities against detection and punishment, as the vilest of men desire. The good can never need such securities, and the bad do not deserve them, nor is it safe for society, that they should have them. If a man is always obliged to act *openly*, he is strongly induced to act *honestly*. But give him an opportunity to act *secretly*, and the security against punishment, which masonry guarantees, with great strength and a dreadful energy, and he will act more agreeably to the selfish propensities of a sinful heart. Continue in existence your society, and many will be disposed to cultivate the bad principles of their nature; abolish it, and they will be disposed to cultivate the better principles. Thieves, robbers, and counterfeiters, do not mature and discuss their plans in open assemblies, but in *secret*, "neither come they to the light, because their deeds are evil." They may cultivate the "friendships and honor" peculiar to themselves, as masons may cultivate the dispositions peculiar to their unlawful compact, but on the whole, the *character* is generally impaired, and society is injured.

3. In maintaining your views, you hypocritically say, page 9, "if these secrets injure no one from their very nature, they must be referred to the day when all secrets will be disclosed." But we reply, that such is the *nature* of your secrets, when joined with the *selfish nature* of man, that they will be injurious to society. To this rule there may be exceptions, but the rule itself is founded upon the broad and philosophical view of the *human character*. A *dagger*, from its *very nature*, injures no one; but put daggers into the hands of such men as those with whom you have confided your secrets, and they are dangerous instruments. We do not approve of their being worn, for the purpose of practising upon others who wear them not. Harmless as the instrument of masonry is in itself, good men ought not to wish for it—and bad men do not deserve it. Our safety in lives, character and property, in our prosperous application to business, and in our various privileges, guaranteed to us by the government under which we repose, requires that this instrument be *wrested* from the hands of bad men—and consequently from all—because in constitutional provis-

ions, distinctions are impracticable. As the case now is, with masonic magistrates, jurors, &c. &c. if we must appeal to such a court, with a *mason* for an antagonist, we go not with equal hopes or privileges for success. We may be wrong in such a manner as to obtain no redress by legal process; because perhaps, we cannot show that these masonic officers have, in a *tangible* manner, violated the *letter* of the law, although its *spirit* has been corruptly disregarded.

We have another remark to make on the manner in which you are disposed to express yourself, concerning these secrets—that "they must be referred to the day when all secrets will be disclosed." What is your *meaning* here? Is it, that your secrets cannot be known? Deceive not yourself, nor vainly attempt to deceive others—for they *are* known. Or, do you mean, that if they are known, the public cannot touch them now—that they are not to enjoy the liberty of examining the *nature* of this extraordinary code, thus thrown out before their gaze? And if so, by what legitimate authority is this liberty abridged, and this silence of the tongue imposed? In our view, these revelations *are things of this world*, and men will judge them according to the light which God hath given them.

But you proceed page 9, and make the following declaration, in favor of the *lawfulness* of your society, "that I know nothing in our secrets which appears to one contrary to the word of God or the rights of men—and that I never had the least suspicion that there was any masonic penalty worse than expulsion."

With respect to this first clause, we have already remarked in substance, what we deem sufficient—on the last clause, we say, that such assertions are by no means new things to us,—we have, long since, understood them. We know what is pledged to those who are about to be initiated, when in the preparation room, that nothing is to be imposed which will injure their "religion or their politics." We also understand how masonry is "explained" to some candidates, who are horror struck at the oaths; we grant that there is a favorable commentary on such passages—yet we also understand the commentary on those same oaths, whenever there is an intended revelation of your secrets—we have the commentary in the murder of Morgan—it is written in blood. Perhaps you and your conscience rest easy under the *one* comment, but *we* cannot under the other. But on this point, there is a wide difference of opinion in the interpretation of those tremendous oaths, among your own brethren; the most of them understanding the penalties according to the legitimate construction of language While therefore there is the difference of opinion on this fundamental article, among your brethren, and while you are still disposed to defend masonry in the gross, you cannot expect to feel satisfied with the continued existence of an institution which contains such provisions; for whenever a great occasion arises, the penalties are inflicted by some of your brethren, (the rest standing by,) and if the deed comes to light, nothing is more convenient than for you to say, that those executioners did not *properly interpret their obligations*, and still you go on and support the institution! An institution from which such outrages will proceed more or less frequently, as naturally as water runs down hill. Where are the men to be found who will support your institution? We reply, that they must never be found among the number of those whom we may in future ordain to the work of the ministry. Now, sir, with all these facts and considerations before you, can you not possibly see any thing against the "intrinsic lawfulness" of such secret societies? But such is the strange infatuation of men on some questions and on particular occasions that possibly you will come out again and attempt to say some plausible things in favor of *masonry in the gross*—that the conduct of a great number of your brethren has fallen below their "avowed principles" and that we here only discover the abused principles of masonry, as in many instances we may notice the abused principles of Christianity—all this may pass off with the negligent and superficial as being very fine; though in our estimation, it is neither *s lid* nor safe. For you may grace the hilt of the *dagger* with as many sparkling diamonds as you please, but they do not blunt the point.

But masonry, like the responses of the heathen oracles, is on some points exceedingly indefinite and flexible—with some it is a very mysterious thing indeed, and with those who look upon it with a stupid and unsuspecting wonder, there is nothing which takes so happily as your fine eulogiums coming from "a full heart." It is so ancient, so venerable, such great names on the list of membership—so much like Christianity!! But when we ask, what man has it made wise? what is the answer, but silent confusion? The *general* rule is this, that could the nature of this mysterious thing be known before hand, wise and good men would not have been juggled into it. On the unsuspecting, it has played off more tricks, and practised more impostures than any thing else excepting the church of Rome. See the simple, the wise and great ones of this world in their passage from one degree to another, hoping to catch something by and by, and sometimes thinking they were close to it—one more step—and then! and what then? why then, all this reminds us of the ludicrous chase of our childhood to catch the rainbow.

We have only to add here to the preceding remarks, on the "intrinsic lawfulness" of your institution, that if you permit the question to be decided by scriptural maxims, the decision will be against you. Every thing which is thus secret, does not meet with the approbation of the New Testament. The principle which induces any company to perpetual secrecy, must be selfish and corrupt—or it would not have received the direct denunciation of our Lord, who knew what was in man—and therefore renders the true reason for secrecy, when he said "neither come they to the light, because their deeds are evil."

By order of the Consociation,*

JOHN TAYLOR, *Moderator.*
SILAS PRATT, *Clerk.*

---

* Names of members of the Consociation.

Rev. *John Taylor*, Mendon; Rev. Mr. *Jones*, Mendon; James Saxton, Mendon; Rev. *Wm. P. Kendrick*, Shelby, Orleans Co.; Rev. *Milton Huxly*, Stafford, Genesee, Co.; Rev. *Jabez Spicer*, N. Penfield, Monroe Co.; *Abel C. Ward*, Bergen, Genesee Co.; *Ezra Coon*, Byron, Genesee Co.; Rev. *Elihu Mason*, Bergen, Genesee Co.; Rev. *Herman Halsey*, Bergen, Genesee Co.; Dea. *Joseph Bloss*, Brighton, Monroe Co.; *Abijah Gould*, Henrietta, Monroe Co.; *Theodore Ingersoll*, Ogden, Monroe Co.; Rev. *E Raymond*, N. Bristol, Ontario Co.; Rev. *Julius Steel*, East Bloomfield, Ontario Co.; Rev. *John F. Bliss*, Gainesville, Genesee Co.

REMARKS ON SECRET SOCIETIES.

*Addressed to the Anti-masonic Convention, held at Dedham, Mass. January 1, 1828. By Benjamin Waterhouse, M. D.**

Being called to the unusual station of presiding over a large, deliberative assembly, the novelty of the situation calls, of course, for your indulgence.

As a retired man, I may not be exactly acquainted with the precise views, and predominant feelings of the numerous delegation here convened. I know, generally, that it has been occasioned by certain alarming events, which have roused the universal attention of one of the largest States in the Union; and that this agitation was excited by deeds of cruelty and bloodshed, instigated, it is said and believed, by a very numerous and growing *secret* society of active and aspiring men, knit together by solemn vows, and unusual OATHS, with shocking penalties annexed, unknown to our laws, and repugnant to our feelings as men and Christians; and that this serious state of things has called us together, to look into the disorder; and if we cannot at once, devise and apply the remedy, to prevent, at least, its spreading. Let me promise, however, that the task is not an easy one, from the very nature of the disease; it being "*a pestilence that* WALKETH IN DARKNESS."

My observations, at this time, must be of a *general* complexion, and not of a particular nature. It appears, from the earliest records of mankind, that there has existed in almost every country, little combinations of restless men, like what is now called *masonry*. In the EIGHTH chapter of the book of *Ezekiel*, (who lived 590 years before Christ,) you will find mentioned "about five and twenty men," in a secret recess, "with their backs towards the temple of the Lord, and their faces towards the east, worshipping the sun."

There was a combination of great influence and celebrity in Greece, that generally met at Athens, denominated

* B. Waterhouse, M. D. formerly Professor of the Theory and Practice of Physic in Harvard University; and Professor of Natural History in Brown University.

the *Eleusinian Mystery*, conducted with deep solemnity and secrecy. If any of the initiated revealed the secrets of it, it was thought unsafe to live in the same house with him, lest it should, by the wrath of the gods, be struck with lightning, and the wretch was put to death. Yet the sagacious *Socrates*, that wonder of his age, that light shining in a dark place, denounced that secret masonry of the Grecians, as impious towards Heaven, and mischievous towards the community at large, and it is well known that for this attack on their *secret society*, he was condemned to drink the fatal hemlock.

Men of a certain cast of mind are prone to wrap themselves up in a cloud of mystery, that they may more easily govern their fellow creatures: a striking instance of which may be seen in the history of the first Popes of Rome, who, during several hundred years, bound in chains the human understanding, till *Martin Luther*, and other reformers broke the spell, and freed the human mind from a degree of slavery and thraldom that is scarcely credible. Reason was confounded by mystery, image worship, awe, dread and ignorance; while the most degrading superstition, and priestly violence upheld, for ages, a debasing system of mental oppression.

If we recur to the oldest book we have, the BIBLE, we shall find that the Jewish system was made up chiefly of ceremonies, types, and figures, denoting intellectual things, and moral duties. This mode of teaching morality was, at that early period of the world, necessary—absolutely necessary—and why? because then, not one person in ten thousand, beside the priesthood, could read. The people were not then able to *exhibit thoughts to the eye* by means of writing, hence the necessity arose of teaching by *signs* and *symbols*, that when these struck the *eye*, they should raise corresponding ideas in the *mind*, and thus convey moral truths and duties by the sight and by the operation of tools, and mechanic instruments. This is the fulcrum on which rests and turns the first, and most fascinating part of masonic instruction, which, from its simplicity, and manifest adaptation, delights a young and uninformed mind, predisposed to wonder.

The pleasing analogy between things material and intellectual, strikes with admiration the imperfectly educated mind; and MOSES was permitted, if not enjoined to use it, in governing the six hundred thousand Jews whom he led out of Egypt: and modern masons have imitated the lighter parts of it. I say the *lighter* parts of it, for the *Persian*, if not the Egyptian mode of teaching the most weighty and important truths, was of a higher standard, and of a more sublime nature. This was the secret literature of the ancient kings, taught them in strict confidence by the *Magi*, or "*wise men of the east*," who were the GRAND-MASTERS of the symbolical school. While modern masons make a structure or temple, the symbol or emblem of society, the *Magi* made the order, and government of the *material world, a mirror or looking-glass for the political government of a state*. In the highest grades, they took their emblems from what they knew of the *solar system*,—the sun, moon, and stars—the succession of day and night—the beautiful variation of the seasons, and their delightful consequences; in which the SUN, the *eye* and *soul* of this lower world, afforded them a glorious, and exhaustless emblem! It is worthy of notice that the Peruvians and Mexicans on this continent, have the same ideas interwoven with their religion.

But all this typical, or mechanical morality was swept away by CHRISTIANITY, which substituted *intellect* in its place. Instead of tangible and visible things, it made the Christian's heaven, not a *material structure*, the *work* of a slowly progressive *architect*, laying one *hewn*-stone upon another, (which the Bible forbids,*) but a "temple not made with hands," and therefore "*eternal*."

We neither censure, nor deride those who are enraptured with a system that addresses itself, like the worship of images, to the eyesight. Yet we may, I hope, be allowed to express surprise and wonder, and even astonishment, that clergymen—ministers of the Christian *protestant* religion, should be so attached, as some are, to a system of ceremonies—forms—types—figures and instruments, and be aiding in getting up a sudden, theatrical contrivance, to effect amazement instead of exhibiting the inward man of the heart!—We lament that any

* Exodus, ch. xx. 25.

teacher of a *spiritual* religion should take up with the *husk* and *shell* instead of the *meat;* or that he should ever mix the words of Christian worship with the jargon of masonry, since it is forbidden in the Bible to mix *linen* with *woollen*, or to plough with an *ox* and an *ass!* *

But I forbear, lest we should be thought to tread on forbidden ground, and intermeddle with any one's religion, which is, with every individual, a sacred thing, while that of FREEMASONRY is, and ought to be open to the decent examination of any man, at this time of apprehension, and well grounded alarm for the safety of the citizen, and the free and righteous course of justice in judges and in *jurymen.*

Your aim, if I rightly comprehend it, is to induce each member of the mystical society in question, to *think*, so as to satisfy himself whether he has built his house on a sandy foundation, or upon a rock; and whether, in selecting his mental food, he has been sufficiently careful to strip off the *husk*, retaining only that part which constitutes solid and wholesome nutriment; and this sort of food is to be found in Christianity—a system purely intellectual, that has no need to have recourse to *fright* or to shocking OATHS, which the New Testament positively forbids, and strictly enjoins to "*do violence to no man.*"

There are mysteries enough in the creation around us, without presumptuous, short-sighted men getting together, in the night, to contrive new ones, the tendency of which is to make straight things crooked, instead of making the crooked path of life straight.

The human faculties cannot comprehend many things in creation. In the vast frame of nature, some of its parts are placed so high up, that we cannot examine them, and must remain ignorant this side the eternal world. But it is not so with the affairs of men. In human society nothing ought to be mysterious to a wise man, seeing, by due care, pains and *industry*, he can understand every thing. Hence, every mystery between man and man, is "*a mystery of iniquity*," whether it be in government, in the arts and sciences, or in teaching morality, or in illustrating religion.

---

* Deuter. ch. xxii. 10.

What then are we to think of a very widely spread association, planted, and watered by ample funds, in every village, town, city, and district of the United States, marshalled by numerous grades of officers, bearing royal, military, and *hierophantical* titles, the very cement and essence of which is *secrecy?*—whose meetings are never held until the sun has sunk beneath the horizon, and the curtain of darkness shrouds the earth; and whose door is guarded by a drawn sword?—a system whose soul and substance is close concealments; a scheme, which, at every ascending round of the ladder, covers the aspirant with a thicker and darker veil of ambiguity, surrounding every thing with a fearful *halo* of mystery, generating solemn doubt, or imperfect satisfaction—just sufficient to create a thirst for more light and information; and yet the encouragers of these gropers in the dark call this anxious progression—"going from west to *east* in search of *light!*

I conceive the object of this Convention to be, to discourage the growth and continuance of ALL *secret societies* whatever, without casting harsh reflections on any man, or holding up individuals to public odium. Your wish, I presume, is to entreat the fraternity of masons not to be led away by dark and delusive tradition; but to view the thing as it really is, by the steady light of philosophy and the Christian religion, and in a spirit worthy the present day, and the country we live in; and not mistake mystery for wisdom, and solemn professions for morality, or, in other words, *darkness* for *light.* Our ardent wish is to aid the hasty and unthinking in divesting their partial system of those enticing ceremonies, those fascinating figures, and captivating metaphors, "*which give to airy nothing a local habitation and a name.*"

To a moral people, situated and circumstanced as we are in these United States, all *partial* illuminations are injurious The thing to be desired is—THE BRIGHT AND SHINING LIGHT OF TRUTH, which may illuminate all things around it, and put an end to our conflict with shadows.

Let the lights of masonry continue burning, unmolested. But let the people outside their lodges be so informed and instructed, that the boasted lights of the fraternity shall appear *like candles in the day time.* The period in which we live, the government we enjoy, and the country we inhabit, demand this homage to the human understanding.

One word more, and I am done.—We are all citizens of free States, in which every man has a *right* to *think* and to *act* without hindrance; and we are all disposed to guaranty to him this privilege, provided he do not stand an armed man in the avenue to Justice; and provided he attempt not to shelter himself behind OATHS and *strange obligations*, unknown to our laws: and, above all, provided he do not contaminate the sanctity of a *verdict*,—the VERUM DICTUM of conscientious men.

ADDRESS OF REV. MOSES THACHER,

Before the Anti-masonic Meeting, in Faneuil Hall, on the evening of September 8, 1829.

MR. CHAIRMAN,—It has been stated, that the object of this meeting is, "*To investigate the secret principles of Freemasonry.*" The first question therefore, which demands our attention, appears to be this: ARE THE SECRET PRINCIPLES OF FREEMASONRY BEFORE THE PUBLIC? If the secret principles of Freemasonry are *not* before the public; then the interest, which has been excited in the public mind, relative to this subject, is without foundation, the object of our meeting is chimerical, and we have no subject before us, either worthy, or capable of investigation.

The issue of the question, which I have stated, must turn upon these THREE POSITIONS: *First*, Can the secret principles of Freemasonry be communicated?—*Secondly*, Is the evidence plenary?—*Thirdly*, Are the witnesses competent?

In the first place, then, *Can the secrets of Freemasonry be communicated?* That the secrets of Freemasonry can be communicated, is evident from the very fact that *there are secrets*. A *secret* always consists in *something*. To say that a secret consists in *nothing which can be commu-*

nicated, is a contradiction in terms. If I impart anything to another with the injunction of secrecy, it necessarily implies, that what I have committed to him as a secret, can be revealed to a third person. Otherwise, why the injunction of secrecy? No man ever commits *nothing* to another, with the charge of secrecy. If then we admit, that there *are* secret principles belonging to the masonic institution, we must admit that those principles *can be revealed*. But, that there have been secret principles belonging to the masonic institution, has always been avowed by masons themselves; and they have professed to be under obligation to withhold those principles from all persons who are not received as members of the masonic society. This fact is also confirmed by the highest masonic authority. "The Book of Constitutions" for Massachusetts, compiled by Rev. Thaddeus Mason Harris, D. D., says, (p. 37,) "The virtue indispensably necessary in masons, is SECRECY. This is the ground of their confidence, and the security of their trust. So great stress is laid upon it, *that it is enforced under the* STRONGEST PENALTIES AND OBLIGATIONS!" Now it would be absurd in the extreme, to communicate anything to another as a secret, "UNDER THE STRONGEST PENALTIES AND OBLIGATIONS," when, at the same time, that thing *could not be revealed* to a third person. It is indisputable, then, that there *are* secret principles belonging to the masonic institution, and that those principles *can be communicated*.

In the *second place*, Is the evidence PLENARY, that the secret principles of Freemasonry are now before the public? If the fulness of evidence, is depending upon the number of witnesses, there can be no doubt that the evidence in their case is PLENARY. What evidence, then, have we, that the secret principles of the order have been divulged?

1. We have Prichard's "Masonry Dissected," first published as early as 1730; and which professes to be a full and fair disclosure of the first three degrees, which were the whole of Freemasonry in existence at that time.

2. We have the disclosures contained in the publication entitled, "Jachin and Boaz," which testifies substantially to the same things, with this difference, that the institution has become more complicated in its ceremonies, with additional clauses to its several obligations.

3. "Illustrations of Masonry," by William Morgan. This publication, in *diction*, differs sufficiently from "Jachin and Boaz," to show that it is the genuine work of its reputed author; and yet confirms the testimony of the preceding, in such a manner that masons have said, "It is nothing but the old story 'newly vamped.'"

4. We have the explicit testimony of THIRTY-EIGHT SECEDING MASONS, at the first Le Roy Convention, who have averred, that Morgan's "Illustrations" are substantially correct, and have also given a revelation of succeeding degrees, if I mistake not, up to *fifteen.*

5. We have the testimony of ONE HUNDRED AND TWENTY-NINE, some of whom had received at least *twenty degrees*, who signed the Anti-masonic Declaration of Independence, certified to the correctness of Morgan, and who also confirmed the revelation made by the Le Roy Convention.

6. We have the evidence of FIFTEEN of different degrees, in Genesee county, New-York, who have given their affidavits before the civil magistrate, that the "Illustrations of Masonry," made by William Morgan, are substantially true.

7. The public have, by estimation, at least FIVE HUNDRED seceding masons of different degrees, and in different parts of our country, who have not only certified the same thing in respect to Morgan, but have also confirmed the disclosures made at Le Roy. In addition to these, they have perhaps not less than TWO THOUSAND, who have *virtually* testified the same thing, by withdrawing from the institution.

More than all this, we have THE KIDNAPPING AND MURDER OF WILLIAM MORGAN!! Here, the evidence is written in BLOOD. It is "*marked, cut, carved, stained* and *engraven*," by *masons themselves*, in crimson lines, too legibly to be obliterated; and too deeply impressed upon the mind of every *free* American citizen, ever to be forgotten. If Morgan has made no *disclosures* in the opinion of masons, detrimental to their institution, why was the village of Batavia filled with strangers, afterwards found to be Freemasons, passing and repassing, from "high twelve at noon, till low twelve at night," assembling in conclave, and concerting measures for his destruction? Why were six Royal Arch Chapters, and every lodge in that vicinity, engaged, either directly or indirectly, in that horrid conspiracy? Why was Miller's office enveloped in flames, and its unfortunate occupant *taken*, and *retaken*, and *taken again;* before sufficient strength could be mustered effectually to rescue him from the hands of this lawless banditti? Why was Morgan transported from Batavia to Canandaigua, and from Canandaigua to Niagara, there to be first *imprisoned*, and then *butchered?* These questions, and ten thousand more of the same nature, are unanswerable, except on the ground, that, in the opinion of masons, Morgan had violated his obligations, and made disclosures, which they considered masonically illegal.

Again; The conduct of Freemasons themselves, affords unequivocal testimony that the secret principles of their institution are before the public. What is it that has shaken, to its very centre and foundation, every Lodge, and every Chapter, and every Encampment, from Maine to the Mississippi, and from the Lakes to the Atlantic; if Morgan and other seceders have not made a full and fair disclosure of what have been called masonic secrets? We may indeed, well ask, partly in masonic language, not, "what occasions the alarm" *without?* but "what occasions the alarm" *within?* Why have Freemasons used every possible exertion *to defame and destroy the reputation of seceders;* if the "secret mysteries" of their institution have not been developed?

But the strongest argument, that has yet been presented to prove the affirmative of our main question, is, what we have seen and heard in this Hall, this evening!!* I hope it will not be considered that I intend to cast reflections; for I am certainly *surprised* as well as *gratified*, that Freemasons themselves, on this occasion, should, so

* The speaker here alludes to *the hissing of the fraternity.* So soon as he touched "the Morgan affair," the Freemasons, throughout the hall, raised such a clamor and hissing, that his voice was drowned for some minutes, and he was obliged to stop, until the Chairman, who presided with great decision and dignity, succeeded in restoring order. The *hissing*, however, instead of disconcerting the speaker, as was intended, afforded the most favorable opportunity possible to illustrate what he had at first stated.

unexpectedly, put into my mouth an irresistible argument in favor of my position. It cannot be denied, then, that the evidence is *plenary* that the secret principles of Freemasonry are before the public. The only remaining question, is,

Are the witnesses competent? That they were *Freemasons,* there can be no dispute. This, Freemasons themselves do not pretend to deny. They must, therefore, have known whether or not they were telling the truth. They must have known whether or not they had passed through these ceremonies, which they describe as the secrets of masonry. For, *they were men of common sense.* Otherwise it can argue nothing in favor of the institution to have received them as members.

Many of these witnesses *are known to the public,* as men of sterling talents, and strict integrity. They were certainly acknowledged as such, by Freemasons themselves, until the moment they left the institution. If then these witnesses were *ever* worthy to be believed, they were worthy of credence when they dissolved their connexion with the masonic institution. A man's character does not change in a minute. It always takes *time* for any person to become "a drunken, worthless, miserable vagabond;" as masons have represented some, if not the most of their seceding brethren, who were in acknowledged good fellowship with them, until the moment of their secession.

Nor do these witnesses come forward under the crime of acknowledged perjury, and then, as has been alleged by masons, ask you to place confidence in their integrity. How have they perjured themselves? Not, certainly, against the laws of our country. No person will presume to say, that there is any thing in any of our civil institutions to sanction masonic oaths; but, on the contrary, many of these oaths, as they have been divulged, *are in direct opposition to our civil rights.* It is equally evident that they have not perjured themselves against the law of God. That perfect rule of moral conduct, which allows no man to *forswear himself,* and which is recognised and sanctioned by Him, who said, "*Swear not at all,*" must certainly *condemn* such oaths, as masons are said to take upon themselves. There is nothing in the whole Word of God, which warrants the administration and observance of such oaths, any more than that of Herod, to kill John, or than the curse that the Jews imprecated upon themselves, "that they would neither eat nor drink until they had killed Paul." On this subject, I fear not to appeal to the common sense of any enlightened, intelligent and impartial citizen. Indeed, there has been but *one opinion*, with jurists, divines and laymen, who have attended to the subject, and who are not biassed in favor of Freemasonry, that what seceders have alleged to be masonic oaths, are neither *morally* nor *legally* binding. But, if seceders have perjured themselves against the masonic institution, and not against the laws of God and our country; why, then, the masonic institution is in *opposition* to the laws of God and of our country.

You, fellow citizen, are a Freemason, and *you* say, These individuals are *perjured*, and, therefore, *not to be believed*. Why? Because they have violated their masonic obligations, and have divulged something that is unlawful. This *you* admit; and, in admitting this, *you* virtually say, that the secrets of masonry are before the public, and hence, *you* are perjured, *ipso facto*, as much as they, and that *on your own confession*.

The secrets of Freemasonry, then, *are before the public*. Freemasons *know* that they are before the public; and every intelligent citizen, who has attended to facts, has just as good evidence, that he is in possession of what *were* the secrets of masonry, as that there is such a place as London, or that there was such a man as Alexander the Great. It is, Mr. Chairman, an insult to your understanding, for Freemasons to assert, that you know nothing about their secret mysteries. It is a species of falsehood for any one to attempt to *evade the subject*, and the grossest imposition upon the public, for any Freemason to say, that the witnesses who have testified, are either incompetent, or that they have not told the truth.

Now, if the secret principles of Freemasonry are before the public; then the public have a *right to examine them*. The free citizens of this country have the same *right* to examine *this* subject, that they have to examine any other, which affects our religious and political interests. The clamor, raised by Freemasons, in order to suppress free inquiry, or to check the freedom of the press, or to silence the warning voice, is altogether unreasonable, and an infringement of the rights of every free citizen.

We may as well submit reason and conscience to the decisions of an ecclesiastical hierarchy, or be under the domination of Cæsar, as be denied the *right* and the *privilege* of investigating any subject which affects the public mind. This is a right, indeed, which freemen *cannot* relinquish. The moment they relinquish this right, they are *no longer freemen*, but *slaves*. Masons might first bind, and then *gag*, William Morgan; but they must first *gag*, before they can *bind* a *free people*.—They may continue to raise the cry, and to sing the song, "Political Anti-masonry,—Anti-masonry and Orthodoxy,—Anti-masonry and Unitarianism,—Anti-masonry and Priestcraft,—Anti-masonry and Federalism,—-Anti-masonry and Democracy;" but they need not think to close the eyes, nor the ears, nor the mouths of an intelligent community, any more than the lullaby of the nurse can sooth to rest the motion of the elements. Those who watch over the religious and political interests of our country, and with untiring zeal and vigilance seek the general good of the great whole, cannot be satisfied with the mere outcry of Demetrius and his "fellow craftsman,"—"Great is Diana of the Ephesians." They must have *strong reasons* and conclusive *arguments*, that their "image which fell down from Jupiter" is of real, intrinsic value; or they will never consent to let it remain in the temple of their liberty.

The citizens of this community not only have the *right* to examine the principles of the masonic institution; but they are under *obligation* to examine those principles. Who, in this country, can secure the rights of the people, but the people themselves? Every free citizen ought to feel himself highly responsible for the public welfare. It is the duty of every free citizen, therefore, to examine every subject which affects the public weal. But who can suppose that the masonic institution has no bearing of any importance upon the general interests of our country! Who can suppose that a society of *three hundred thousand* members, in the very heart of our country, with a fund, *unlimited* and *unrestricted*, at their control, can be capable of doing neither good nor hurt.

If the secret principles of the masonic institution are before the public; then the public *can judge of their nature and tendency*. The time *was*, perhaps, Mr. Chairman, when you might be disposed to inquire of masons, respecting the political and moral tendency of their institution. But this inquiry of them, is now no longer necessary. Every intelligent citizen can examine for himself, and form an opinion *for himself*. An enlightened community will not *now* be satisfied with the bare assertion of Freemasons, that theirs "is a noble, scientific, moral and charitable institution;" because every citizen must feel *competent* to examine and determine for himself.

The public can judge of the *morality* of the masonic institution. They can judge, for example, whether the following clause in the Master Mason's oath, is founded upon the broad basis of Christian purity, or, is the legitimate offspring of licentiousness, checked only by self-interest. "Furthermore do I promise and swear, that I will not violate the chastity of a master mason's wife, mother, sister, or daughter, I knowing them to be such, nor suffer it to be done by others, if in my power to prevent it."—Now, if a Congregationalist should enter into such a covenant respecting the wives, mothers, sisters and daughters, of his own particular communion, would not the Episcopalian, and the Catholic, and the Baptist, and the Methodist, and the Friends, have just reason to be jealous? Would they not draw the natural inference, that the Congregationalist intended to restrain his passions only so far as his own denomination was concerned, and to make common game of the wives, daughters, mothers and sisters, of all others? Would it not be an insult to common sense to say, that such a covenant as this maintained the principles of sound morality? It is, also, easy to determine whether an institution, in which the sacred names, titles and attributes of Jehovah, are used as pass-words, and mock miracles are wrought as signs; and in which the Word of God is used with the most shocking familiarity, does tend to cherish that veneration for the Supreme Being, which becomes rational, moral, and accountable creatures.

Having the principles of the masonic institution before them, the people can determine whether those principles are *dangerous* or *salutary* to a republican government. They can also judge, whether or not extra-judical oaths have a tendency to bind mankind to regard the oath of God, which is necessarily imposed by civil authority.

It must be acknowledged, that these are subjects of vital importance to this community; and it cannot be, that the people of these United States will pass them over, without a critical, thorough, and impartial examination. It cannot be, that the citizens of Boston, whose fathers were among the first to throw the gauntlet, and to "bid defiance to the gigantic greatness of the British power," can be indifferent to the welfare of our country. It cannot be, that the citizens of Boston, who have been nursed in the lap, and rocked in the "Cradle," of the American revolution, will refuse to investigate first principles, the suppression or prevalence of which may prove the salvation or destruction of our civil and religious liberties.

REASONS WHY THE CHURCH OF CHRIST SHOULD DISFELLOWSHIP FREEMASONRY.

Extract of a Sermon by Rev. Henry Jones, of Cabot, Vermont.

"And I heard another voice from heaven, saying, come out of her my people, that ye be not partakers of her sins, and that ye receive not of her plagues."

It will not be expedient for me to say, that this voice from heaven must be considered, as uttered with special reference to the connexion of the church with the masonic institution as it now exists in this country, but rather it becomes me to fall in with the prevailing opinion of our commentators, that it was in view of another abomination, which has long had its principal seat in Italy, rather than in this part of the Zion of God. Still it is not the manner of the Divine Spirit, in his warnings to the people of God, to have exclusive reference to one evil, when there are others of a similar nature which might be included in one, as well as to have separate warnings given against each of them. Therefore if the masonic institution, in its obligations and principles, be of that wicked and anti-christian character, which has now, for some time, been considered in fact the case, by many who have given the subject the most impartial investigation, the correctness of whose decision we are not prepared to disprove; most certainly, that Being who spake from heaven, saying, "Come out of her my people," having the same view of this institution from eternity, which he has at present, must have had allusion to this, as well as other evils and abominations, in which his people are ever entangled. On the present occasion, then, we may feel authorized to lay aside every other interpretation of this command, and treat upon it, as though it were spoken with exclusive reference to the present connexion of the church with the institution of Freemasonry. Taking this view of the subject, which I must feel authorized to do, the people of God, or church of Christ, as a body are called upon, as by a voice from heaven, to come out of this institution, in order to escape her sins and her plagues.

To illustrate this command I propose to show that the Church is at present so entangled, or in fellowship with this institution, as to render the command in the text to come out of it, suitable.

On this point, but little need be said; and it will not be necessary to show, that there has ever been any such thing as a formal act of the Church or any branch of it, acknowledging a communion or fellowship with Freemasonry. The connexion which exists at present, between the two institutions, has been accomplished by slow and imperceptible degrees, by the uniting of the members, each with the other, while the Church has continued till of late, to tolerate these connexions, with scarcely the least suspicion of treachery on the part of her pretended and accomplished friend, Freemasonry.

Although I have no knowledge but that ever since masonry has existed, it has been common for those connexions, more or less, to take place, I believe it to be quite a late thing, according to the recollection of the most aged, for any very large number of church members to be connected with that institution, and more especially are we to consider it a late thing for any considerable number of the clergy to be connected with it. But during a few years past, in the growth of our Churches and increase of ministers, it seems that a large proportion, particularly of the clergy, by the remittance of the initiation fees generally, have been induced to join, so that, in New-England, I should not think it strange if among the various denominations, one fourth, or one third of their number have been drawn into the institution, while it is presumed, there is scarcely a Church to be found, if we except those of a very few denominations more careful than others in this thing, which has not in its connexion more or less of that fraternity, and perhaps, scarcely a lodge to be found without more or less of the members of the Church in its connexion. Whether the godly are willing or not, to acknowledge this relation, or fellowship for the masonic institution, there is certainly no way, at present, to evade the fact. Masonry has frequently displayed her banners, her splendid array, and glittering ornaments in the house of God, and many times she has claimed the holy Sabbath for this purpose on funeral occasions, while the Church has not only yielded up her rights to her demands, but has seemed to manifest unqualified approbation and complacency; in addition to which, many of the Church have put on the masonic badge and walked in the procession. More than this, many of our clergy have officiated and taken the lead in these masonic exhibitions, as it were, and in eulogizing the institution, thus manifesting, in the strongest and most public manner, their fellowship for its laws and principles. Then while so large a portion of Christian ministers and members of Churches, are thus fellowshipping that institution, and the Church knowingly fellowships them in doing it, is it not, on the part of the Church, a practical acknowledgment that the two institutions can walk in harmony and fellowship with each other? And how can this practical fellowship for the institution be separated from its corruptions and wickedness, which are now known to be attached to its character? Then is not the Church in a dreadful bondage and entanglement, so connected with that institution, while her blessed laws of discipline must be trodden under foot, to make way for the execution of masonic laws?

Many of the members of our Churches, who have recently become acquainted with these facts, are looking on, with the most bitter grief, because their brethren generally seem so backward to suspect any mischief from this source, that they cannot be persuaded to behold and turn away from such a deadly evil, justly feeling that, so long as the Church continue to fellowship Freemasonry, they must themselves be implicated in the anti-christian character of that institution. Can any one show, how this melancholy inference can justly be avoided? while now there is quite a threatening aspect upon the face of this institution, speaking a language not difficult to be understood, that if the Church will not peaceably retain her in fellowship, she will array all her forces against the Church for its overthrow. This threatening aspect of the institution, from which I would exonerate the character of our masonic Christian brethren, seems to be, perhaps, the most important reason, why there is such an apparent trembling and reluctance to come forward, with many of our brethren in important stations, who appear to *see* the danger of the Church, and yet stand looking on, as though they were disinterested spectators; or waiting for a general alarm to be given, that all may act in concert, and with the greater safety. This being the situation of the Church, in regard to the masonic institution, how reasonable the command from heaven, "Come out of her my people."—I pass now to urge some reasons for a compliance, on the part of the Church, with this important command of heaven.

The first reason which I shall notice, for the separation of the Church from the masonic institution, in addition to what may be considered as implied under my former proposition, is that which is first mentioned in the text, "*That ye partake not of her sins,*" that is, that the Church, and its members may not be looked upon, and dealt with from heaven, as participating in the present manifested guilt of Freemasonry. We have already taken something of a view of the evil deeds of this institution as they have, of late, been exhibited, since its veil of darkness and secrecy have been so entirely removed.

Although there have been no small number of men, of moral and religious principles, who have been deceived by the alluring pretensions of that institution to become its members, who, by their goodly lives, have seemed to enstamp upon it outwardly, the appearance of a humane, moral, and almost a religious institution, yet, from its true character as it has exhibited itself of late, separate from what it has borrowed from the Church, and the character of good men who have been drawn into it, I should think we are safe in considering some of its legitimate fruits to be, falsehood, deception, pride, office, power, profanity, perjury, deism, defamation, murder and treason. Can the Church, living in fellowship with this institution, while such of its characteristics are exhibited to public view, prosper any better than Israel could, when defeated and slain before the inhabitants of Ai, merely because one of their number, Achan, had pilfered a wedge of gold and hid it, while this, no doubt, was a secret to Israel generally? Although it is often said, that the Church has never flourished more than within thirty years past, which is during the very period of the principal growth of Freemasonry in this couutry, as an argument to convince us, that they ought not now to be separated; the argument appears to me unsound, though it is, perhaps, as good as any other which could be produced for the same purpose.--The argument is evidently unsound, because, until a very short time past, the evil or anti-christian character of Freemasonry has been concealed, like a serpent in the grass, so that the Church has not had occasion to suspect but that its professions of humanity and benevolence, were hearty and sincere. Thus it appears, that "*God winked at*" her "*ignorance*," in her continuing so long to walk hand in hand with that institution, but now, since her true character is exposed, should the Church continue this fellowship, she must inevitably be a voluntary partaker in all the guilt which is proved against that institution.

A second reason which I would now urge for a compliance on the part of the Church, with the command to come out of the masonic institution, is that which is also contained in the text, "*That ye receive not of her plagues.*" Nothing, perhaps, is more sure, than that plagues sent from God, are the just and natural consequences of unrepented iniquity. Such plagues have sometimes been experienced in this world, rather as a premonition of that "*fearful looking for of judgment and fiery indignation which shall devour the adversaries.*" Though we are not to suppose, that God will so abandon his real children, even in their wanderings from him, as finally to give them over to the kingdom of Satan, they may be called to experience very severe sufferings in consequence of their wicked conduct, and feel as though they were actually forsaken of God forever;—and by their examples of wickedness, may be the means of bringing plagues upon their companions and posterity, which shall include the dreadful judgments of the eternal world.

Were I to speak of the temporal plagues of the masonic institution as being alluded to, in the text, I should say, from present appearances, that in connexion with its sins, some of which have been mentioned, as having appeared to public view, they appear to be, *alienation, contention, division among the members*, or *a house most strikingly divided against itself*, and an *inevitable falling.* It is devoutly to be hoped, that the Church may not be called to experience things like these, but I confess, that however some may differ from me in judgment, who are much wiser than myself, I am unable to see, from a long and close examination of the subject, any way by which, these very plagues can be averted from the Church only by her unreserved coming out from that institution according to a command from heaven. I know that this represents the Church and its members as being in a peculiar and trying situation; but certainly, not so apparently beyond remedy, and dangerous to individuals, as in the reformation, when it became necessary for it, to escape the plagues of heaven, to come out from the Romish Church.

In further urging reasons for a compliance with this command, on the part of the Church, I will here notice one fact, which must appear obvious to all who have examined this subject and its bearing upon the Church, and that is, such a general cessation of revivals of religion in our land, since the disclosures of the secrets and character of masonry. Though there may be a few exceptions, I think it will be admitted generally, by those who are familiar with these things, that in all our Churches where Freemasonry exists, and her character is examined by the brethren, they have seemed at once disqualified for any further special manifestation of the Divine Spirit, in the awakening and conversion of the impenitent among them. And is it not apparent, that the Church must sink, and continue to sink, until there shall be a deliverance effected from this melancholy evil? I am well aware of the responses of thousands of voices, where such a question as this may be asked, from those who yet think favorably of Freemasonry; and I shall not question but that multitudes of well meaning persons, who acknowledge and deplore the evil now before us, as much as ourselves, do honestly believe at the same time, that it is *not* masonry, but *anti-masonry*, which is the guilty cause. But certainly, if this must be taken for good logic, though revivals in many cases have been observed to be checked, so soon as the masonic question began to be examined, or anti-masonry appeared there, so to speak; then surely it must be equally good reasoning, if there should be some of the most scandalous wickedness, secretly introduced into a Church, perhaps, ignorantly at first, by some of its well meaning members, and should for some time lie concealed, from the Church and the world, while the place might be experiencing a refreshing from the presence of the Lord, to say as before, after this wickedness and scandal shall be uncovered to all the people, if any of the Church shall protest against it, and refuse any fellowship for it, then *these* are the guilty individuals who have put a stop to the revival, if it shall cease, rather than others who might have introduced the scandal at first, and still persist in retaining and justifying it in the Church.

Must it not be agreed by all, that the Churches of our land, which have began to experience trouble from the subject of Freemasonry, cannot expect to enjoy the smiles of heaven again, until it can somehow be disposed of among them? Then how shall it be disposed of, but by a general withdrawing from the fellowship of the institution? Sure, it can no more be hushed up and forgotten, where it is, and the Churches thus be restored to peace, than the earth can be stopped in her revolutions and the sun prohibited his shining. But a separation from the masonic institution, is practicable, and expedient, and in my opinion the only way which can be devised, whereby the church can here rest and be built up.

Again, shall not the express commands of heaven be regarded? "*What concord hath Christ with Belial? or what part hath he that believeth with an infidel? and what agreement hath the temple of God with idols? Wherefore come out from among them, and be ye separate saith the Lord.*" So in our text, "*And I heard another voice from heaven, saying, come out of her, my people.*"

ADDRESS OF THE WATERBURY ANTI-MASONIC MEETING.

At a numerous meeting of Freemen opposed to the principles of Speculative Masonry, holden at the Meeting-house in Waterbury, Washington county, Vt. on the 27th of October, 1829, *the Hon.* EZRA BUTLER, *Ex-Governor of Vermont, was chosen President, and* CHARLES CALKINS *and* ELYMUS S. NEWCOMB, *Secretaries. The following Address was submitted to the meeting, and adopted.*

FELLOW CITIZENS,—In addressing you, we would freely and fearlessly express our views concerning Freemasonry—not for the purpose of creating prejudices in your minds against Freemasons, but to show you the nature and tendency of their institution. Our objections to Freemasonry are founded principally on the masonic oaths, such as have been revealed, and are not now denied by masons who adhere to the institution. On a fair construction of these oaths, the following conclusions are deducible:—

"It exercises jurisdiction over the persons and lives of its members.

"It arrogates to itself the right of punishing its members for offences unknown to the laws of this or any other nation.

"It requires the concealment of crime, and protects the guilty from punishment.

"It encourages the commission of crime, by affording the guilty facilities of escape.

"It affords opportunities for the corrupt and designing to form plans against the government, and the lives and characters of individuals.

"It destroys all principles of equity by bestowing its favors on its own members, to the exclusion of all others equally meritorious and deserving.

"It creates odious aristocracies, by its obligations to support the interests of its members, in preference to others of equal qualifications."

It requires a spirit of malevolence in its members, contrary to the precepts of the gospel.

An institution fraught with such principles as we find in Freemasonry, we cannot view with complacency.—When all its doings are secret, it must excite the jealousy of a free people. Its members may resolve no evil, or it may resolve the overthrow of our liberties. Abroad, revolutions have been effected by Freemasonry, and they may be effected by it here as well as there; for it is admitted that the principles of Freemasonry are the same the world over. Then ought we not to be jealous of this institution, and more especially now, than formerly, as its shocking principles are fully revealed? It is a knowledge of these principles that is calling forth the energies of the people in opposition to Freemasonry. In these principles the people can see nothing to approve, but much to censure. It is these principles which give an odious character to the institution.

Because Washington, Franklin, and other worthies have been members of it, it by no means follows that the institution is not corrupt: bad men have been members of a good institution—and good men have been drawn in to become members of a bad institution. While we venerate good men who have been, or are, nominally, Freemasons, we would fearlessly oppose the institution, and the doings of those men who are governed by its pernicious principles. Not that we expect by our exertions, suddenly to overthrow Freemasonry, which is so deeply rooted in our soil; but we hope to check its growth by exposing its deformities.

Very lately our attention has been called to an Appeal

to the people, *issued from the Grand Lodge of Vermont*, and signed by 168 masons. In this appeal they say—"Were we to remain silent, we should be guilty of inflicting no less an injury upon you than upon ourselves; for were we quietly to submit to the dispensation and dissemination of error, and suffer a political party to be built up on it, destructive of the liberties of the people, when we possess the power to expose the falsity of the representations, we should, to say the least, display an unwarrantable and reprehensible disregard for the safety of the free institutions under which we live."

Here the *appellants* declare, that they have not only *the power, but the disposition, to disclose the error*, upon which anti-masons would build up a political party. Now what have they disclosed? They have told the people that they "are *guiltless* in any manner of shedding human blood—*guiltless* in any manner of conspiring against the liberties or privileges of the people, or endeavoring to monopolize an unequal portion of those privileges to ourselves, or to abridge the rights of others—*guiltless* in any manner of impeding, retarding, or diverting the course of justice—*guiltless* in any manner of an intrusion into the three great departments of our government—*guiltless* in any manner of attempting to identify the subject with politics, or making the latter a subject of discussion or remark—*guiltless* in any manner of performing any act, immoral or irreligious—and *guiltless* in any manner of entertaining the remotest suspicion, that the life of a fellow being was subject to our control." This *appeal* is signed by some of our most worthy citizens, and we never entertained the least suspicion, that they had been personally guilty of what they say they are *guiltless*. They are honorable men, and their word is to be taken, where there is no proof to the contrary. If they have been personally charged with committing the aforesaid crimes, we can view it in no other light than gross slander. We know *that they have been charged with taking the masonic oaths*, such as have been revealed to the public. To this charge they have not plead *guiltless*. From their silence on this subject, we have a right to infer, and do infer, that every mason has taken one or more of these oaths, according to the number of degrees to which he has advanced.

If the appellants could truly make the declaration, and would make it, that they are *guiltless of having taken these oaths*, it would go far to show a fundamental error in the reasoning of anti-masons. It would be a denial of the premises from which they draw their conclusions. But so long as their premises are not denied, their reasoning must have weight with the people.

If the *appellants* have not done these things which the principles of masonry would warrant, it does not prove that masonry is any better than it is represented by anti-masons. It does not prove that among 150,000 masons in the United States, there are not 100,000 who are *political*, and would vote for a brother mason before another person of equal qualifications; and it does not prove that there are not 50,000 masons, who would take the life of a brother for disclosing the fundamental secrets of the order.

What else, but the fear of death, prevented the disclosures of these secrets from a thousand tongues, before Morgan disclosed them? And wha. has been the fate of Morgan for making the disclosures? We attribute his abduction and death to masonry. But no mason, who participated in the abduction, has been expelled the lodge. Many masons have, by the laws of the land, been convicted and imprisoned for the crime; but the laws of masonry have not been violated, and the convicts remain worthy members of the lodges! We say these things to show the principles of masonry, and not to accuse the *appellants* of shedding human blood.

Fellow Citizens:—Political masonry should cease from among us, or political anti-masonry should be tolerated. We hear masons declare that there is no such thing as *political* masonry. Let us see what facts prove. One masonic obligation requires, that a *mason shall vote for a brother in preference to any other person of equal qualifications*. Is not this political masonry? The masons in Vermont are about one twentieth part of the freemen, and they hold about three-fourths of all the important offices in the State. Is this owing to their superior fitness, or to political masonry?

This state of things is produced by *political* masonry. There are no masons in the State so well qualified for any office, but that there are other freemen to be found, who are not masons, as well qualified for the same office; yet the mason must always obtain the office. We would not recommend the adoption of any rule to prevent masons obtaining office, but the freeman's oath. We will, however, act according to this oath, in resisting their shameful monopoly of offices, whenever and wherever called to give our suffrages.

In the fifth Congressional district, in this State, *political* masonry, for twelve months past, has effected wonders: masons have combined, in so many different shapes, to secure the election of a mason, to represent us in Congress, that their zeal and shame are now without a cover. They have presented to us four masons in succession for the office, and spared no pains to slander the patriot and statesman, WILLIAM CAHOON; but the freemen have done nobly; they have, thus far, sustained him for their Representative through seven successive trials.

And do we not see *political* masonry in the *appeals* to the people, one after another, issued from the lodge-room in Montpelier? Were not these appeals designed to have a political effect! If masons in their lodge, can unite to make an appeal to put down anti-masonry, we see no reason why they might not unite on some other political subject as well; for instance, *to stand by, and assist each other to office.*

There is nothing in their obligations that restrains masons from acting on political subjects. In their lodges they have matured political plans which have made kings tremble on their thrones. They always have been, and always will be political, when circumstances require it, for their own security or aggrandizement. Not that we believe that masons would introduce party politics into a lodge; for this might occasion contention in the body. A union in thought, and in action, is a principle of *political* masonry; therefore, party politics are excluded.

Political masonry, in and out of the lodge, cries aloud that anti-masonry is *political*, because she peaceably, and without previous concert, goes to the polls, and has the audacity to vote down political masonry. It is submitted to the people to say, whether this be a crime.

Political masonry says, anti-masons *proscribe* masons.

It is true, anti-masons resist masons, when they attempt to monopolize offices. And is this a fault? Anti-masons have, and will oppose ARISTOCRACY, in whatever form or shape it presents itself. They call no man in these United States, King, Lord, or Most Worshipful—they disclaim all titles of nobility. They are free citizens, and claim equal rights and privileges.

Fellow Citizens:—We look with astonishment, when we behold the rule in Freemasonry that requires its members to point a masonic brother out to the world as an unworthy and vicious vagabond; to oppose his int rest, to derange his business, to transfer his character after him wherever he may go, to expose him to contempt during his whole natural life. This rule is wholly opposed to the gospel, which teaches us not to render evil for evil, but good for evil; to love our enemies, and do good to those who injure us. But why does the masonic rule require these things? Because the brother has offended. He has offended, perhaps, by withdrawing from Freemasonry. We fear that the principles of this rule are applied by some professing Christians, who are masons, to pious clergymen, who have honestly seceded from the lodge. And other clergymen, who have had the boldness to raise their voices against Freemasonry, we believe, have been dismissed, or threatened with a dismission, or to have their living taken from them on that account. The preachers of the gospel are to be awed into silence, and the truth is not to be told about the anti-christian principles of Freemasonry, although these principles, at this day, are as well understood by others, as by masons themselves. Is iniquity to be covered over? Does not the prosperity of the churches require plain preaching on this subject? We would give thanks to the Lord that so many pious persons have shaken off the shackles of Freemasonry, and it is our heart's desire, that a great multitude may soon follow their examples. We are religiously opposed to many things in Freemasonry; and wholly condemn the application of the principles of the above masonic rule to any offending brother, by an offended brother in the church. We consider the gospel rule in Matthew altogether preferable. Is it not decreed in high heaven, that Freemasonry shall soon cease to be revered by all the saints on earth? She has already fallen, with her robes stained in human blood. Many of her sons are astonished, and are exclaiming, " It is not I; it is not I, who have done this wicked deed." If you are guiltless in this matter; if you have not done any thing " immoral or irreligious," then no longer advocate Freemasonry, but be ye separate from her.

EZRA BUTLER, *President.*

C. CALKINS,
E. S. NEWCOMB, } *Secretaries.*

REPORT

Respecting the Authenticity of the Masonic Disclosures.—Made to the New York State Convention, Feb. 21, 1829.

The committee appointed to inquire whether the ceremonials, obligations and secrets of the masonic order, as disclosed by the late William Morgan, before his abduction and murder, and the convention of seceding masons at Le Roy, on the 4th and 5th July last, are substantially correct and true, &c. respectfully Report:

That the subject of inquiry allotted to your committee, has received that mature deliberation, which its importance seemed to demand. Your committee are of opinion, that in the exercise of their legitimate powers, it does not appear proper to introduce in their report animadversions upon masonry, and they therefore confine the report strictly to the evidences, in relation to the disclosures, reference to which has been had.

In regard to the correctness and truth of the three first degrees as disclosed by the late William Morgan before his abduction and murder, your committee deem it unnecessary to multiply proofs—no further evidence would seemingly be necessary on that point, than what has been heretofore laid before the public. The murder of the author has effectually and conclusively impressed the seal of authenticity upon his revelations. But, if further proof be required by any, it may be found in the clearly expressed concurring testimony borne by some hundreds of seceding masons—and also, by the ready admission of many of the order, who still adhere to the precepts and principles of masonry, and who not only admit the truth of the degrees published, but likewise the murder of the author for a violation of his obligations in writing those degrees.

In relation to the truth of the disclosures made at Le Roy, at the period stated in the resolution, your committee have been enabled to receive from the lips of three persons of high reputation, who have taken all the degrees, such a statement of attendant facts and circumstances, as that none can doubt the general correctness and truth of the disclosures. Your committee, in preparing their report, have studied to make it as brief as the nature of the subject, and the mass of information obtained would admit. They respectfully submit the following as a statement of facts authenticated to the entire satisfaction of your committee. The Royal Arch Degree as published, was obtained through an authentic source, directly from Jeremy L. Cross, Grand Lecturer of the United States. That differences in the manner of work, and in the lectures had sprung up among the lodges and chapters, to check which, and produce uniformity, this Mr. Cross was appointed to the office he now holds—that in administering the obligation of the Royal Arch Degree, as he instructs, the words "*murder and treason not excepted*," are expressly used, while some chapters before had only required a companion's secret to be kept "in all cases without exception"—that instances have often occurred where the recipients of the Royal Arch obligation have refused to attest to certain parts of it, and that such parts, after fruitless and artful attempts to explain them to the satisfaction of the candidate, have been omitted. That on the trial of S. D. Green, of Batavia, before an ecclesiastical tribunal, three witnesses on oath, stated that the degrees as disclosed by the Le Roy Convention of the 4th and 5th July last, were substantially true—that affidavits of some ten or twelve persons to the same effect, were made and attested to, for the purpose of being used at a meeting of the Presbyterian order held in Bergen, Genesee county, in December last—five of which deponents had received all the degrees—that on numerous occasions during the pendency of trials in courts of justice, some of the seceding Masons at Le Roy were subpœnaed to attend such trials as witnesses, to sustain objections against masonic jurors, when called in a cause where a brother or companion was a party—that they did attend, that objections were interposed on the ground of the existing obligation between the juror and the party, and that the objected jurors have uniformly been dispensed with, rather than submit to a trial of the objection.

With respect to the correctness and truth of the degrees of Knights of the Red Cross—Knights Templars, and Knights of Malta—Knights of the Christian Mark—and Knights of the Holy Sepulchre, the evidence is *written*, and a reasonable doubt cannot be entertained—a ritual of the degrees in manuscript was left with those who made the disclosure by a high masonic officer, known to have been authorised to confer those degrees.

This ritual formed the basis on which the publication was made, and still remains in their possession. There has also been a ritual in manuscript, left by a high and authorised mason, who came among them to establish a council, called "The Holy and Thrice Illustrious Order of the Cross," and grant diplomas, headed "The Ancient Council of the Trinity, by their successors in the United States of America"—from the rituals, were the degrees of Knighthood taken and published. Your committee therefore are of opinion, that the evidence in relation to these latter degrees is conclusive.

The progress in masonry, of one of the informants, was thus given masonically.

Regularly *initiated* into the degree of entered apprentice mason.

Passed to the degree of fellow Craft.

Raised to the sublime degree of Master.

Advanced to the honorary degree of Mark Master.

Presided in the chair.

Acknowledged and received as Most Excellent Master, and exalted to the sublime degree of Royal Arch.

Degrees in the Encampment.

Knight of the Red Cross.

Knight Templar, and Knight of Malta.

Knight of the Christian Mark, and

Knight of the Holy Sepulchre.

In the Council he received the degree of Illustrious, Most Illustrious, and Thrice Illustrious Order of the Cross.

The offices he held were, Worshipful Master.

Secretary of the Chapter, and Generalissimo of the Genesee Encampment.

That in addition to the three degrees of masonry revealed by William Morgan, and the twelve degrees disclosed by the convention of seceding masons at Le Roy, on the 4th and 5th of July last, your committee would beg leave to state that ELDER DAVID BERNARD, late Intimate Secretary of the Lodge of Perfection, and one of the seceding masons at Le Roy, is about to publish the "*Eleven Ineffable Degrees*" conferred in the Lodge of Perfection, and also, Seven French Degrees of a still higher order of masonry; the authenticity of which your committee think cannot reasonably be *doubted;* that in one of these degrees now revealed, namely, the "*Knights Adepts of the Eagle, or Sun!*" DEISM is plainly avowed, and a dagger aimed at the Christian Religion.

BATES COOKE, *Chairman.*

Resolved, That in the opinion of this convention, the authenticity of the thirty-three degrees of masonry revealed, is satisfactorily established.

REPORT

Of the General Central Anti-Masonic Committee upon the progress and condition of the Anti-Masonic cause.—Made to the New York State Convention, holden at Albany.

IN rendering our grateful acknowledgements to the Dispenser of all good, and congratulating our fellow citizens upon "*the signs of the times*" which indicate a great moral and political revolution in the coming overthrow of Freemasonry, it may not be unprofitable to glance backwards over the relationship which that institution bore to the people and the country, at the period when the overt acts were committed, which are leading the American Republic to re-assert and confirm its Independence.

The masonic society by its arrogation of all the science, wisdom, patriotism, and virtues, which illumine the age, endow and sustain the institutions of the country, and adorn the human character, had conciliated the esteem and won the confidence of public opinion. It had grown under these general influences, unsuspected of other motives than those which it professed, into enormous wealth and gigantic power. Professing strict obedience to the laws, and a wedded affinity to the religion of the country, it had implanted its roots, extended its arms, and established its laws all over the land. The suspicions and apprehensions that had watched and overcome all other secret associations, by the soothing pretensions and specious bearings of Freemasonry were quieted and disarmed.

At this crisis of popular credulity, the masonic conspiracies and outrages which have aroused the moral energies of this State, and promise to interest the whole nation, were matured and perpetrated.—Voluntary investigations were speedily undertaken : but the people were slow to entertain evil thoughts of an ancient and honorable institution.—The great, the wise and the good, of every age and country, were claimed to be among its votaries and patrons. Investigations, embarrassed and crippled by the influence and stratagems of the fraternity, proceeded with slow and uncertain steps. The laws were relaxed and the ministers of justice lingered in their course. The constitutional reliances of the people, for protection and safety, were soon found too weak to discharge their functions; and the public press, which, on all other occasions of existing evil or approaching danger had asserted its high prerogative, was now awed into silence.

A general alarm spread through the western counties. The people met and appointed committees of investigation. It was soon discovered that the outrages had not been unadvisably perpetrated by irresponsible members of the fraternity, but authorised by the institution and impelled by its principles. The conspiracy, from its origin to its conclusion, embraced a period of more than four months, and the knowledge of it extended from the immediate actors in it, to the highest authorities pertaining to the Order.

The results of the first six months' investigation, are embodied in a narrative, and published by the Lewiston committee. The facts and developements therein set forth, have withstood the "*test of truth, and the scrutiny of time.*" With a view to possess the people of information which so deeply concerned their individual rights and the public safety, the committee caused five thousand copies of this narrative to be gratuitously circulated through this and adjoining States.

Finding the ordinary tribunals of justice, in some instances disinclined to discharge their duties, and in all cases too feeble to resist the mysteriously powerful influence of Freemasonry, the people memorialized their Representatives for relief. Their petition respectfully detailed the alarming facts now so well known to all, and earnestly praying that the arm of the law might be strengthened, scarcely received the decent forms of legislative interment. The same irresistible power which had misruled our public officers, sealed the lips of witnesses, tampered with the consciences of jurors, and suspended the sword of justice, now closed the halls of legislation upon the people.

Turned out of Court and repulsed by their Representatives, the people of the western counties appealed, not to the weapons which God and nature had put into their hand, as would have been the case in a less enlightened country, but to public opinion, lawfully and understandingly expressed, through the BALLOT BOXES, for protection and redress. Every other avenue was *closed.* This was the only constitutional *last resort.* Truly auspicious results, and salutary influences, are vindicating the wisdom of this appeal, and all coming experience will sanction its justice.

Meantime the public eye, and the committee, more especially, turned inquiringly from individual offenders, towards the institution itself. A keen desire was manifest to know the real character of Freemasonry, and the true tendency of its principles. Morgan had made a full revelation of the three first degrees, the truth of which was attested by his abduction and sealed with his blood.

Masonry, however, professed to be a "*progressive science*," and further developements were necessary to the formation of a correct estimate of its character. These were not long withheld. An encampment of Knights Templars at Le Roy, after a violent and protracted struggle with that portion of their companions which approved of the outrages, resolved to restore themselves to society and their country, by renouncing the principles and exposing the secrets of the institution. This solemn duty was discharged, in convention, at Le Roy, on the 9th of February, 1828.—The horrid oaths, unearthly penalties, profane orgies, and blasphemous rites, of the higher degrees, were made public. Freemasonry, stripped of her seeming vestal garments and gorgeous attire, now stood bald naked, exposed to the scorn and abhorrence of a long deluded, but finally disabused people.

The committee continued their investigations, and were in constant attendance upon the several courts, where indictments were pending, vainly endeavoring to accelerate the tardy and fettered footsteps of justice.

Near the close of the winter session of 1828, the executive and legislative departments of the Government became suddenly impressed with the propriety and necessity of affording the relief which was so promptly denied the preceding session. An act was passed, authorising the appointment of special counsel, to prosecute the investigation of the masonic outrages. The then acting Governor appointed Daniel Moseley, Esq. to discharge this responsible duty.

That gentleman entered immediately into the investigation, which he continued to prosecute, diligently, until called from the discharge of the duties, to a seat upon the bench, in the 7th Judicial District.

Mr. Moseley has collected and arranged an important mass of complicated testimony, evidencing a wide spread of conspiracy, and an accumulation of crime, fearful, dark and atrocious. This fulfilling measure of guilt grows out of the necessity, from which the *institution* cannot escape, of protecting those who, in obeying its mandates, violated the laws of the land. The masonic conspirators *acted under the advice of their chapters*, the *principles* of which, in *letter* and *spirit*, cover the whole ground. Even the murderers of Morgan, can open their Freemason's Monitor, and *demand their reward for executing the traitor.*

If any thing were wanting to prove that these outrages were the natural offspring of masonic PRINCIPLES, we would refer to the fact, that the persons notoriously concerned in them, not merely stand fair with their lodges and chapters, but have been *elevated to their highest honors and offices!* Those too who fled from justice, have been *protected* and *supported* by the fraternity. And we have strong reasons to believe, though unsupported by positive testimony, that monies have been furnished by the *grand chapter* for the relief and defence of the conspirators, who are distinguished by the mystic brotherhood, as the "*Western Sufferers.*"*

The *time* and *manner* of Morgan's murder has been ascertained, by those who were immediately connected with the investigations.—Most if not all the persons by whom the foul deed was perpetrated, *are satisfactorily known*—but when, and by whose agency, their guilt will be *judiciously* established, remains with the great disposer of all human events.

Edward Giddins, whose testimony would go very far in developing the *finale* of this extended conspiracy and foul murder, has been rejected as a witness, in the Ontario court of Common Pleas, by a rule, in relation to the soundness of which the most distinguished jurists entertain conflicting opinions. Had the objection went to Mr. Giddins' *credibility*, he would have been fully sustained —for few men have passed through life with a more blameless reputation.

Elisha Adams, into whose hands Morgan passed from Mr. Giddins, and who continued to feed and guard him until the night of the murder, was sent by its confederates to Vermont, from whence he was demanded as a fugitive from justice. Adams was a reluctant agent of the

* This fact has since been *directly established* by the declaration of Mr. Yates; who gives *names* and *sums.*

c nspirators, and during his seclusion, had determined if brought to the bar as a witness, as he himself repeatedly averred, to "*make a clean breast of it*" by telling the truth. He continued in this wholesome frame of mind, until he found himself surrounded by his guilty Royal Arch Companions, who soon succeeded in re-establishing their mysterious influence over his conscience; and subjecting him to that obligation of their peculiar code, which, under the most fearful penalties, enjoins the keeping of a companion's secrets, in all cases, "murder and treason not excepted." William King, who professed to have returned to Niagara county, for the purpose of confronting his accusers, swore off his trial, and has retraced his steps to Arkansas. Howard, of Buffalo, who applied the torch to Miller's office, fled to Europe, and has not since been heard of. John Whitney, of Rochester, who following the councils of more wary conspirators, went fearful lengths, after hiding in distant States for nearly two years, has returned and awaits his trial. Loton Lawson, who pleaded guilty to the conspiracy indictments, to prevent the production of testimony, that would inculpate him for a higher offence, has completed his two years imprisonment, and taken up his abode in the State of Pennsylvania. It is known that a masonic friend of Lawson's preceded him on his route from Canandaigua to his destined residence, summoning the chapters to meet—but for what purpose we are left to conjecture.

The case of Eli Bruce, late sheriff of Niagara county, who was *convicted* in Ontario of receiving and confining Morgan in Fort Niagara, was referred, on a question of form, to the supreme court. Eighteen other persons concerned in the outrages have been indicted, but the public prosecutor *has not been able to bring on their trials.*

Nothing but the intelligence and virtue of a great proportion of its members had so long restrained Freemasonry from open misrule and violence. Its signs, grips and obligations, afford every facility for the protection and escape of masonic offenders. And these facilities are far from having been unimproved. Depredations to a greater amount and conspiracies of a more formidable character, have been committed and concealed under the ripening influence of Freemasonry, than the public, aided by recent developements, would be willing to believe.—The institution exerts a mysterious and pernicious influence over all the relations of life. The obligation which binds masons to warn their brethren of all approaching danger, and to keep inviolable their guilty secrets, is a direct bribe to the vicious propensities of our nature.—And that obligation which compels a mason to assist a mystic brother out of difficulty, "right or wrong," furnishes the widest latitude to crime. It is not unknown to those who have given the subject their attention that the numerous gangs of counterfeiters who have so frequently flooded the State with spurious notes and base coin, were almost wholly composed of Freemasons. With this knowledge, it is no longer a mystery how they so frequently eluded the ministers of justice, or escaped through the meshes of the law.

But there is an evil of a more alarming nature to which we feel constrained to draw the public attention. Freemasonry has cast her broadest mantle over legislative corruption and bribery.—The attempt of John Anderson to bribe the Hon. Lewis Williams, chairman of the committee of claims, in the House of Representatives, has led to a brief examination of transactions of a similar character in our State legislature. Col. Anderson attempted to bribe Mr. Williams as a "*man and mason*," but being no mason, Mr. W. was at liberty, not only to reject the bribe but to expose the culprit.* This incident is full of in-

* COL. ANDERSON'S LETTER.

The Hon. Lewis Williams.

Honored Sir: I return you thanks for the attention I received to my claims to pass so soon. Mr. Lee will hand you some claims from the River Raisin, which will pass through your Honorable Committee; and I have a wish that the conduct of the British in that country may be related in full, on the floor of Congress; which will give you some trouble in making out the Report and supporting the same. *I have now to request that you will accept of the small sum of* FIVE HUNDRED DOLLARS as *part* pay for the extra trouble I give you; *I will present it to you as soon as I receive some from Government* (*!*) This is CONFIDENTIAL, that *only you and me may know any thing about it;* or, in OTHER WORDS, I *give* it to you as a man and a MASON; and *hope you belong to that society.* Sir, should it happen that you will not accept of this small sum, I request that you will *excuse* me; if you do not accept, I wish you to drop me a few lines; if you accept, I wish no answer. I hope you will see my view on the subject, that it is for extra trouble. [!!!!!!!!!!] JOHN ANDERSON.

Washington, Jan. 6, 1818.

struction. Had Mr. Williams been a mason, though promptly rejecting the bribe, he was not at liberty to expose a mystic brother to shame and punishment. A Freemason approaches his legislative brother, with the wages of iniquity in hand, in the full assurance that if his bribe is rejected, his guilty secrets will be inviolably kept. This reason is fortified by an extended train of facts. The history of all the known corruption practised in our legislature, from the briberies committed with the Merchant's Bank in 1804, to those of the Fulton and Chemical Charters in 1824, is pregnant with testimony against Freemasonry. The fact that almost every man known to have been disreputably concerned in those transactions, was a Freemason, admonishes the people to guard these avenues against the corrupting influence of that institution. And that ancient, if not honorable fraternity, the Lobby, which still infests the seat of government, and beleaguers the capitol, stands conspicuous in the lists of Freemasonry. Of all the horde of mercenaries who hang year after year upon the legislature, let even one be named who is not a bright Freemason. These assertions are not brought upon slight or insufficient testimony. The evidence of their entire truth may be obtained by all who make proper inquiries.

But the institution puts forth on all occasions, as a shield and defence against her, the names of eminently virtuous men, who in their youth, misled by her false pretensions to science and wisdom, "*took her for better or for worse.*" The sainted name of WASHINGTON, though his recorded admonitions to "*beware of all secret self created associations, under what specious garb soever they appeared,*" forbids the profanation, is imprudently used to patch up the tattered vestments with which a detected imposter still seeks to cover her deformities. The stainless reputation of a contemporary,* whose charities have engraved his name upon the hearts of thousands, and whose munificence is even now unfolding the treasures of knowledge to the humblest citizen, and extending the boundaries of science to the remotest section of the State, is daily pressed into the service of Freemasonry, to give false lustre to its character, and posthumous currency to

* Hon. Stephen Van Rensselaer.

its principles. It is due to this distinguished gentleman to state, that although the swelling titles and empty honors of the fraternity have been continuously lavished upon him, he never could be pressed beyond the third degree of Speculative Freemasonry. And a confiding hope is entertained, based upon our knowledge of his virtues and patriotism, that ere long he will feel constrained to inhibit the use of his right name in beguiling the footsteps of our youth into the dark and devious recesses of the lodge room. More than four hundred initiates, within our own State, including members of every Degree, from an Entered Apprentice to the Thrice Illustrious Knights of the Holy Trinity, have publicly renounced the institution. Thousands have silently withdrawn, and it cannot be presumed that any good man who received it upon trust, will continue his connexion with the fraternity after he has thoroughly examined the tendency of its principles.

Freemasonry is deeply anxious to conceal the truth in relation to herself and her steadfast votaries. It will require much zeal and labor to expose and dissipate the falsehoods and delusions which the fraternity have so industriously spread abroad. Time and truth, however, will ultimately encompass these ends. All there is of Freemasonry, pertaining to the lodges, chapters, and encampments, may be gathered from Morgan's Illustrations, and the Le Roy revelations. But the inquirer for real Freemasonry, divested of its gaudy trappings, and its traditionary fable, must seek out other sources of information. The work of Abbe Barruel, and Professor Robison's Proofs of a Conspiracy to overthrow all Religion and Government, present a faithful and alarming picture of Freemasonry, and commend themselves to the deliberate consideration of the American people. Of the various writers who are now developing, with fearless pens, and surpassing powers, the legitimate tendency and aims of Freemasonry, Henry Dana Ward, of New York, and Elder John G. Stearns, of Oneida county, have attained a proud eminence, from which they are dispensing floods of light and knowledge. These gifted and enlightened men were members of the masonic fraternity. They had, however, sifted its pretensions, and eschewed its principles, previous to the murder of Morgan. The writings of these gentlemen ought to be speedily procured and extensively circulated through every town in the State. We hazard nothing in saying, that no intelligent man or mason can read Mr. Ward's volume, entitled, Freemasonry, without being convinced that the institution is a rank imposture and dangerous cheat. * * * * *

Entirely erroneous opinions have been propagated, far and wide, in relation to the views and conduct of antimasons. We are represented as persecuting and oppressing all the members of the masonic society, thereby confounding the innocent with the guilty. Nothing but Freemasonry itself, is more fallacious than this accusation. Freemasons have violated the laws of the State and taken the life of an unoffending citizen. The influence of the fraternity has impeded, and continues to impede, the course of justice, and the offenders stalk abroad in the community, cherished and supported by the institution, unmolested and unpunished. The secrets and principles of the institution, which have been fully exposed, are positively and undeniably bad and dangerous. We therefore ask Freemasons to renounce them. If they refuse to accede to a request so reasonable, are we made obnoxious to the charge of persecution for withholding our support from them? How are the people to redeem their halls of legislation, to purify their temples of justice, or to re-establish the ascendency of their laws, if the supporters of Freemasonry are not dispossessed of place and power.

The progress of truth, and the developements of time, have refuted many of the fictions, and turned back some of the calumnies with which the fraternity so long held public opinion in suspense.—It is no longer gravely asserted that Morgan is selling his books, that he has retired beyond the Rocky mountains, or that he has joined the standard of the false prophet, at Smyrna. All who do not egregiously undervalue the intelligence of the people, are constrained to admit that this citizen, blameless of all offence to the laws of the land, *after five days confinement, was deliberately murdered at Fort Niagara, and cast into Lake Ontario.* The same calumny which represented the just indignation of freemen, as an excitement got up for the temporary purpose of aiding a party, has spent its malice, and passes, with the mass of falsehoods which that fruitful occasion for private and public defamation provoked.—The deep sensibility and awakened interest which ten free States are manifesting, by unequivocal demonstrations of hostility to the masonic institution, repels the accusation of the fraternity which confined their belligerents to an infected district of madmen and fanatics in the western part of the State of New York.

But we turn from the past to contemplate the future—where hope is unfolding her bright visions to the eye of patriotism, and promising her treasured rewards to the aspirations of piety. The quiet, but resistless power of public opinion, is accomplishing a great moral and political revolution. This work, which moved forward with cautious and faltering steps, through its incipient stages, is now rapidly spreading all over this and the neighboring States. We cannot yet fix its boundaries, or estimate the time that it will require to accomplish its high purposes. But one thing is certain. The fire will burn while the fuel lasts; and the disenthralled spirit which has gone abroad, will not return until the Republic is effectually redeemed from the unhallowed grasp of Speculative Freemasonry.

SAMUEL WORKS,
HARVEY ELY,
F. F. BACKUS,
F. WHITTLESEY,
THURLOW WEED.

Rochester, Feb. 15, 1829.

REPORT

Of the Select Committee of the House of Assembly of New-York, on the Abduction and Murder of William Morgan.—Made Feb. 16, 1829.

The select committee to whom was referred so much of the message of his excellency the governor, as relates to the abduction of William Morgan, and the proceedings under the act passed the 15th day of April, 1828, respectfully report, in part;

That they have endeavored to give the subject that attention which its importance demands, and to pursue their investigations in that spirit of candor that should characterize an inquiry into matters of so much delicacy; and respecting which, there exists great public excitement. They cannot flatter themselves, however, that they have carried nothing of feeling with them into the investigation of the subject; for, coming, as most of them do, from what has been sometimes termed the "infected district," it is hardly to be supposed, that they should be indifferent, in the midst of a community greatly agitated. Still, they trust, that they have so far succeeded in discussing it dispassionately, as to lay before you no facts, except such as have the impress of authenticity, and to draw no inferences which are not fairly deducible from established premises.

The message of his excellency the governor treats the subject as one which may require the interposition of the legislature, and to your committee has been assigned the task of ascertaining what legislation is necessary. It being highly important that the legislature should be in possession of the facts in every case, respecting which they may be called to legislate, your committee believed it to be their duty to collect and spread before this house a statement of the circumstances of this extraordinary affair, together with the causes which produced them, so far as the same have been ascertained. For this purpose, they directed their chairman to address letters to the Hon. Daniel Moseley, special counsel, appointed by the executive of this State, under the act passed April 15, 1828, and to Bowen Whiting, Esq. district attorney for the county of Ontario, requesting from them a statement in detail of such particulars of the transaction as may have come to their knowledge, in the discharge of their official duties.

Your committee were aware, that the circumstances relating to the Morgan outrages, had been collected and published in a pamphlet form, and in some public newspapers, by a number of respectable gentlemen, selected for that purpose, by their fellow citizens in public meetings; and that notwithstanding these gentlemen, some of whom have seats in this house, affixed their own signatures to these publications, no attempt had been made to disprove their statements. Still, as there exists a disposition in our country to discredit statements which are made through the organ of the periodical press, and it being desirable to lay before this house such data as might with proper safety be relied upon, by those who may be called to act in this grave matter, your committee thought it better to refer you to statements emanating from those whose official duties have made them acquainted with these singular transactions. It has too long been the opinion of many, that the "western excitement" belonged more properly to our newspaper, than to our judicial history; and events more alarming in their character, when viewed in all their bearings, than any that have transpired in the course of many years, have been regarded rather as a romance than as solemn matters of fact. In making this statement, your committee mean no reflection upon the intelligence of this house or this community. The state of feeling and the incredulity that have existed in many places with regard to this matter, have proceeded from an honorable confidence in our free institutions, and in the integrity of our fellow citizens, which bespeak great elevation of sentiment and nobleness of spirit; but which at the same time show with what ease our good nature may be practised upon by the artful and designing.

The call for information made upon Mr. Whiting, was answered. And your committee would take the liberty of expressing their acknowledgements to this gentleman for his promptitude and frankness in preparing for them, in the midst of pressing professional engagements, a statement so full and satisfactory.

From this statement it appears that in the summer of 1826, a notice was inserted in the Ontario Messenger, a newspaper published at Canandaigua, by the procurement of those who were afterwards concerned in the outrages, representing Morgan to be guilty of bad conduct, and that particular information might be had respecting him, on application to the lodge in that village. During the summer of that year, it was reported that Morgan was writing a book on Freemasonry, to be published by David C. Miller, of Batavia, and this report was confirmed by subsequent events. Much feeling was excited amongst many members of the masonic fraternity, in consequence of this report; and meetings were held in many places, to consider of measures, by which the publication of the book might be prevented. A Canadian whose name is Johns, and who is said to have belonged to the British fur company, was introduced to Miller, under pretence of assisting him in the publication, but in reality for the purpose of acquiring information where Morgan's writings were to be found. Through his aid, the conspirators were enabled to obtain the possession of a part, at least, of Morgan's manuscripts.

On the 11th of September, persons from Lockport, in the county of Niagara, 90 miles distant from Canandaigua, applied at Fort Niagara for a place of confinement for Morgan, because he was about "to reveal the secrets of masonry." The day before, Ebenezer C. Kingsley of Canandaigua, by the persuasion of Nicholas G. Cheesebro and others of that place, made a complaint against Morgan, before a magistrate, for stealing a shirt and cravat, the property of Kingsley. A warrant was issued on this complaint by the magistrate, directed to Cheesebro, as one of the coroners of Ontario county, or to any constable of that county, for Morgan's arrest. It was delivered to Cheesebro, who hired a post-coach and procured Hallaway Hayward, a constable, and three or four others, to accompany him to Batavia, where Morgan resided. The party arrived at Batavia the same day, and the next morning the warrant was served by Hayward, it having been first endorsed by a magistrate of Genesee county. Immediately after the arrest, the same party returned to Canandaigua, and arrived in the evening. Morgan was taken before the magistrate, examined and discharged from the arrest, the charge of larceny appearing to be unfounded, the shirt and cravat having been borrowed from Kingsley.

Immediately on his being discharged, a demand of two dollars was presented to the justice against him in favor of Cheesebro, as assignee of one Ackley. Morgan confessed a judgment, and an execution was forthwith issued. He took off his coat and offered it to satisfy the execution, but it was refused, and he was arrested and locked up in prison.

Information that Morgan was in custody, was immediately sent to Rochester to certain persons there, or to use the language of Cheesebro, to Morgan's *friends* in that place, some of whom came to Canandaigua the next day, for the purpose of carrying him off. A carriage was stationed a few rods from the gaol, where it might be ready to start at a given signal. Previous to this, Loton Lawson had been at the gaol, had seen Morgan, and proposed to Mrs. Hall, the wife of the gaoler, (he being absent,) to pay the debt out of friendship to Morgan, and release him from prison. Mrs. Hall at first refused to comply, but on Cheesebro and Sawyer's recommending it, she consented to release Morgan. As she went towards the prison, Lawson went to the street door and made a signal. She turned, and saw a man come up the steps. She released Morgan, and on going to the door, saw him between Lawson and the man who came up the steps, struggling and crying *murder*. His mouth was stopped, and he was forced off down the street. In the struggle, Morgan lost his hat. One of the party made a signal by rapping on a well curb, when the carriage started after them, took them in, and went towards Rochester.

The carriage was driven by Hiram Hubbard, who has testified, that he drove the party a little beyond Hanford's landing, near the east end of the ridge road, where he arrived about sunrise; and that they got out at a place, distant from any house. On his return, and a short distance from the place where he left the party, he met a carriage with a pair of horses. The same day, a carriage was procured from Ezra Platt, of Rochester, under pretence of going to Lewiston to the installation of a lodge. Mr. Platt has been examined as a witness, and denies recollecting who hired the carriage. He says that it was applied for before daylight, and that the driver has left the country, but that he does not now recollect his name. On that day, a carriage passed along the ridge road to Lewiston, under peculiar and extraordinary circumstances, not stopping at public houses, drawn by horses belonging to persons living on the road, which were changed in bye places, and driven by men who would not ordinarily be engaged in that business. This carriage stopped in a back street at Lewiston; and on the morning of the 14th, at a very early hour, another carriage was procured to go to Fort Niagara. The latter carriage was driven by Corydon Fox, a stage driver, who was directed to go to the one standing in the back street for his passengers. Fox states that he did so; that four or five men left that carriage and got into the one driven by him. One of the men had no hat, and appeared to be helpless. He then drove towards the Fort, called by the way at Col. King's, took him in, and when near the Fort, left the whole party in the road, and returned to Lewiston. It is proved, that on that day, a man was in confinement in the magazine, attached to the Fort. Mr. Whiting adds, that it can now be proved that Morgan was in the carriage that passed along the ridge road on the 13th of September, 1826.

He also subjoins a statement of the testimony of Edward Giddins before the grand jury of Ontario county, and which said Giddins has published. Mr. Giddins, on the trial of Eli Bruce, Esq. late sheriff of Niagara, was offered as a witness, and rejected, on the ground of religious belief. Mr. Whiting, however, seems to credit his statements, which, he says, are corroborated, in some important particulars, by other witnesses. From his statement we learn that Morgan was confined in the magazine at Fort Niagara, and if we give his statement credence, we must come to the conclusion that he was finally murdered. Mr. Whiting comes to that conclusion, independent of the testimony of Giddins; and your committee believe that he is fully warranted in so doing, by the facts and circumstances which he has detailed. Mr. Moseley, in his communication to your committee, states, that he has ascertained material testimony, in relation to the abduction, since the making of this report to the executive, and adds, that he has been put in possession of some information of a *graver* character, from a source entitled to credit. Your committee, therefore, feel justified in saying, that there is very little reason to doubt, but that a free citizen of this State has been deliberately put to death by highly respectable individuals, and that many men in high standing were privy to the designs against him, and assisted in the preliminary measures, although, perhaps, but few directly participated in the final catastrophe.

It may be proper to mention in this connexion, that at a trial at Batavia, not particularly referred to by Mr. Whiting, three men were convicted of a daring outrage upon the person and liberty of Col. Miller, who was associated with Morgan in the publication of the book on masonry. This outrage was committed on the same day that Morgan was forcibly carried away from the gaol at Canandaigua. A principal actor in this affair was the Canadian, Johns, who, eight days before, had suddenly disappeared from Batavia. But your committee will not tax the patience of this house, by a recital of the particulars of this outrage, and of several others committed or attempted against the persons and property of Miller and Morgan, and in which many persons are known to have participated.

Although the special council, appointed by the executive, has interposed a caution against speaking of "societies and denominations of men" in relation to the subject of these inquiries, your committee feel bound to state, that in their opinion, if the abduction of Morgan is chargeable upon individuals, acting "as such," it is likewise chargeable upon them, as members of a powerful society, existing in our State, claiming a high character, on which has been bestowed many marks of public favor, and whose annual convocations and dazzling honors have been regarded with great interest, and sought for with much avidity. Your committee are not insensible, that they are preferring a grave charge against an institution which has many bright and honorable names enrolled among its votaries. Still they conceive, that the true character of the transaction, and its relative importance are to be ascertained by adverting to the cause which produced it, and the motives which actuated the perpetrators.

The active and persevering district attorney of the county of Ontario, who has carefully investigated the whole matter, states it as proved, "that the motives which actuated those who conspired against Morgan, were to prevent the publication of his book on Freemasonry. The same objects were avowed in the meetings in Genesee county, by those who visited Fort Niagara, by those who acted in Canandaigua, and by those who came to Canandaigua, in consequence of the information sent to Rochester. So far, therefore, as their motives were then avowed, the suppression of Morgan's publication was the object to be effected, and the abduction of the man was the means by which that object was to be accomplished."

"The abduction of Morgan," says Mr. Whiting, "is a singular and striking event in our history; and as in case of other irretrievable evils, it is easier to lament it, than to find a remedy. I have no hesitation in saying, that it has resulted from the confidence which members of the masonic society have felt in its power and influence; from a false estimate of the value of that institution, and from an opinion, that they were bound to preserve it from violation and injury." And he adds in conclusion, "It is worthy of remark, that it has been proved or conceded, that all those who have engaged in these outrages were members of the masonic fraternity; a fact not without meaning in reference to the subjects of the conspiracy."

A proper consideration of these facts, fully established by solemn judicial investigation, will lead to a due estimate of the subject referred to by your committee. Some have wondered why the abduction, or even the murder, of a comparatively obscure individual, should be considered of so much importance. Had he fallen in deadly strife with his fellow, or had a single assassin planted a dagger in his heart, the event and its circumstances would long since have ceased to interest the public. It is the offence against the dignity of this State, and the just grounds of alarm, indicated by the character of the transaction, which gives it its relative importance. Many cases of personal suffering may be pointed out in our history, which, if the individuals only are to be taken into consideration, must be regarded as much more afflictive, than the case of the American seaman who was shot by British authority in the harbor of New-York, and whose death caused such great sensation. Still, his death was justly considered a matter of national concern, whilst others, who fell by private assassins, were soon forgotten. A wound was inflicted upon our national honor, which awakened the sensibilities of this whole nation. We felt, that such aggressions on our sovereignty should be repelled, and that the permanence and stability of our institutions could only be secured, by showing our neighbors that such acts could not be committed with impunity. If the spirit and feelings that were then excited were just and proper; if that event was considered an alarming outrage, principally in consequence of the source from which it proceeded, does it not follow that the offence committed against the majesty of the people, in the case of William Morgan, should excite general interest. The members of a wide spread association, whose principles and operations are studiously concealed from the public view; who claim for their body high antiquity and distinguished renown; who assume imposing titles, and display the badges of royalty, feeling themselves bound to preserve their own institution from violation, have violated the majesty of the laws, and trampled upon those fundamental principles, on which are based our free institutions.

Your committee believe, that such an act, from such a quarter, is to be regarded as more alarming in its character than a simple outrage, committed by the agents of a foreign government. It is much more easy to repel the assaults of a foreign enemy, than to counteract the wiles and machinations of a domestic foe. The security of our free institutions, in a great measure, depends upon their due estimation by those who enjoy their benefits. If our honorable, learned, and influential citizens consider themselves bound to an invisible power, existing amongst us, by stronger ties than their allegiance to that country which so amply protects them in the enjoyment of life and liberty, and in the prosecution of those pursuits which they deem essential to their happiness; if reckoning upon the strength and influence of that power, and with a direct view to its preservation, they venture upon the exercise of the highest acts of sovereignty, thus contemning the sovereign authority of this State, have we no just ground for alarm?

Your committee are sensible that they have stated a strong case, but have they stated a stronger one than is detailed by Mr. Whiting, if we allow that he has not mistaken the true character of the transaction, and the motives of the actors in that sad tragedy? What have they alleged, that is not fully said by a faithful public officer, who has had every opportunity to judge in this matter, and whose relation to those concerned, precludes the idea that he has misconstrued their motives? Well might the distinguished public officer,* who now presides over the other branch of the legislature, say, that those who perpetrated this outrage, 'have disturbed the public peace, have dared to raise their parricidal arms against the laws and constitution of our government, and assumed a power which is incompatible with a due subordination to the laws and public authority of this State.' Following up the idea of the same distinguished individual, your committee add that such attacks upon the sovereign power, of which every citizen is a constituent member, should be resented and guarded against.

Your committee believe that an idea has too long prevailed, that this is a trivial affair; and therefore they have dwelt longer upon this branch of the subject than would otherwise have been necessary. They forbear to descant upon the reasons that have given currency to this idea, and the cold indifference with which it has been regarded by a body of men whose members, for a series of years, have filled a great proportion of the responsible stations in every department of the government. The citizens of those counties where these outrages were perpetrated, when they discovered the intimate connexion between them and Freemasonry, expected that the members and officers of that institution would have been foremost in ferreting out the guilty individuals, and unwearied in their exertions to wipe from its escutcheon so foul a stain. It was certainly reasonable to suppose that an institution laying claim to the greatest purity of principle, would have made liberal contributions of its funds and exertions, in bringing to light this dark, nefarious and alarming transaction; that at least they would have affixed some mark of disapprobation upon those whose conduct was so criminal, and so directly calculated to bring their fraternity into disrepute. Your committee cannot learn, however, that any such measures were deemed necessary by the institution. They cannot but think that this apparent apathy solemnly admonishes us, as a people, to inquire into its causes; and why is it that when members of this society are frequently debarred from its privileges, for offences which are not cognizable before our courts, the perpetrators of these flagrant enormities should not be

* Judge Throop.

considered guilty of "unmasonic conduct," and treated accordingly. The inquiry naturally suggests itself, was that confidence in the power and influence of their society which led these men to the commission of such crimes, such as the principles of that society warranted them in entertaining; and was their construction of their masonic obligations that which is fairly inferable from the tenor of those obligations? The standing of these men in society and with the *craft*; their numbers; their avowed motives, with reference to this affair; and the treatment they have received from their brethren, certainly justifies the presumption that they were not mistaken; and would, if we had no other evidence, afford the strongest grounds for suspicion. But on this subject we are not left to conjecture. The principles and obligations of masonry are well known to at least one member of your committee; and they afford a complete solution to this inquiry. Several of the obligations, taken by members of this society, as published by a convention of seceding masons, who were led to an examination of the principles of the institution, in consequence of the outrages committed in their neighborhood, were laid before the legislature at their last session, for the consideration of this house. These obligations taken in connexion with those published by Morgan, (for the authenticity of which we have evidence of the most *conclusive*, as well as of the most painful kind,) too plainly show the truly appalling fact, that those deluded men whose hands are probably stained with a brother's blood, though politically and morally wrong, were *masonically* right. This, in the view of your committee, is the most distressing and alarming feature in the whole transaction.

To the sincere patriot, to every citizen, it affords matter for *grave* reflection, that those men, some of whom have seats in this house, and hold high and responsible stations, should have calculated with so much confidence on being shielded from public vengeance, although guilty of high enormities, by the power and influence of a secret society. Whether they supposed that this society afforded facilities for the commission of crimes without the possibility of detection, or whether they calculated on corrupting the fountains of justice, the fact is equally interesting to every lover of his country. Did these men suppose that masons in high stations would interpose the broad shield of their authority to protect them in their high handed villany, in their " preconcerted and deliberate " attack upon the laws and constitution of their country ? Did they suppose, that witnesses and jurors, feeling themselves bound by masonic obligations, would lose sight of their duty to their country and their God ? Your committee take no pleasure in dwelling upon this subject; still it is one which requires a thorough investigation. A society of men who meet in secret, embracing all ranks of life, comprising many men of talents, and a very large proportion of those who hold high and responsible stations, is looked up to with confidence by its intelligent and respectable members, as affording a sure protection from the consequences of the most infamous and dangerous crimes. Yet this society boasts of her charities, professes to teach the most expansive benevolence, and carries in her public processions the volume of inspiration. Why this confidence ? How do they expect protection in such cases, except by trampling under foot all that is dear to us as freemen ?

Whether the existence of such a society, holding her meetings in secret places, guarding the entrance to her conclaves with the instruments of death, binding her votaries with such ties, affording them protection when in difficulty, " right or wrong," regarding her own laws as paramount to the laws of the land, is compatible with our free institutions, should be taken into serious consideration. The subject addresses itself to our love of country in the most imposing form ; and however disagreeable it may be, we should not shrink from the examination.

Your committee are aware, that any measures which may be taken, with the view of removing this evil, will be called intolerant. It will be said, that the society or sect of Freemasons, are entitled to the same protection as other associations for charitable purposes and mutual improvement. There can be no question but that Freemasons have a right to assemble and transact their business in their own way, so long as their business is lawful, and they in no way injure others, or endanger the State. But that men may meet for any purpose, and form associations whose tendency is to screen the guilty and sap the foundations of civil liberty, is inconsistent with the genius of our government. Every government has the right to provide for its own safety, and to prohibit any thing that tends to its own subversion. A government without such right could be of no value to the community that adopted it.

If Freemasonry has dangerous features, there can certainly be no doubt of the right of the legislature to require those features to be expunged. If it is, as its friends contend, merely an association to promote charity and social intercourse, it has no occasion for such obnoxious oaths, of a character so different from the real objects of the institution. Why such horrid penalties to enforce the practice of such duties, and to effect such objects?

Your committee cannot believe that the rights of any citizen would be abridged by forbidding him to put himself under such obligations, or to partake in rites directly calculated to corrupt the public morals. We have not only a right to prohibit crime, but to prevent men from binding themselves to its commission.

Your committee believe, that the institution of Freemasonry owes its dangerous character to its obligations which are imposed as they are informed, upon noviciates, without making known to them their nature. Destitute of their sanctions, and the bond of union they produce, (the sure consequence of the barbarous penalties that are interwoven into their texture,) it would lose its mischievous tendency, and be completely shorn of its locks. Its boasted cement, which owes its influence to one of the strongest, though not the noblest, passions of the human heart, would lose its power; and the mighty edifice that affects to defy the "world in arms" would fall by its own weight. If Freemasons are tenacious of their ornaments, badges, and vestments, let them continue to use them, and to display them in public, if it will afford them any amusement or pleasure. But certainly it is asking too much of this community to require us to tolerate them in the use of oaths which tend directly to sap the foundations of our free institutions, and to subvert the citadel of liberty.

Your committee believe that the passage of a law, prohibiting the administration of extra judicial oaths, would produce many salutary results, disconnected with the masonic institution. The committee, who, at the last session, reported the bill to prevent the administration of such oaths, say, with great force and justice, that "the frequent unauthorized and irreverent administration of oaths has a powerful influence to destroy that religious sensibility to their nature, and that scrupulous and conscientious regard to all their requirements, which alone entitle them to confidence. Great and enlightened men have, with one accord, condemned the multiplication of oaths, with or without the sanction of law, as immoral and impolitic." If such remarks are correct with respect to oaths administered in the usual form, what shall we say of those presented to the consideration of the house, and which are said to be taken under circumstances of peculiar degradation? It must be perfectly obvious to every one, who will make himself acquainted with their nature and provisions, that they must frequently put it in the power of men, desperate in principle and depraved in morals, to exercise a commanding influence over men of pure principles and upright intentions; that not unfrequently the virtuous citizen finds his known duties clashing with his masonic obligations. Cases must frequently occur which require a conscientious individual, either to disregard an oath imposed by the authority of his country, or one he has taken in a masonic assembly. Cases so distressing and embarrassing should always be prevented if practicable, as they serve to ensnare the conscience, to blunt the moral sense, and weaken the security which is sought to be obtained by requiring the confirmation of an oath.

Your committee forbear to enlarge upon the case with which an institution, constituted as Freemasonry is, might affect our elections and keep its influence out of sight. The citizens of the western counties, when their attention was called to the subject, by the strange transactions which took place amongst them, were surprised to find that nearly every high judicial and ministerial station, in that section of the State, was filled by members of the order. In fact they almost literally filled "every department of the government." It should also be remembered, that one of its votaries has asserted, when speaking in the name of his brethren, on a public anniversary, (and whose boastings, not altogether idle, perhaps, have been extensively circulated in masonic newspapers and publications,) that "masonry has the power of cooperating in the desk, in the legislative hall, on the bench, in every gathering of men of business, in every party of pleasure, in every enterprise of government, in every domestic circle, in peace and in war, among its enemies and friends, and in one place as well as another." This idea of masonic influence, it will be seen, accords with that "confidence," to which an able and faithful officer of the government ascribes the untimely fate of the unhappy Morgan.

In directing their inquiries towards that part of the subject which has relation to the legislation that may be necessary in reference to this subject, your committee have deemed two things important: first, to provide for the detection and punishment of those who committed the outrage, and then to guard against similar offences. Taking into consideration the circumstances of the case, your committee are persuaded that the act of April 15th, 1828, should be continued in force. The reasons given by Mr. Whiting for the adoption of such a course are, with them, conclusive.

In order that the subject may be fully investigated, it may be necessary to make some provision for those witnesses who are required to attend the courts in distant counties. The frequent delays that have occurred, in the legal proceedings that have been had, have rendered it extremely burdensome on those witnesses who have been called to a considerable distance from their homes. Mr. Moseley recommends that provision should be made for their relief, and your committee, believing that it would promote the ends of justice, by preventing the difficulty of procuring testimony, have incorporated a provision to that effect, into a bill which they ask leave to introduce, to continue in force the act entitled "An act to provide for the employment of counsel for the purposes therein mentioned."

They also ask leave to introduce a bill to prevent the administration of extra judicial oaths.

The subject referred to your committee, being one of

first impression and of vast importance, they do not feel fully prepared, at present, to say what legislation may be necessary, in relation to its full developement, and the furtherance of justice. They do not, therefore, ask to be discharged from the further consideration of the subject, but wish to be indulged with further time for reflection, on the measures which should be devised for the more effectual investigation of the outrages committed on the person of Morgan, and to provide against the recurrence of events, so alarming in their character, so destructive of the peace of society, and the safety of its members.

A. HAZELTINE, *Chairman.*

REPORT

On the Abduction of William Morgan.—Made to the Senate, (New York,) Feb. 14, 1829.

THE select committee, to whom was referred so much of the governor's message as relates to the abduction of William Morgan, and the proceedings under the law of the last session upon that subject, beg leave respectfully to report in part:

That they have attentively examined the message of the Executive, of March 18, 1828, and the law appointing a commissioner, which was thereupon enacted; as also the recent message of the present governor referring to the same subject. They have also perused with especial care, the report of the commissioner, which is to be presumed a fair and correct statement of what has been transacted by him, during the laborious duties of the last ten months; they cannot nevertheless abstain from expressing their surprise at the meagre character of the commissioners' report, when they call to mind that the first duty specified in the law creating that office was "to institute inquiries concerning William Morgan and his fate subsequently, and all the incidents connected therewith." That the report, coming as it does from a man of reputation, and high official standing, should be thus jejune and bare of incident, confirms an opinion long entertained by individuals composing the committee, that all those criminal transactions, whenever an attempt should be officially made to bring them to light, would from causes of a peculiar character, be shrouded in a veil of impenetrable darkness.

Your committee have come to the deliberate conclusion, that the evils intended to be remedied by the legislation of 1828, were not at that period fully understood; that their character was misconceived, and their importance underrated. That legislation seems to have been based upon the supposition, that the administration of justice was feebly dispensed, in the western section of the State, and that the deputation of a special counsellor or attorney, to give it tone and energy, was alone sufficient to remedy the evils complained of by the people. However much the appointment of such a commissioner might in different ways expedite and facilitate the trials growing out of the fate of Morgan, still such commissioner has been, and will hereafter be powerless, in bringing to merited justice the guilty individuals, who have been chiefly concerned in the transactions, that have so much disturbed and afflicted the community. In the judgment of the committee, the past evils cannot now be reached by any legislation within the range of our constitutional powers, and it is their opinion that remedial enactments having regard to the recurrence of similar evils, ought chiefly at this time to attract the attention of the Senate.

To entitle this opinion to its just weight, some of the reasons which have led to its adoption will be briefly stated.

At no period since the revolution, has the public mind been so severely agitated as by the abduction and subsequent unhappy fate of William Morgan. The great moral shock has been felt with few exceptions, by people of every age, sex and condition. The high-handed violation of law, the great number concerned, the cheerless and desolate condition of his bereaved wife and children, the uncertainty that for a while attended the whole affair, were all calculated to arouse the public mind to an unexampled state of sympathy, indignation and abhorrence. But these passions, although intense at that period, are in their nature evanescent, and before this time, would have spent their force, had not the attempt to bring the offenders to the bar of justice, produced a developement of facts, circumstances and principles as lasting in their effects as the love of liberty in man.

The committee think it proper to observe that a just regard for the wishes and feelings of their constituents, and the other requirements which grow out of the occasion, will compel them to lay aside all that delicacy in treating this subject, which is incompatible with a just and manly discharge of their duty—and reluctant as they are to give just cause of offence to any man, they feel themselves compelled to designate classes of men by the names they have seen fit to adopt, and to animadvert freely upon their conduct, when such animadversion comes within the legitimate scope of their duties.

The people of this State are distinguished by their attachment to a pure administration of justice as connected with the trial by jury—by their love of self-government, and by their aversion to every thing which directly or indirectly tends to thwart the operation of the democratic principles, which are the basis of our political compact. They are distinguished by their jealousy of powerful and talented men, and especially of the combinations of such men for purposes either unknown, or known to affect improperly, the even and healthful current of our political affairs. They have learned that concentration of feeling, of interest and of effort, are to the moral and political, what the lever and the screw are, to the mechanical powers, and they dread their operation.

The order of the Jesuits, whose discipline secured unity of design and secrecy in action—which used the solemn sanctions of the most high God, to subserve purposes the most selfish and profane, presented to the 16th century a moral power greater than the world had ever known. It penetrated with the silence and certainty of fate, the secrets of every Court in Europe, and subjugated, without the force of arms, one half the continent of America to the dominion of the Pope. This order has been crushed, but within the last 120 years another has arisen—the society of free and accepted masons.

This institution, professing to be of ancient and even

of divine origin, adopting sanctions similar to those of the order of the Jesuits, and commanding a secrecy still more profound, have recently made demonstrations of a power, astonishing in its effects upon the social and political compact, and of a character such as the friends of free institutions cannot fail to deplore.

The powers manifested by the masonic institution which may have been exercised in its unlawful restraints of human liberty, or pretended jurisdiction over human life, are not now so much the occasion of alarm, as its fearful moral influence, exerted upon the public press, and its facility in controling results in the tribunals of justice. The public feeling at the West, which has borne the ridicule and sarcasm of those interested in quelling it, is not, as they would have it believed, the mere animal sensation indicated by brutes, whose bellowing marks the spot where some victim has been slaughtered;—but is the result of sober, calculating reflection, looking to causes and their consequences; to existing evils and the remedies to be applied; to posterity, and not the present generation alone. The life of one man, or even a thousand, in a republic consisting of 12,000,000 of inhabitants, politically considered, is of but little moment. But that the streams of justice should flow pure and uncontaminated, is matter of infinite concern not only to the people of the West, but to the whole State; not only to the State, but the Union.

But they have lost the confidence they formerly reposed, in the tribunals of justice. They believe that masonry exerts its influence, in civil, as well as criminal cases; in arbitrations, references, and in trials by jury, before justices of the peace, as well as in the higher courts. Formerly from one half to two thirds of their justices belonged to the fraternity of masons—now not one in twenty are initiated; and this change has been chiefly produced by their entire conviction of the fact that masonry pervades and influences the courts of justice.

During what have been called the Morgan trials, and other civil cases which owe their origin to his abduction and subsequent fate, the people have crowded the courts of justice to overflowing. They have watched the deportment of masonic witnesses upon the stand; some of whom, of good repute in society, have sworn to facts, which in the opinion of by-standers, were not credited by a single one of the hundreds of persons who were present. It is believed that grand juries, a majority of whom were masons, have omitted to find bills of indictment when there was proof before them of outrages, not surpassed in grossness and indecency, by any committed in the country since its first settlement. Those outrages were committed upon a mason, who had been in the daily habit of exposing in lectures, what were once called the secrets of masonry. Grand jurymen have said while assembled for the discharge of their duties, and when it was apprehended their masonic brethren would be implicated, " we must not let our brethren suffer." In a case of recent occurrence, a defendant who had been sued by a mason, not willing to have his case tried by masonic jurymen, challenged them ; stating to the court his readiness to prove the character of the masonic oaths, and to show that the obligations assumed by them were of a description, unfitting them to sit in judgment between the parties ; and of such a nature as to disqualify them in point of law. With the assent of the circuit judge, the masonic jurymen left the box, and the trial proceeded. The counsel for the defendant, entertained no doubt, upon the law and the facts he could prove, that the challanges were well taken.

The committee might multiply cases of this description, but they are omitted for others of more public notoriety, and tending to the same point.—The case of Col. King, is one fully known to the public, and partly from information contained in his newspaper communications. The committee therefore recur to it, the more readily, but without any intention of expressing an opinion of his innocence or guilt. He had been suspected of having had a concern in some of the transactions affecting William Morgan. He went to Washington in the fall or winter of 1826-7 ; applied for public employment, and obtained, with the assistance of some of his masonic friends, the place of Sutler to the United States' troops in the territory of Arkansas. The suspicions resting upon the public mind in regard to him increased : and Messrs. Garlinghouse and Bates were despatched by the Governor of this State for the purpose of arresting him, and perhaps some others who were supposed to be fugitives from justice. They ascertained that King was at cantonment Towson, and procured an order from the Secretary of War, to the commander to surrender him forthwith.

The fruit of this sovereign exercise of the State and United States power, in procuring the return of this humble sutler to answer in the courts of this State for the misdemeanors charged upon him, was precisely such as might have been anticipated upon the supposition that the obligations of masons to each other, are such as they undoubtedly must be, upon the proof that has been presented to the public. Bound to protect each other by the tenor of obligations in their view of higher import than those they owe to the State or country which gives them protection,—the officer of the Fort, instead of obeying the order of the Secretary of War, notified King of his danger; and Garlinghouse and Bates soon found by the escape of King, that their labors, arduous as they had been, were defeated by the machinations of masonry.

The annals of criminal jurisprudence furnish no parallel in many respects to the case of William Morgan. The majesty of the laws and the powers of masonry have been brought into conflict. What may be the result of the mighty struggle none can tell. But the events of the two last years during which the conflict has been maintained, induce the belief that masonry will be victorious. The history of Morgan's fate is short and simple: On the 11th day of September, 1826, he was taken by several masons in broad day, by force, from the village of Batavia to Canandaigua, a distance of 50 miles, and there upon a process originated for the occasion, confined in jail. While on his way from Batavia, one of his kidnappers who had him in charge, said with an oath, Morgan should not be taken from him alive. After a short confinement in the prison at Canandaigua, he was taken out on Sunday the 12th, at evening, and amidst his distressing cries of murder, was forced into a post coach. He was then driven through a densely populated country, 110 miles to the United States Fort, on the Niagara river, and there confined. The horses and coaches used in conveying him from Canandaigua, were owned or procured by masons. And the owner of a livery stable kept at Rochester, who at that time and now is a royal arch mason, actually charged the *Grand Chapter* for the use of his coaches and horses to Lewiston. Pains were taken to obtain masonic drivers. The last driver, however, accidentally was not a mason. It was Corydon Fox. He drove the prisoner, attended by three masons to the grave-yard, about 80 rods distant from the Fort, and was directed to halt. The party dismounted, and Fox was told to return to Lewiston. This was in the night time. Shortly after Fox made some observations about his trip to the Fort, which excited fears in the minds of the brotherhood, and within a short period, a special lodge was called, and Fox was initiated as a member of it. An unusual number of masons were at Lewiston, and in the vicinity of the Fort, during the three or four days of Morgan's confinement there, and nightly visited the Fort. The sufferings of Morgan were probably terminated on the night of the 18th of September, 1826.

Morgan was fifty years old; in point of talents and manners was above mediocrity—had fought in the defence his country at the battle of New-Orleans, and immediately preceding his abduction from Batavia had unfortunately for himself and family been concerned in writing a book upon masonry, disclosing its usages, oaths and obligations.

It has been fully established by the testimony in the various trials that have been had, that a great number of masons have been directly or indirectly concerned in the abduction and subsequent fate of Morgan. But notwithstanding the publicity of this transaction arising from the great number necessarily concerned in it—notwithstanding the thousands of dollars offered as rewards by the executive of this State, as well as the governor of Canada, to those who would give information of his fate, and the thousands contributed and expended by humane and patriotic citizens to ferret out the iniquity; and notwithstanding too, a commissioner has been sent by the legislature, to add his talents and industry to that of the courts in the country, still no record tells us whose hands have been stained with the blood of this masonic victim.

The committee assume the fact, that the life of Morgan has been destroyed; they are compelled to do so, from the irresistible weight of circumstances tending to fortify that conviction. The love of gold, incited by the great rewards which have been offered; the love of character stimulating individuals implicated, and indeed the fair fame of whole classes of men reproachfully assailed; the fear of punishment operating on the agents more immediately concerned; and in fact every consideration, that should influence men, pressed them to a re-deliverance of Morgan to his friends and to society, if it had been possible for them to do so. The people of the western counties, fully aware of the leading circumstances of this transaction, and having had more than two years for inquiry and reflection, have arrived to the decision with unexampled unanimity, that this man has become a victim and a sacrifice.

It is conceded that the facts herein detailed to show the interference of masonry in the administration of justice, come chiefly under the head of circumstantial evidence—of its weight and conclusiveness, the Senate will judge; but it is entirely certain that it fully justifies the opinion of the commissioner, Daniel Moseley, Esq., expressed in a paragraph of his report to the Senate, in which he states that, "as to his fate subsequently thereto, it is not yet developed, nor can it be anticipated with much confidence, to be judicially determined by any tribunal over which men have control."

The committee will now proceed to remark upon other evidence which has come to their knowledge, in reference to the subject before them, of a different but highly alarming character, and calculated more directly to impress upon the Senate the necessity of ulterior legislation. Many masons at the west, whose feelings had been aroused by the enormities of the institution committed in that quarter, learned from witnessing the temper of the people, that they should be protected in any infractions of its laws. They were satisfied beyond controversy, that the strange oaths of an institution, governed by iniquitous principles, and used for evil, and sometimes for murderous purposes, ought in no respect to bind the consciences or conduct of those, who had imprudently taken them. They saw the absurdity of supposing that any human being could be bound by an oath appealing to the Supreme Being, when that very oath enjoined an obligation to do that, which is in opposition to the laws of both God and man. They finally assembled at Le Roy in convention, on the 19th of February, 1828, and frankly and truly stated to the world, the substance of the masonic oaths and obligations.

Several of those masons who have seceded from the institution, are personally known to a majority of the committee, and they deem it proper to assure the Senate, that they are men of standing in the community, whose characters for veracity are beyond the reach of calumny.

* * * * * * * * * *

In the remarks which His Excellency has been pleased to make, in his message to the legislature, in regard to the abduction of William Morgan, and the excited state of public feeling consequent upon it, the committee have observed, not without sensibility, that just appreciation of the purity and intelligence of the western population of the State, which distinctly commands our acknowledgments. This merited eulogium from so high a source, is doubly welcome at a period when the opposers of masonry at the west have been nearly overwhelmed by the torrent of misrepresentation, reproach, and ridicule, heaped upon them without measure, by the friends of that institution, in all parts of the State and country. In this condition they have sustained themselves, and triumphantly too, by the force of their own moral feeling, and without the ordinary means of defence. The public press, that mighty engine for good or for evil, has been, with a few most honorable exceptions, as silent as the grave. This self proclaimed sentinel of freedom, has felt the force of masonic influence, or has been smitten with the rod of its power. His Excellency further observes in that part of the message referred to the committee, and in relation to the public feeling aroused at the west, that "it would not be extraordinary if attempts should be made to pervert this honest indignation of the people to selfish and sinister purposes. But the character of those who really feel what they profess upon this subject, affords the best security that the success of such unworthy schemes, cannot be great, or of long duration."

In ascertaining the meaning of this paragraph, the committee have not deemed it proper or expedient to go beyond the plain and obvious import of its terms. Any different sense, arising from a different sort of construction, would be gladly avoided, inasmuch as its adoption by the committee, would at once put them in the attitude of entire disagreement with His Excellency, and render it doubtful whether the message in this part of it, manifested that high regard for dignity of station, which is due from every officer of the government.

Nothing is more proper than that all republican legislation should be characterized by the highest degree of frankness and simplicity; and under the guidance of this spirit, we take the liberty to re-assure the Senate, that the committee entirely concur in the opinion expressed by His Excellency, in the paragraph quoted above. The political movements at the west, to which His Excellency no doubt alludes, have been characterized thus far, and we trust that they will be hereafter, by a great devotion to principle, and activity and firmness in the pursuit of the objects they have proposed. They have proceeded so immediately from the bosom of the people, that the ordinary restraints of parties and their discipline, together with the efforts of those politicians, who have heretofore influenced public opinion, have been laid aside and regarded with utter indifference. Satisfied beyond all question, that the evils inflicted on the State and country, by secret, self created societies, were a thousand fold greater than any that for many years past had been conjured up by the devices of cunning politicians, the people have sought with wonderful unity of design, of principle, and of effort, to destroy, by the peaceful exercise of their rights at the polls, the existence of the masonic, as well as all other secret associations.

The wisest and best men among them, who have neither held nor desired office, have not been able to discover any *better*, or indeed any *other*, mode of effecting this most interesting object. This peaceful mode of overthrowing an institution of such amazing power, by withholding political support from all its members indiscriminately, until they shall sunder their obligations to that institution, and to each other, and return with us upon equal footing into the social compact, furnishes, perhaps, one of the highest illustrations of the inherent energy and excellence of our republican form of government, that has ever been presented. The Autocrat of all the Russias has exerted the force of his edicts against masonry, but without having been able to extirpate it from his dominions. Its existence is suffered in Great Britain, but a member of the Royal family is always at the head of the institution, ready to repress any attempt affecting the government. In France, no lodges are allowed to sit, without an agent of the government to watch their proceedings; and in Spain, the meeting of the members of a lodge to admit, and actually admitting a new member, is made felony of death. But in this free country, to effect similar objects, no cruel punishments, no governmental force, no state surveillance, is at all necessary. Here, every citizen exercises a portion of the state and national sovereignty, and if this is done with a faithful regard to his own interest and that of his posterity, by withholding that, which no one has a right to demand, the great object will be effected. Legislation therefore, brought to bear immediately and directly upon the existence of the institution, if such could be exerted in conformity with the spirit of the constitution, as expounded by a majority, might, nevertheless, be considered as a measure of doubtful expediency; but that legislative enactments, of somewhat different character, and more prospective in their operation, ought to be adopted, seems evident from the fearful relation in which the masonic institution stands, in reference to the rest of the community.

There are now in this State, as appears by a late, and it is believed accurate, enumeration, more than 500 lodges of Freemasons, and about one hundred chapters. These lodges and chapters have a probable average of 60 members. The whole number of masons then, cannot be less than 30,000; and these are scattered, in pretty nearly equal portions, throughout the whole population of the State.

The efficiency of such a body, and so located, none will doubt. Controlling as it does common funds, and possessing the advantages of secrecy and activity almost unexampled; using the language of signs, and a character for a written language; its members bound by the most solemn obligations to God and their brethren, they can surmount all difficulties. These men can effect every thing within the compass of human effort. If the order were to exert itself in aid of charitable objects, not an individual in the State could be either hungry or naked; want would be a stranger in our borders; and vast funds would still remain unexpended. If their zeal and industry were turned to the occult sciences, to which they have professed a devotion, the driest and most abstruse problems of the geometricians, the algebraists and the astronomers, would, long before this, have been as familiar to us all, as the road to market. But if unmindful of charitable objects, and neglecting the pursuit of the arts and sciences, which they have professed as their leading measures, they should like the rest of mankind, be tempted by the allurements of power, to make an effort to acquire it; all will confess, they must be irresistible, so long as the people remained ignorant of their secret designs. Nothing but a belief or knowledge of those designs, and public opinion brought to bear upon them at the ballot boxes, in countervailing measures, would at all check this otherwise resistless power.

The opposers of masonry at the west, entertain no doubt that this institution was originally intended, and is now kept up, for the sole purpose of securing to its members, unjust advantages over their fellow citizens, in the various concerns of life, but chiefly with the view of facilitating their acquisition of political power. To change this opinion of our western population, is utterly impossible. It is fortified by their own observation. Their masonic neighbors confirm it, by talking with freedom of their principles and practices, until they become as familiar to them, as the highway act, or the act regulating common schools. But if they still doubted, they have only to call to mind that when they undertook the great work of reform, three-fourths of all the offices in the country, were filled with members of that institution. The operating causes, in producing the success or defeat of a particular candidate, are not always of easy discovery. But when for a long series of years a large proportion of political and public employment, is in the hands of any given order of men, it is natural that suspicions should be entertained, that every thing is not right; and when the disproportion of offices held by the members of that order, becomes extravagant and enormous, and continued through a long period of time, notwithstanding the revolutions of political power, then suspicion yields to the moral certainty, that there is a principle of evil in operation of fearful and dangerous import.

At the annual election last fall, 270,000 votes were given in this State. If the computation that we have 30,000 masons is correct, they will amount to one-ninth part of our voting population, and are of course entitled upon the principle of numbers, to one-ninth part of all offices. If it should be granted, that the members of the order, have double the talent, and fitness, in proportion to their numbers, they even then, would not be entitled to one-fourth of the power of the State, and yet they have held for years, three-fourths, or very near it. Supposing them to possess on the average no higher qualifications than the rest of the community, which is presumed to be correct, with the exception of that practised talent and facility in business, arising from the actual possession of so great a share of official power, it then becomes a mathematical certainty, that if they hold only two-thirds of all places of power and trust, in the State, their proportion is precisely six times greater than it ought to be, upon the just principle of equality. The state of things here presented, astonishing, and conclusive, as it may appear to some, is, after all, not surprising when the obligation of the higher order of masons to each other is properly considered and understood. One of their oaths explains the whole matter, and renders the existence of masonic political action, not only certain, but proves beyond the shadow of a doubt, that such action is obligatory on all those masons, who give to the oath a binding force.

To all these high charges, tending so strongly to inculpate and disgrace the masonic institution, no defence has been offered, at all satisfactory to the undertaking. It is true the question is sometimes asked, and with much plausibility, is it possible, if the institution is as corrupt and wicked as has been represented, that distinguished and meritorious men, and many such are admitted to be members, would continue parties to such a nefarious compact? To this it is answered, that masonry, in the day of its power, allowed none of its members to recede and express their opinion of its principles and practices, without exposing themselves to punishment, more horrid and inhuman, than any known to the criminal codes of the civilized world. That there are virtuous and excellent men who belong to the institution, can be doubted by none of us, who look around upon the circle of our relatives, friends and acquaintances. How this fact is compatible with the opinion we maintain, of the character of the institution, neither time, nor the occasion, will permit us to explain. But now when masonry totters in doubtful empire; when her countenance is blanched with fear; when the rod of her power is broken, and she no longer dares inflict the punishments of her inhuman code, it is believed those men will feel that they have a duty to perform, of great moment to themselves, to posterity, and their country.

The committee have now laid before the Senate, in a plain and simple manner, some of the principal reasons which have produced a conviction upon the minds of the western population, that masonry meddles in the administration of justice, and is subversive of the republican equality, guaranteed by the constitutions of the State and Union. In doing this, they trust they have not been led beyond the limits of parliamentary usage, by discussing subjects not referred to them, or others not german to those topics, which it became their duty to consider. They have carefully abstained from examining the influence of masonry, whether it be deleterious or otherwise to those social and moral relations, which so vitally affect the prosperity and happiness of mankind. They have avoided also, any inquiry into the nature and amount of its influence, over the religious feelings and propensities of the members of that institution. These matters, however intensely they may interest the moralist and theologian, are beyond the reach of legislation, and therefore, are not, in the opinion of the committee, proper topics for their discussion.

The committee are sanguine in their hopes that the Senate will think it expedient, from the views of the subject herewith presented, to adopt farther legislative measures for the special protection of the rights and liberties of the citizens of this State, against the secret and insiduous encroachments of a self-created society, to which they have had occasion so often to allude. A declaratory and remedial law, by its terms preventing a reputed mason officiating as juryman, in any case where either party belongs to the fraternity, while the other is not a member, might do much in quieting the apprehensions of those opposed to secret societies. And although no doubt is entertained, that the principles of common law, would without alteration, exclude a mason, in such circumstances from acting as juryman, yet the difficulty of procuring, upon the urgency of the occasion, the full legal proof that the juryman proposed is actually a mason, when such is the fact; together with the further difficulty of proving, at all times, the nature and character of the masonic obligations, is so great, that the law as it now stands, affords but little relief against the evil it is intended to remedy.

That the oaths are of such a character and tendency as to require the interposition of penal laws, to prevent their future administration, is obvious from every consideration that should influence a republican legislature.

The English Stat. 37, George III., Chap. 123, contains some provisions in regard to oaths of this description and tendency, which might perhaps with great propriety be engrafted into our statute book. The 1st section, among other things provides, " that any person who administers or causes to be administered any oath, whereby another becomes obliged to obey any orders or commands of any committee or body of men, not lawfully constituted, or of any leader or commander, or other person, not having authority by law for that purpose ; or not to inform or give evidence against any such associate, confederate or other person, or not to reveal or discover any unlawful combination, or not to reveal or discover any illegal oath or other engagement which may have been administered or tendered to, or taken by such person, or by any other person, or the import of any such an oath or engagement, shall on conviction be adjudged guilty of felony, and may be transported for not exceeding seven years."

While the committee observe in this otherwise wholesome statute, some of those severities which mark the character of British penal legislation, and which ought always to be avoided, they cannot abstain from expressing their entire conviction, that if like so many other British statutes, which we have adopted as our law, it had been re-enacted in this State ten years since, the immolation of Morgan, with all its afflicting incidents, would never have happened, to arouse the sensibility and indignation of the people of this State.

But the committee have abstained from reporting, at this time, any bills embracing either of the objects to which they have alluded. They cannot now be apprised, from the recently deranged and morbid condition of the public press, and other causes, what is the state of information, and of opinion of gentlemen of the Senate, upon this new presentment of an unusual subject of legislation. They are not aware how the whole subject matter of the report, they have now the honor to submit, will be appreciated. They are duly sensible of the importance of the subject, and that it is one of new impression, and are therefore inclined, in this stage of their labors, to ask respectfully, the further direction of the Senate. With this view, they submit the following resolutions :

Resolved, That the select committee to whom was referred so much of the governor's message, as relates to the abduction of William Morgan, and the proceedings under the law of last session upon that subject, be instructed to report a detailed statement of the evidence they may now possess, or may hereafter obtain, confirming the leading opinions, and principal facts, contained in their report presented the 14th day of February instant.

Resolved, That said committee be provisionally instructed to report to the Senate, a bill or bills to carry into effect the objects specified in said report of the 14th day of February instant, to be acted upon, in case the facts to be reported shall, in the opinion of the Senate, be sufficiently confirmed.

M. HAYDEN, *Chairman.*

AN ADDRESS

Delivered at Lyons, N. Y. Sept. 11th, 1829, in commemoration of the outrages committed on that day, and subsequently, on William Morgan, and other citizens, by Freemasons; exhibiting the criminal conduct of the fraternity; and containing an exposition of the true principles of Anti-masonry. By Myron Holley.

Fellow Citizens:—We are now assembled, to consider and commemorate facts and principles which we deem vitally hostile to the great interests of our country. These facts are of recent occurrence, and the principles have been gradually disclosed by examining into the nature, tendency, and origin of the facts. Together, they constitute an unparalleled emergency in our national experience; and while they challenge our best faculties of reflection and judgment, they should be canvassed in the spirit of universal good will, and with becoming moderation. In proportion to the weight of responsibility cast upon us, in every case, should be the impartiality and completeness of our deliberation, the singlenesss of our motive, the firmness of our decision, and the perseverance of our resolution.

In the summer and fall of 1826, a train of events transpired, in this community, oppressive, criminal, and alarming—involving the most atrocious violation of private and public right. Of these events it is impossible to give a minute detail in this address. That can never be done fully and adequately, till a festering consciousness of grievous wrong, and a brave devotion to truth, shall untie the tongue of Freemasonry. The events alluded to are known to have included successful abuse of the forms of law, treachery to earnest professions of friendship, cruel slander, conspiracy, robbery, arson, kidnapping and murder. And, shocking as these outrages were, to the moral sense of an enlightened people, they would, probably, have been punished, lamented, and forgotten, like many other enormous offences, had it not been for the very extraordinary circumstances following their commission, and attending all attempts lawfully to investigate them.

No sooner had the feeble cry of those, who suffered from them and yet lived, begun to reach the general ear, than intelligent and respected men, were found adroitly engaged in practising the arts best calculated to disguise their character, and, as far as possible, to conceal them. The victims were represented as infamous, and unworthy of sympathy, if they did suffer. But their sufferings were denied, and the rumors of crime, which it was found impossible to hush, were imputed to them as fraudulent inventions which they had originated and imposed upon the public, for pecuniary objects.

These arts were partially successful. The whole community, for awhile, yielded to them. Many individuals are still under the delusions, which they produced. But all are not. The sagacity and habitual inquisitiveness of some of our fellow citizens soon enabled them to discover irresistible evidence, that foul deeds had been committed. And entertaining the generous sympathies of freemen, with an enlightened conviction, that the safety of all depends upon the protection of each, they called public meetings, in several places, at which committees of inquiry were raised to aid the operation of our legal authorities, in detecting the criminals.

With the exertions of these committees, patriotic and public spirited as they were, commenced those disclosures, which have justly filled our country with alarm. The crimes had been committed by Freemasons. Freemasons were endeavoring to conceal them. Forgetting all the obligations of self respect, of civil duty, of social benevolence, of morality, of religion, Freemasons of extensive information, wealth, and reputation—men, who had possessed largely the honors and confidence of their unsuspecting country, were found to have been consulted on the subject of these crimes before they were committed, and individually and collectively to have sanctioned them; and this, not casually, ignorantly, or inadvertently, but after months of deliberation and frequent counsel. Considering the nature of these enormities, the means employed, and the restraints which were broken through, in their perpetration, such dangerous outrages upon the principles of liberty, were never attempted before, since the commencement of regulated associations. No human ingenuity could array before you all their evil consequences.

We have a government to which we cannot be too strongly attached. The privilege of establishing it was obtained through trials, sufferings and achievements, which have secured to our sage and heroic fathers, imperishable renown. Its principles have been combined with the most considerate wisdom. And if its administration has not been perfect, it has been conducted with unequalled virtue and success. Under its benignant influence, religious and civil freedom, were multiplying, extending, and securing all their benefits. Its power to withstand the seduction and defeat the assaults of foreign governments, has been severely, but triumphantly exemplified. Its reputation abroad is honorable ; and its example every year becoming more attractive. It is rapidly preparing the public opinion of the world, for the general introduction and enjoyment of freedom.

Why is our government so effective for good? Why does it attract the grateful regard of all our enlightened fellow citizens, and the admiration of every independent mind? Because it was instituted by the whole people, and not by a part of them only ; for the protection of the rights of all, and not for the protection of the rights of a part merely. Because, while it presents no impediment to the useful exertions of any, it encourages the honest and strenuous efforts of all, by offering its rewards to *merit and to merit only*. Because it intends to secure the safety of all, by enforcing, universally, and without partiality, its penalties, upon all offenders—and because its agents are responsible, its proceedings are public, and it is *free*. Religion, knowledge, charity, are its open friends, the pillars of its strength, the objects of its veneration. It delights in every exercise of benevolence, in every discovery of science, in all the advances of piety. It is impossible to name any attainable good, the pursuit of which, it would not cherish and honor. But this government is eminently a government of law. All its benefits result from the adoption, administration and enforcement of its laws. Humility before God, and before the laws of such a government, are kindred and exalted virtues. With what a proud homage should the laws be obeyed ! Where their dominion is universal and supreme, what a cheap defence do they set up, around the great treasure-house of human rights ! And how detestable is rebellion against them !

Yet such a rebellion Freemasonry has raised. It has violated the dearest rights of nature, and the most sacred enactments of our laws, and this, in a spirit manifestly treasonable, for it has done this, in pursuance of solemn, deliberate, and voluntary obligations to a foreign government,—I mean its own,—a government more alien to that which claims our allegiance, than any that has ever afflicted mankind. Fellow citizens, let me beseech you to look into the government of Freemasonry. Examine it fully. You can easily comprehend it. You will have to encounter no arduous labor—you will involve yourselves in no perplexing inquiries; and you will arrive at no doubtful conclusion. You will find it a monstrous compound of monarchy and hierarchy, pursuing its objects with all the badges of fraud and guilt. Its power you will justly dread, but that is not invincible. Its distinguishing characteristics, you will certainly abhor, but these you can abolish.

To faithful citizens, all that belongs to Freemasonry must be odious. Its pompous titles, they will scorn; its ceremonies, indecent, profane or fantastic, they will contemn; its habiliments, they will deride, as the harlequin frippery of a barbarous antiquity; its emblems and tokens, innocent when innocently used, they will regard with compassion, as very imperfect means of communication, to which honest ignorance may sometimes justifiably resort; its cipher, they will deem evidence of knavery; its pretensions, its secrecy, its oaths, its principles, and its power, they will reprobate and oppose. * * *

From the first machination of the recent outrages, through every stage of their criminal progress, to their murderous consummation, the proceedings of Freemasonry have afforded a practical exposition of the principles deduced from their oaths. And the distinct and full operation of every one of them may be obviously traced, by those who have been attentive to these fatal transactions. Even to this day, Freemasonry conspires against the laws, and defies their authority, in the very presence of our courts of justice. Individual members, by advisement with others, spirit away witnesses from the trial of indicted brethren,—refuse to testify because by so doing they must criminate themselves,—conceal the crimes of their masonic coadjutors, by perjury,—supply delinquents of their order with information of their being in danger of persecution, and with counsel and pecuniary aid to escape from the penalties of law,—maliciously slander and persecute those, who in obedience to the most sacred injunctions of truth and honor, oppose them,—and prefer the interests of the fraternity to those of their country.

Notwithstanding these foul exertions and the extensive prevalence of the nefarious principles, on which they are founded, that justice, which was well nigh suffocated, has overtaken a few of the felons, and consigned them to the awards of law, and the detestation, which high crimes unrepented of, should always find. But the guilt of these convicts, the infamous punishments, to which they have been justly doomed, and the execration of honest men, which they must encounter, seem only the more strongly to have secured to them, the fellow-feeling and attachment of their unconvicted brethren.

Why is this, my countrymen? Why have not these convicts been discarded from the sympathetic favor of the titular kings and priests of the order? I will tell you. The reason is obvious as the sun at noonday. It is not in thewit of man, to assign but one reason for such conduct. The convicts had violated no law of Freemasonry. They are the victims of unflinching adherence to its requirements. They were unhappily sustained, in all the dark and loathsome steps of their iniquity, by an assured confidence, that they would be protected, upheld and justified, by the society. Nothing but the firmest conviction of this could have induced men of previous good standing in the community, industrious, wealthy, intelligent and influential, to violate the binding ties of domestic life, and the consecrated securities of civil blessings. This is the reason, which has effectually prevented the dignitaries of Freemasonry from expelling, or even censuring, a single individual of these convicts. It has not been because they were fearful of exercising their authority to expel or censure; for the men who have bravely and worthily revealed their crimes and secrets, for the common good, they have expelled, they have censured, they have slandered, and persecuted with a malice peculiar to their order.

What is the power of Freemasonry? One of its most

eloquent orators, in Connecticut, in the year 1825, represented it as follows: "It is powerful. It comprises men of rank, wealth, office, and talent, in power and out of power, and that, in almost every place, where power is of any importance. And it comprises, among other classes of the community to the lowest, in large numbers, active men united together, and capable of being directed by the efforts of others, so as to have the force of concert throughout the civilized world. They are distributed too with the means of knowing one another, and the means of co-operating, in the desk, in the legislative hall, on the bench, in every gathering of business, in every party of pleasure, in every domestic circle, in peace and in war, among enemies and friends, in one place as well as in another! So powerful indeed is it, at this time, it fears nothing from violence, public or private; for it has every means to learn it in season, to counteract, defeat, and punish it. It is too late to talk of the propriety of continuing or suppressing masonry, after the time to do so has gone by. So, good or bad, the world must take it as it is. Think of it, laugh at it, hate it, or despise it; still it is not only what I have told you, but it will continue to be; and the world in arms cannot stop it."

Such are the claims of a permanent self-created society, which connects the aristocratic part of this community into a brotherhood, with the Princes, and Nobles, and Priests, and Generals, of every region of the globe, by cords, which no power of man, in the proud opinion of such as are encircled by them, is sufficient to sunder. And to sanction the existence and pursuits, in our country, of a power so expansive and redoubtable, and yet, though political, unknown to the government, the well meaning part of the fraternity have fondly believed, the illustrious names of Warren, Franklin, and Washington, could be adduced.

"To err is human." There has been but one name given under heaven, in which no indiscretion, or stain of sin, could be found. Many of the patriots of the revolution, especially among the officers of the army, did join the masonic society. In the number of such, were the exalted benefactors of mankind before alluded to. But little advantage can the society, in our times, derive from this fact. Their great authority, will in no way serve to cover the accumulated folly and guilt of the higher degrees of the fraternity, nor indeed of any degree at this day. And the attempt to use it for such a purpose, it can be shown, without drawing upon them the imputation of crime against their country and the rights of man, will only serve more strikingly to illustrate the dangerous designs of the institution. For hear it, ye friends of equal rights, and of the government established by your renowned forefathers, these patriarchs of civil liberty, when they entered the fraternity, had cast off the oaths of allegiance to the tyranny under which they were born, and were battling for the great privileges of self-government. Under no bonds of established authority, in a crisis most momentous to all the cherished interests of life, and threatened with all the calamities of anarchy at home, and of the most formidable and vindictive power from abroad, an institution offering social ties, of which they were destitute,—great means of secret communication, which they needed,—and many subduing motives to obedience, indispensable to their objects, was adopted, by them, and made successfully instrumental to the overthrow of the government, against which they used it.

If such men, under such circumstances, in such a cause, used Freemasonry, not yet clothed with its most alarming principles and most censurable obligations, against a kingly and tyrannical government, shall their example be cited, to authorize its use against a government of their own establishment,—a government which they and their associates contrived, and set up, as the perpetual storehouse, and sanctuary of all the principles of freedom ?

Fellow citizens, you will not allow such an abuse of the inestimable inheritance of their immortal names. In your offices, in your shops, in your fields, in all your resorts of business or amusement, you have thought too reverently of the blessings of equal laws, and the rich enjoyment which their universal and unobstructed administration secures, for this. Participating all the fruits of your honest and protected industry, in the bosom of thriving and cheerful families, you have felt your hearts burn within you as you reflected upon the great founders of your national family, and these reflections have turned the gentle currents of your domestic affection into the broad and swelling tide of patriotism ; but patriotism cannot rebel against freedom.

Long association in toils and dangers, produces lasting friendships. Washington found it difficult, altogether to withdraw himself from Freemasonry, at the close of the war. It was natural for him to recollect, with complacency, many of the events which it had been made to assist. And its claims were frequently pressed upon him, by old companions. He did not, therefore, wholly renounce it. It had been used by him only for good, and courtesy and consistency required him, not violently and suddenly to cast it off. He did not patronize it after the objects of the war had been obtained. It fell into neglect upon the restoration of peace, and remained so until his death. He was undoubtedly opposed to its renewal. In 1794, he said to several of his confidential friends : " The real people occasionally assembled in order to express their sentiments, on political subjects, ought never to be confounded with permanent, self-appointed societies, usurping the right to control the constituted authorities, and to dictate to public opinion. While the former was entitled to respect, the latter was incompatible with all government, and must either sink into general disesteem, or finally overturn the established order of things."

The greatest masonic authority* in this State, with all the honors of the institution thick upon him, about four years ago publicly declared, that masonry was sometimes abused to political objects. In our own village, before one of its most respectable magistrates, when in the exercise of his official duty, we have seen a bold attempt to use it for the purpose of procuring impunity from all the legal consequences of imputed crime. In forty counties of this State, being all from which authentic information could be obtained, it was ascertained, by the anti-masonic convention assembled last winter in Albany, that, in the year when Morgan was martyred, there were in office thirty-three masonic Sheriffs. More than half of the important public offices in the Union are filled by Freema-

---

* De Witt Clinton.

sons, though they do not count one in four of the whole number of persons equally well qualified and eligible to fill them. Inquire for yourselves as to the number of masons, who have filled the town, county and state offices, within your knowledge; and you will not fail to discern a striking effect of the inequality produced, by the obligations of Freemasonry.

If you have read the statements of respectable men, who have renounced it, you have learnt, that in ordinary times and in many cases, it has successfully assailed the great duties, upon which all our social advantages depend. Its obligations are utterly destructive of that equality of right, which our constitutions and laws are intended to maintain. They are inconsistent with the oaths of legislators, judges, grand jurors, petit jurors, sheriffs, and every other public functionary, because they enjoin illegal and unrighteous favor to brethren, and unjust and oppressive opposition to the uninitiated, in a vast variety of the most important exigencies of life. They are now, and have long been fatal to that political equality, which every freeman should most highly prize, because it is the only efficient means of suppressing all wrongful inequality.

No man would dare to take upon himself the obligations of Freemasonry in public. Or if he did, no man would expect public favor afterwards. And shall we permit their existence, because they are taken secretly? Shall we yield up all our rights as a boon to Freemasons, for the favor they have conferred upon us, by fraudulently usurping most of them, through the fatal efficacy of their secrecy, their tokens, their cipher, and their oaths? Have we free hearts, free minds, self-respect, social love, intelligence to look before and after us, and shall we be hewers of wood, and drawers of water, for an institution rotten to the core?—of which the principles and deeds have covered all over with blisters, the fairest body politic that ever was presented to the admiration of the world?—of which the only practical use is to forge, in its gloomy fires, and fasten upon us, and all the unitiated forever, the chains of a degrading servitude? Will you submit to this? I know you will not submit to it. I know the hour draws nigh, when the whole country will be arrayed in opposition to it,—when the Dagon of these Philistines, who have come upon us,—when the kings and priests of Freemasonry, with all their courts, their altars, and their gods, shall sink together into everlasting oblivion, and the gavel of masonic vengeance, shall be the weapon of official oppression no more forever.

To abolish the evils of Freemasonry, open and concealed, is the object of anti-masonry—and what considerate citizen will not approve it? If masonry be the Pandora's box from which all possible evils to ourselves and country, are to be feared, let us shut it up. If it be a noisome seed bed of the most pernicious weeds, let us eradicate the weeds, remove its smothering enclosure, introduce the cheerful light and the wholesome air—dig it over, through all its compartments, and sow it with healthy and nutritious wheat. Whatever it may be likened to, let us take effectual measures to exclude its evils.

How can this be done? By resorting to the ballot-box, and by that alone. And shall we be slanderously and maliciously assailed with insinuations of sinister purposes, and with opprobrious epithets, for betaking ourselves to this resort? Is it not peaceable? Is it not honest? Is it not lawful? Is it not consistent with all the rights of others? If it is not, then their rights are wrongs to us, of which we must take the redress into our own hands.

The right of election is the paramount right of all freemen. And the place where it is exercised is the holiest, in the temple of liberty. Shall we not be permitted to go up, and offer pure homage there? There can be no acceptable homage, but what is pure. Purity of election consists in exercising the unmolested right of voting for the men, whom we think wise to know, and faithful to pursue, the best interests of the community. The best interests of the community in which our lot is cast, are the constitutional and equal rights of the citizens. These are invaded by Freemasonry. Shall not those who are opposed to Freemasonry, repel the invasion? Yes. We will repel it; and that in the most majestic court, that has ever been known among the sons of men,—in the grêat court of the whole people, which announces its sentences from the ballot-box.

Why should we not go into this court for the decision of our cause? Shall we not find it as respectable as any other court? Shall we not find it as honest as any other court? Shall we not find it as much under a sense of the necessity of upholding the essential rights of the people, as any other court? Shall we not find it as inaccessible to all the biasses of partial influence, as any other court? We shall. And the interests of this court, which may God in his goodness perpetuate, are our interests. Truly we might go into the subordinate courts, established in our land. But we have a right to choose; and we choose the court of the people. Is this disreputable? Or shall we be held to trial, in those courts only, where a large proportion of the officers have taken oaths against us?—where we have found it impossible to proceed to a righteous result, of the whole matter, though such a result has been sedulously pursued, for years?—and where we now know jurisdiction of the whole case does not exist.

You may repel the invasion upon your rights, (we are told, by a small number of our fellow citizens, running all over with candor and liberality;) but take care not to avail yourselves of political means, in doing it! You may repel it, by expressing gentle opinions against it! You are not obliged professedly and directly to aid the invasion. Only hold your necks still till the foot of the invader presses them to the earth, and fair opposition, by courteous words, may be permitted! Men there are, who hold this doctrine; and they go in and out among us, without the marks of conscious shame, or undisguised fatuity, upon them! Of what race are they? They come not from the true-hearted, investigating, devoted stock of the asserters of our freedom. They have no alliance with that class of men into whose bosoms, all the oppressions of tyranny serve only to burn their abhorrence of it,—and all the gladdening results of liberty, to hallow their love of it.

It is merely hypocrisy, and shallow hypocrisy too, for men of common sense to pretend opposition to the existence of any thing, which they would not take the most effectual honest means to destroy. The reproach cast upon anti-masonry, for its being political, springs from attachment or subserviency to masonry; and can spring from nothing else. And its taking a political character, would not be objected to, by those who cast upon it this reproach, only because, by being political, it will be successful. Political character, in the sense of adherence to the just policy of our government, which is the sense we entertain of it, is the highest character, which can be acquired by man, in reference to things terminating with life. And I glory in political anti-masonry. Anti-masonry is political; it must be political, or all is lost.

As citizens, our liberties are political, our rights are political, our duties are political. Let us all perform our duties, in accordance with our rights, and the rights of others, for the advancement of the just policy of our government.

But it is said that anti-masonry is bigoted, and persecuting. Bigotry is an obstinate and blind attachment to a tenet, ceremony, creed, or party. Anti-masonry is opposed, and will forever be opposed, to every tenet, ceremony, creed, or party, which infringes upon the universal rights of man. It is the real democracy of our country, embracing in its good will, as objects of its protecting care, every interest, right, duty and enjoyment, of every individual in the nation. Persecution means withholding rights, or inflicting injuries, unjustly. Such persecution is precisely what has called anti-masonry into existence; and this name of democratic freedom, will cease to exist, as soon as it has made adequate provision to secure the rights unjustly withheld, and to redress the injuries unjustly inflicted, by Freemasonry. Shall anti-masonry be accused of bigotry and persecution, then, by those too, who have invoked, upon themselves, all the wrath of the Almighty if they cease to exercise an obstinate and blind attachment to the tenets, ceremonies, creed, and party of Freemasonry, or cease to withhold rights, and inflict injuries, unjustly, upon their renouncing brethren and countrymen?

Wanting nothing, expecting nothing, and fearing nothing, from the public, but what pertains equally to the rights and securities of every citizen, I have come before you as the representative of freemen. With no bonds upon my soul, but those of obedience to my Maker, (would that they were always felt with greater intensity,) and with a yet unfettered body, I have spoken to you freely and indignantly of an institution, which I deem desperately wicked. But *I* entertain no hostility to its members. I have spoken from a regard to interests, from which I would by no means shut them out. Among them are numbered some, who partake of the same life-stream with myself, and who are as dear to my heart, as the ties of nature, early affection, and enduring sympathy, can make them. There are others to whom I owe all that can be required or given, in honor. And I should consider it as a stigma upon my character to cherish malice towards any human being.

But ours is a cause of comprehensive benevolence. It includes the interests of Freemasons as well as our own. And the most reflecting among them, are already with us, in their secret convictions. Nothing but a pride, reluctant to acknowledge error, and some fear of the vindictive hostility of the fraternity, prevents them from openly avowing it. They should avow it. Washington would pursue that course. In the path of renunciation, you follow his example, my countrymen. With him no private feelings or interests could supersede the public good. Even to what appeared to be envious clamor, injustice, and persecution to all but the high sighted eye, and all encircling hearts of patriotism, he, and the great men of the revolution, gave up the society of the Cincinnati, to which they were fastened, by all the strong links struck out in the welding fires of a glorious warfare. Follow their example. Do yourselves the great justice to discard Freemasonry. By all the unutterable privileges of life and immortality, by your most precious connexions and attachments here, and hereafter, by your undying thoughts, by your unfading hopes, renounce it.

ADDRESS

Of the Republican Anti-masonic Members of the Legislature of New York, to their Constituents.

FELLOW CITIZENS,

IT is the proud boast and consoling reflection of Americans, that the free institutions of their country have triumphed over all the dangers that have beset them. Whatever have been the perils that have threatened their existence, the virtue and inherent energy of the people have been adequate to every exigency.

Recently the people have been awakened to an alarming internal danger, of the existence of which they were unconscious. The abduction and murder of a free citizen, without crime, with the attrocities that attended and followed it, have excited their inquiries, and revealed the fearful fact that there is in the midst of a confiding community an institution, the existence of which is incompatible with liberty. When the outrage first became public, the efforts of the neighboring inhabitants were directed to the enforcement of the laws, the detection and punishment of the guilty offenders. In the simplicity of their hearts, they expected universal co-operation. In the prosecution of objects so just and patriotic, for purposes so high, holy, and humane, they, with entire confidence, expected the powerful aid of the Press, and the united exertions of their fellow citizens. Far from them was the thought of arraying a *party* for any purpose whatever. Their astonishment was greater even than at the perpetration of the outrage, when they discovered the appalling truth, that it was the work of a conspiracy, embracing large numbers of conspicuous citizens; that the PRESS was silent as the house of death, or spoke only to defame and mislead; that a whole fraternity, claiming irresistible power, regarded the outrage with cold indifference, or engaged in active efforts to screen from punishment the guilty perpetrators.

When they met opposition at every step of their progress; when they found their objects belied, and their motives impeached; all their acts subjected to misrepresentation, and their characters consigned to obloquy and vituperation; when they perceived that the perpetrators of the outrage and their abettors were men of peaceful lives, elevated and unsuspected characters, bound to the performance of their social duties by all the ties that exist in civil society, the unwelcome conclusion was forced upon them that the deeds they had done were not perpetrated as the acts of individuals, but as members of their fraternity; and that it was *the institution* that had sinned through their instrumentality. When the people, excited by the Morgan outrage, perceived that all efforts to vindicate the majesty of the laws, by the punishment of the atrocious violators, were resisted and rendered abortive; when they saw that the fraternity possessed the power to silence or pervert the Press; to stop the mouths, destroy the memories, or extract the consciences of witnesses; to extend its baneful influence into courts, and poison the fountains of justice; UNION became indispensable to the further prosecution of their righteous objects. The Republican Anti-masonic party arose from necessity, and not from design. Opposition caused its formation, and opposition by assisting to develope the true character of the masonic institution, is constantly increasing its numbers, and will finally insure its triumph. Believing it to be in accordance with your wishes, we have acted together as a party, upon every befiting occasion.

The attention of the legislature was called, by the executive, to the Morgan outrage, as a subject of legislative inquiry. The reports made to the senate and assembly, contain the material facts comprising the history of that transaction. Other "matters" "embracing" information of a graver character, "exist, which could not in the opinion of a high judicial officer, with propriety be made public," as they would tend very much "to prejudge the guilt of persons indicted." After the reports were made, additional evidence of the extent of the conspiracy was obtained, but it was deemed unnecessary to make a further report, as no attempt was made to controvert the statements of those presented to the legislature, and as the whole subject is in a train of thorough judicial investigation. A gentleman was then appointed to conduct the prosecutions, at our unanimous recommendation, and we look with anxiety and confidence to the result of his indefatigable and able exertions.

Although the excitement caused by the Morgan outrage is universally applauded, with sincerity or affectation, the objects of those who obey its impulse are opposed and misrepresented. The objects of the Republican anti-masonic party are plain and freely avowed. They are to bring to merited punishment, the perpetrators of an outrage which has no parallel in a civilized community; to annihilate the institution that has filled the land with crime, and thus to vindicate the laws, purify the fountains of justice, and rescue liberty from the dangers that beset it. The people, constrained by unwonted opposition, rushed together by a spontaneous impulse, to give concert and strength to their efforts. This party, thus obviously and necessarily formed, seems recently to have excited fearful alarm. Conspicuous individuals, "in power and out of power," have labored "in season and out of season," to defame its character, and impede its rapid progress. It is manifest that political men have taken advantage of the existence of this party to impress upon honest and unsuspicious republicans, an apprehension of danger; and that designs are in a train of execution to render the "excitement justly caused" by the Morgan outrage, "subservient to political and party purposes," by making it contribute to the sustentation of an existing political party, the leaders of which have never manifested any peculiar abhorrence of the Morgan outrage. A COALITION is formed, embracing many members of the masonic fraternity and those who have been separated by inveterate *political hostility*, to resist the efforts of the people in the work of reformation. However revolting this unholy alliance may be to the democracy of the State, it is not of a nature to excite surprise. It displays the characteristics of the masonic institution. It illustrates the allegation that the order does possess a power by which it can bring political antipodes together, and unite them in efforts for the common fraternal object of mutual protection and preservation. It is natural that the order should extend its influence over those who are elevated to places of authority. It is lavish in its promises of "all-powerful" support.

The possessors of power are usually eager for its continued enjoyment, and readily welcome the aid of adversaries to secure it. They are invariably the foes of reform. They always find it "difficult to believe" that abuses do exist, that corruption triumphs, or that there can be danger to liberty or the peace of society, unless it threatens their own security.

History abounds with illustrious though mournful examples of men, out of power, the bold and ardent advocates of popular rights, having the clearest visions of existing evils, and impending ruin, in possession of power, the blind and "inflexible" adherents of the system they had denounced as full of vice and danger. Democracy, in our country, has been compelled to engage in desperate struggles with the possessors of power. All its past experience banishes apprehension for the result of another conflict. If its energies must be put to new trials, certainty of victory invites to the combat. We have been *reminded* of the far gone days of intellectual darkness and mental perversion, when professing Christians, Catholic and Protestant and unpretending Quakers were consigned to barbarous and ignominious executions for imputed errors in religion. This has been done with the obvious intent to induce the inference that the spirit which caused such abominations was kindred to the hostility now manifested against the institution of Freemasonry. Casuists must determine whether weakness of intellect, obliquity of head, or depravity of heart, is chiefly required to trace a parallel between the relentless sacrifice of Christian Martyrs, for speculative opinions, and the infliction of legal punishment upon kidnappers, incendiaries, and murderers. It manifests a morbid sensibility for crimes, a sickly sympathy for atrocious offenders, to attempt to repress the honest efforts of patriotic zeal, for their conviction, by the hypocritical cry of persecution, and the hollow pretence, that the innocent may be confounded with the guilty. Religious persecution has affixed a deplorable stigma upon the human character and marked the ages in which it occurred for lamentation and abhorrence. It is an imperious duty upon this more enlightened generation not to tolerate an order that attempts a persecution more inexcusable, atrocious and vengeful.

Religious persecution was perpetrated by the sovereign authority of communities. It was in accordance with the spirit of the times, and was the act of the *nation.* The victims were subjected to trials according to *established jurisprudence,* and condemned to suffer penalties prescribed for violations of *laws* intended for universal operation. We have witnessed an institution possessing the power and arrogating the right to inflict the penalty of death upon a delinquent member, for the violation of no law binding upon the whole community or consistent with its safety. If former ages are doomed to reproach for persecutions *according to law,* more ineffable must be the disgrace to that generation that permits or tolerates a persecution more horrid and afflicting to humanity *without* law and in *defiance* of its authority. Since the storm of public indignation has threatened destruction to the arrogant Order, it pretends that the Morgan outrage was not demanded by its requirements or in accordance with its principles. It was long before its proud spirit would submit to the condescension of offering to an alarmed community, even that equivocal vindication which terror has finally extorted. If the allegation be true, the attempted defence is condemning; for it proves that the institution is susceptible of monstrous and dangerous perversion. It is in vain to tell of the original worthiness of object and purity of principle of the institution and of the many good men who are members of it, and of the more illustrious characters who have been, if the influence of all these combined considerations is insufficient to restrain the vengeance of whole bodies of the fraternity, and prevent extensive and powerful combinations for the violation of the laws and the frusration of the purposes of justice. But the evidence from various sources is overwhelming to establish the fact that the outrage with all its attendant enormities was in strict conformity with the obligations and requirements of the institution. That such is the truth, is proved by the testimony of a multitude of witnesses from the fraternity, embracing many "distinguished for their piety, purity of lives and devotion to their country," and corroborated by the acts of multitudes more who still adhere to the institution. The republican anti-masonic party has been accused of *perse-*

cution and proscription. It cannot fail to excite surprise and astonishment that this charge should be preferred by *those* who, at the same time, boldly proclaim a political proscription of all those who do not belong to their own fellowship, although they constitnte a majority of the whole community. If the charge were true, ample justification would be furnished by the declared principles and unvarying practice of those who make it. But it is not true. Anti-masons proscribe and persecute no man. The charge is founded upon the fact that anti-masons resolve *not to elevate to office* those who ADHERE to the masonic fraternity. This is neither proscription nor persecution. No individual has a right to demand the suffrage of another. The bestowment of it is exclusively the right of him who possesses it. To withhold from an individual what he has no right to demand and no claim to possess until it is freely given, is no *persecution.* To annihilate the institution of Freemasonry, or render it harmless, anti-masons have formed the resolution to *withhold* their suffrages from those who adhere to the order. It is no grateful task to make this discrimination. Patriotism enjoins the unwelcome duty. The community have a right to demand, as justice and safety require, that its officers shall be EQUAL and IMPARTIAL as between their fellow citizens. Freemasons have rendered this impossible. They have placed them under obligations which create secret and indissoluble ties, between them and their masonic brethren, *which do not exist in relation to the larger portion of the community.* Under tremendous penalties they have sworn allegiance to an *alien power.* They have voluntarily imposed upon themselves a positive DISQUALIFICATION. Anti-masons, by their resolves, do nothing more than declare the fact and determine to give it effect. By ascribing superior force and sanctity to their masonic obligations, the members of the fraternity declare that they will not be bound by oaths of office in case of conflict. The community can never have full assurance of their fidelity. Unknown instances of conflict between masonic obligations and official duty may occur, and unaccountable results produced. The disability can exist no longer than *they* choose to retain the disqualification. Whenever they *renounce* their partial and secret obligations and mingle with their fellow citizens on terms of equality, their eligibility to every official station is admitted. It is a matter left to their own *free choice*, and if they will continue the disqualification and consequent exclusion, they are their own persecutors.

The objects of anti-masons is the annihilation of the masonic institution, not the disfranchisement of its members. The method they have adopted is peaceful, lawful and will prove effectual. It is the only way in which the people can exercise that sovereign and controlling power with which they are intrusted for the preservation of freedom and all the blessings it confers. The responsibilities of the people are tremendous. The protection of liberty is committed to their charge. In attempting the annihilation of Freemasonry, which threatens its destruction, anti-masons obey the most imperative injunction of patriotism. It is matter of astonishment that any should be found to blame their determination. Freemasonry has now no defenders. When it is alleged that under despotic governments and in barbarous times it may have been useful, a draft is made upon human credulity, for no evidence is furnished of its meritorious performances. But whatever its character, its principles or its deeds may have been, multitudes of the most worthy members who have not renounced the order, admit that it has lagged behind the advancement of the age and outlived the period of its usefulness. It is admitted to be unpromising, unnecessary and worthless: while the great and increasing number whom its atrocities have driven from it, declare the institution to be corrupt in principle, vicious in character and dangerous in all its tendencies. With this mass of continually accumulating testimony of the worthless or awfully vicious character of the Institution, will any lover of his country hesitate to attempt its destruction? Upon republicans the duty is imperious. If Freemasonry could be tolerated any where, it is only in attributing governments, where secret associations may be necessary for the preservation of personal safety. Even there it would be a powerful instrument of revolution and of destruction to existing establishments. But in a FREE REPUBLIC, it is unnecessary and abhorrent. Democracy asserts the EQUALITY OF ALL MEN; on equality in their claim to the enjoyment of social, civil and political rights and to the protection of the laws. It abhors and forbids all artificial distinctions, ranks and orders, "stars and garters and titles of nobility," those "gewgaws that amuse so many children in the shape of men." Freemasonry contravenes the spirit of Democracy. It is monarchical in all its structure; anti-republican in its government, purposes, and all its exhibitions. If republicans wish to prepare for the overthrow of their government, no measure could be more effectual than the toleration of the institution of Freemasonry, which inculcates principles of arbitrary power and slavish obedience the most abhorrent to freedom. Which familiarizes their countrymen to the exclusive pretensions of disgusting aristocracy and the vainglorious distinctions of an arrogant nobility. Democracy cannot exist with Freemasonry. One will inevitably destroy the other. The struggle for supremacy has commenced. It is a struggle not merely for victory, but existence; and the world is interested in the issue of of the contest. The dangers of Freemasonry are enhanced by its *foreign connexions.* It is wholly of FOREIGN ORIGIN. All its new degrees, with their impious obligations and revolting penalties so prodigally multiplied, are wholly of *foreign invention.*

The institution in this country receives with passive obedience, whatever is transmitted from the *foreign* seat of its empire. Here it has formed a confederacy embracing the whole extent of our republic. All our territory is parcelled out, and a branch of the institution established in every section. It has its meetings in the darkness of night and security of secrecy, for towns, counties, states, and the whole Union. The institution is prepared to act throughout the land, with concert, energy and decision, and to receive its impulse from *foreign command.* Its immense resources enable it to attempt the greatest objects. Nothing is too lofty for its ambition or beyond its means of accomplishment. In Europe the institution has been made the cloak of innumerable crimes. In its dark conclaves plots, stratagems, and treason have been designed against government and religion, and the institutions of civil society, and put in a train of successful execution, while its infatuated votaries were unconscious of the object of the master spirits that impelled them to action. What has been attempted in other countries *may* be expected in our own. The organization of the institution here, fits it for the purposes of treason. Its extended confederacy furnishes the opportunity for the widest communication. The masonic cipher gives the instrument of safe correspondence, and its secrecy enforced by horrid obligations, and appalling penalties, affords the assurance of security. The question then is presented to the American people whether they will sacrifice DEMOCRACY or annihilate the institution of *Freemasonry*, which threatens its existence. It is a question interesting to every inhabitant of this land. It summonses him to exertions for the preservation of freedom and its countless blessings. It stimulates him to display the spirit and emulate the patriotic devotion of the revolution who put all that is dear to man in peril to preserve their liberties from foreign encroachment. A FOREIGN DOMINION incompatible with those liberties, exists and exerts its malignant influence for their destruction. The crisis calls for the energies and virtues inspired by reverence for ancestral example. Those manly qualities will ensure to the principles of Democracy, a NEW, a GLORIOUS and ENDURING triumph.

The republican anti-masonic party has the most animating prospect of speedy and complete success. It has experienced great impediments from the silence or misrepresentations of the Press, enslaved by masonic influence. Numerous free presses are now established, and liberally patronized, and greatly increased. Notwithstanding the recent and unfounded statements of THE COALITION, the cause is every where advancing. It is the assurance of this fact that causes such fearful alarm. Republicans are awakening to the fact, that an effort is making to render their honest attachment to principle and to party, subservient to the defence and sustentation of Freemasonry. They are incapable of submitting to such humiliation. The moment the masonic fraternity shall be arrayed in one political party for mutual protection and preferment, universal conviction will be produced, of the nature and power of their obligations, and will be quickly and inevitably followed by the accomplishment of the object of the republican anti-masonic party—the annihilation of the dangerous institution.

To the mind of the humble believer in the Christian religion, Freemasonry presents characteristics that demand his most solemn meditation. Its religious creed is not the creed of any people on earth, who profess adoration for a Supreme Being. It is neither Catholic nor Protestant Christianity, nor Islamism, Judaism, nor Paganism, and yet *equally adapted to all!* Instead of being religion, or the handmaid of it, the masonic creed is a mock resemblance or impious substitute. It teaches its votaries to blaspheme their Maker, banishes all just ideas of the atonement made by the Saviour, and prepares the chambers of the mind for the lodgement of infidel principles.

Those who first engaged in the righteous cause of vindicating the laws and rescuing from disgrace the character of the State, have felt the force of masonic power, and experienced the unmeasured effects of its vengeance. While they have been accused of persecution, they have *experienced* and witnessed its relentless rage. They have persevered amidst innumerable difficulties and appalling perils, and have individually seen and felt too much of the peculiar characteristics of Freemasonry to be insensible of the necessity of exerting all their energies until the overthrow of the institution is accomplished. Foul calumnies have been uttered, and unfounded charges in profusion preferred against them. They have been accused of seeking office and power as though such objects were criminal. And *who* are the accusers? *Those who already possess power, or are greedy for its enjoyment. Those who make politics a trade, charge them with having political designs.* As though it were a heinous offence in one class of citizens to strive for objects to the pursuit of which it is commendable virtue in others to dedicate their lives. Anti-masonry seeks no CONCEALMENT, nor shrouds its operations or designs, in the mantle of darkness or SECRECY. Its objects are proclaimed, and if it desires power, it is because the possession is indispensable to their accomplishment. The sin of anti-masonry, in the eyes of the fraternity, is not solely or chiefly that it attacks the mystic order, but that it threatens to disturb its members in the nearly exclusive enjoyment of office, influence, emolument and power.

Time, that never fails to test the merit of things, will furnish the refutation of the charges liberally preferred against those who are engaged in the anti-masonic cause. To the charge of insincerity, they oppose an inflexible perseverance in the attainment of their avowed objects. To that of persecution, an invariable abstinence from all displays of malevolence and perpetration of acts of outrage and violence. Let them prove themselves, according to their profession, the friends of peace, morality, religion and law. Against the malevolent accusation of being factionists, let them exhibit a uniform and unswerving adherence to the principles and the usages of democracy And to refute the charge of being without a plan or worthy object, let them continue the steadfast and ardent advocates of a liberal, enlightened and judicious policy, calculated to extend and diffuse the blessings of a free government, promote the interests and advance the glory of the State. Public opinion governs the world. The institution of Freemasonry is now subjected to its scrutiny, and its decision will bring to it exaltation or overthrow. The PEOPLE have undertaken the work of investigation, and to them exclusively belong and may safely be intrusted the task of its prosecution. Full confidence may be indulged that they will conduct it in a manner to commend, without apprehension, their acts, their motives and their objects, to the just discrimination and enlightened judgment of a judging world.

Albany, May 5th, 1829.

M. HAYDEN, Ch'n.

ABNER HAZELTINE, Sec'y.

ADDRESS OF THE MASSACHUSETTS ANTI-MASONIC CONVENTION TO THE CITIZENS OF THE COMMONWEALTH.

FELLOW CITIZENS,

"WE hold these truths to be self-evident, That all men are created equal; that they are endowed by their Creator with certain unalienable rights; that among these are life, liberty, and the pursuit of happiness." On these fundamental principles of civil and religious right, the people of these United States not only cast off the yoke of foreign domination, but "the whole people covenants with each citizen, and each citizen with the whole people, that all shall be governed by certain laws for the common good." We consider it therefore, the duty of every citizen to watch for the public welfare; to sound the alarm in view of public danger; and to encourage laudable measures, which may be devised for the safety and interest of the whole.' Although false alarms are never to be created, and existing maladies are to be cured by the best possible remedies; yet, when public evils do exist, free men should never suffer themselves to rest until those evils are eradicated. The common cause of our common country, demands the utmost vigilance of an intelligent community. In order that this vigilance may be maintained, it is necessary that corresponding exertions be used to scatter light upon every subject which has an important political bearing. Light being diffused upon such subjects, and the attention of the people being directed to those things which are either salutary or prejudicial to the public good; it argues either a want of moral principle, or a criminal degree of apathy, not to feel interested; and those who feel deeply interested, must *act*. But men of intelligence and integrity, will act *openly*, *honestly*, *consistently*, *understandingly*, and *perseveringly*. They will not shrink from the scrutiny of their fellow citizens, nor seek to hide themselves from the public eye; and while they adopt and pursue, with a steady, undeviating course, those measures, which they deem for the general interest, they will frankly and ingenuously give the reasons of their conduct, that the public may approve or condemn, as occasion may require.

On this ground, we consider it not only the *right*, but the *obligation*, of citizens of this Commonwealth, in concert with others of our sister States, to assemble for the express purpose of investigating the nature, tendency, and political bearing of Freemasonry.

We are aware that this subject is one of great interest, and, in its own nature, exceedingly delicate; inasmuch as it relates to the opinions and practice of many, who, for talents, learning and integrity, are ranked among the first men in our country. We are, likewise, by no means insensible, that a thorough investigation of this subject must bring us in unpleasant collision with men whom we highly regard for their moral worth, and with many to whom we are bound by the strongest ties of social and relative friendship. We would, therefore, have it distinctly understood, that we have neither collision nor controversy with masons as *men*, but only with men as *masons*.

While however, we are willing to concede to masons, as *men*, all that is just, honorable, virtuous and paiseworthy, on their part; we are *not* willing to admit, that *all* the talents, and *all* the learning, and *all* the moral worth, of our common country, are the perquisite of the masonic fraternity. We are not willing to admit that they "are *the* people," and that "wisdom will die with them." However highly we may respect masons as *men;* we cannot concede, that aprons, sashes, jewels, mitres, secret rites and obligations, or princely titles, can *justly* secure to them prerogatives of honor, profit and trust; or that they are more deserving of public confidence, than any other class of citizens. We cannot stand afar off, and "exceedingly fear and quake," because of the "awful mystery," which, for a century past, has hung over this institution; nor can the venerable locks of some of its members, its pretended claims to sanctity and "holiness to the Lord," nor even the sword of the "tyler," awe us into silence; or hinder our drawing near to scrutinize the foundation, materials, and "cap-stone" of this mystical building.

These things premised, the delegates from several

counties in this Commonwealth, convened for the purpose of investigating the principles of Speculative masonry, now beg leave to place before their constituents, and fellow citizens in general, certain reasons, why they consider the masonic institution as dangerous to our civil and religious liberties.

The first reason which we would offer, relative to this subject, and which demands our serious consideration, is this:

THE MASONIC FRATERNITY HAVE ERECTED FOR THEMSELVES A DISTINCT, AND INDEPENDENT GOVERNMENT, WITHIN THE JURISDICTION OF THE UNITED STATES.

It cannot be denied, that *any* community, arrogating to itself the right of punishing offenders, not recognized by the laws of the land; and, especially, holding in its own power, the lives of its members; must, so far, be considered as claiming independence, and refusing, in these respects, to hold itself amenable to any higher authority. But, that the masonic fraternity have done this, and still persist in their claim to independence, has been made to appear by the most satisfactory evidence. The testimony of their own members has abundantly shown, that they have instituted a code of laws, not subject to the supervision of any civil power; and this code is *sanguinary*. The code of laws in this institution, consists in the several "oaths or obligations" of its several degrees, to every one of which a penalty is annexed; and that penalty is *death*. Every Freemason, in every degree by which he may advance, is made to swear, that he will forever conceal the secret rites and principles of the institution; his acting himself "under no less *penalty*," than to die a most horrid and barbarous death, if he should ever knowingly or wilfully violate any essential part of his obligation. In order to have a fair view of the barbarous and sanguinary nature of this code, it may not be improper to recapitulate the penalties of the first seven degrees. The Entered Apprentice 'binds himself under no less penalty than to have his throat cut across, his tongue torn out by the roots, and his body buried in the rough sands of the sea.' The penalty of the Fellow Craft, is, 'to have his left breast torn open, and his heart and vitals taken from thence, to be thrown over his left shoulder, and carried into the valley of Jehoshaphat.' The Master Mason swears under the penalty of having his body severed in two, his bowels burnt to ashes, and the ashes scattered to 'the four winds of heaven.' The candidate for the fourth degree, 'binds himself under no less penalty, than to have his right ear smote off, and his right hand chopped off as the penalty of an imposter.' The Past Master swears under the penalty of having his "tongue split from tip to root." The Most Excellent Master binds himself under the penalty of having his "breast torn open, and his heart and vitals taken from thence, and exposed to rot on the dung hill." The Royal Arch Mason imprecates the penalty of having his "skull smote off, and his brains exposed to the scorching rays of the sun."

Such, fellow citizens, are the sanguinary penalties, by which the masonic code is sanctioned, up to the seventh degree. Those of the higher degrees, are of the same nature, except, that if possible, they increase in barbarism.

Now it is vain for masons any longer to deny, that these are the penalties by which the laws of their institution are enforced; because those obligations have already become the subject of judicial record, as developed, under oath, in courts of justice.

It is equally vain for them to pretend, that these penalties have received only a *passive* signification. The obligations speak for themselves. No person can read them, with an unprejudiced mind, without receiving the strong, immediate and horrid impression, that they were intended to be put in execution. Some of us, likewise, *know*, from our own observation, that these obligations have been uniformly administered in lodges and chapters, and suffered to stand, as *literally expressed*, without note or comment. The candidate is made to bind himself "*under no less penalty*," than to suffer thus and so, if he "should prove *wilfully guilty* of violating any part of his obligation." But what is a penalty? Johnson says, it is a "*punishment;*" "*judicial infliction,*" "*forfeiture upon non performance.*" It is a contradiction in terms, then, to say, that a *penalty* is merely *passive*. The delinquent also, in the terms expressed, is supposed to prove "*wil-*

fully guilty" of violating some part of his obligation; which could not be the case, if the secrets of masonry were *extorted* from him by persecution. The very terms therefore, "*wilfully guilty*," as expressed in the oath, are a fair exposition of the penalty, and show at once, that it was intended to be put in execution, in case of delinquency. The candidate also, is made to swear, that he "will obey all regular signs, summonses, or tokens, given, handed, sent, or thrown," to him, from a brother, or companion of the same degree, or from "the body of a lawfully constituted lodge" or "chapter of such." This part of the oath too, is left without note or comment. The candidate is to "obey *all* regular signs, summonses, or tokens," whether to be tried and condemned himself, or to try and execute a brother, who may have violated his masonic engagements. This precisely accords with the charge given to the Fellow Craft, as expressed in Webb's Monitor: "our laws and regulations you are strenuously to support; *and be always ready to assist in seeing them duly executed.*"

But, if we had any doubt respecting the design, nature and tendency of masonic laws; we have a fair and direct exposition in the higher degrees. The "Thrice Illustrious Knight" is sworn in the following words: "You further swear, that should you know another violate any essential part of this obligation, you will use your most decided endeavors, by the blessing of God, *to bring such person to the strictest and most condign punishment*, agreeably to the rules and usages of our ancient fraternity." The Elected Knight of Nine swears, that he "*will revenge* the assassination of our worthy Master, Hiram Abiff, not only on the murderers, but also *on all, who may betray the secrets of this degree.*" He also consents, in case of his own delinquency, "*to be struck with the dreadful poniard of vengeance.* The "Illustrious Elector of Fifteen" binds himself under the penalty of having his "body opened perpendicularly and horizontally, and exposed to the air for eight hours, that the flies may prey on the entrails;" and swears "to be ready to inflict the same penalty on all who may disclose the secrets of this degree." The Knight of the East and West binds himself "under the penalty of not only being dishonored, but to consider his life as the immediate forfeiture, and that to be taken from him with all the tortures and pains to be inflicted in manner as he had consented to in his preceding degrees." The "Knight of the Eagle, and Sovereign Prince of Rose Croix De Heroden," is shown a symbolic representation of *Hell*, and then addressed in the following language: "The horrors which you have just now seen, are but a faint representation of those you shall suffer, if you break through our laws, or infringe the obligation you have taken." To the "Knight of the Eagle or Sun," is explained the following emblem: "By the man you saw peeping, and who was discovered, seized, and conducted to death, is an emblem of those who came to be initiated into our secret mysteries through a motive of curiosity, and, if so indiscreet as to divulge our obligations, *we are bound to cause their death, and take vengeance on the treason, by the destruction of the traitor.*" In accordance with this sentiment, the Knight of Kadosh swears "to take revenge on the traitors of masonry," and "to yield *submission and obedience, on all occasions, without any restrictions*, to the orders of the Illustrious Knights and Grand Commander."

Now, if we can attach any meaning whatever to masonic language, or understand the genius of any human government; we must have the irresistible conviction, that the masonic fraternity have intended to assume the power of life and death over their own members. If so, they must be considered as establishing an independent government, within the jurisdiction of the United States. If they are governed by the spirit and letter of their legal code, they must assume the right to punish with DEATH, independently of any other power, offences which are neither known nor recognized by the law of the land. This sentiment corresponds with language used by the grand lodge, in the State of New York; and the same diction, with little variation, is used by the grand lodge of this Commonwealth. "Every grand lodge," says this first mentioned body, "has an inherent power and authority, to make local ordinances and new regulations, as well as to amend and explain the old, for their own particular benefit, and the good of masonry in general, provided always, that the ancient land-marks are preserved, and that such regulations be duly prepared in writing for the consideration of the members. This has never been disputed; for the members of every grand lodge are the true representatives of the fraternity in communication; and are an *absolute* and *independent* body, with *legislative* authority—provided as aforesaid, that the grand masonic constitution be never violated, nor any of the old landmarks removed."

"Here," in the language of one who has written on this subject, "without any reference to the government of the United States, or to any other government, every grand lodge claims to be an 'absolute and independent body, with legislative authority and inherent power' to make what laws they please for their own particular benefit and for the good of masonry, (not for the good of mankind,) in general."

Masonic language and masonic legislation, then, assume as high prerogatives, and as independent authority, as any government on earth; and will cope with the spirit and diction of the United Colonies, when they declared themselves "free and independent States." But, the good judgment of every intelligent citizen must teach him, that it can be neither for the *interest* nor the *safety* of this republic, to have an *independent* and increasing power, springing up within our own territories; making laws for itself; assuming the prerogative to punish with *death*, or otherwise, offences of its own creating; and holding itself amenable to no legislature or executive in the United States. It is on this very principle, that the Executive of the United States has refused to protect some of our Indian tribes. But if the Indians, in a *small local territory*, are not to be countenanced in "creating an independent government;" how can it be consistent to connive at the *existence* and *growth* of a power which has defied "*the world in arms*," in the very heart of our country, and whose members are scattered over the whole land?

Another evil of which we complain, relative to the masonic institution, is, *its unlimited and unrestricted funds.*

Our legislatures, in framing the charters of corporate bodies, have wisely provided, that the funds of such bodies shall be devoted to specific objects, and shall never exceed a certain amount. They have done this, on the principle, that unlimited and unrestricted funds, in the hands of any class of people, are always dangerous. *Wealth* is *power*. It is of vast importance therefore, that funds, in the hands of corporate bodies, be limited and restricted by civil law. Otherwise they may, at the control of ambitious and unprincipled men, prove a most powerful engine against the State, or be devoted to purposes subversive of the public good. But, to what limitation or restriction are the funds of the masonic fraternity subjected? or what support do they lend to civil government? The members of this society may accumulate hundreds of thousands, in secret, subjected to no tax, and responsible to no civil power. Who knows also, the *real*, secret object, for which those funds are created? They *may* be created for purposes of *masonic charity;* and they *may* be created and managed *to the subversion of every civil government on earth.*

It is no less obvious to us, that the masonic institution practises the *foulest imposition.* It *professes*, indeed, to be an institution of *science*, *charity*, and *moral virtue.* But, examining the first principles of the institution, as they have been developed in hundreds of instances, we cannot but be surprised and shocked, at the gross fraud and extortion which it has practised upon our young men. It would be easy to adduce examples in demonstration of this truth; but as the secret rites of Freemasonry have all been laid before the public, we would urge every citizen to examine for himself.

The *immorality* of Freemasonry, is another thing, to which we would invite the attention of the public. Every man of principle, intelligence and reflection, must admit, that the stability of our government, and the security of our rights and privileges, must, in a great measure, depend upon the prevalence of *sound morality*. But, we cannot think, that the secret rites and obligations of Freemasonry, are, in any degree, calculated to enforce the principles of moral virtue. On the contrary, we have the strongest conviction, that they tend to harden the heart, stupify the conscience, and to eradicate every degree of moral sensibility. The frequency and barbarous language, with which *oaths are administered*, in this institution, and the inhuman penalties, with which they are sanctioned, must naturally lead moral beings to trifle with the oath of God, imposed by civil authority. The indecent and ridiculous ceremonies of initiation, intermingled with prayer and reading the scriptures, must tend directly to turn sacred things into contempt. The awful familiarity with which the name, titles, attributes, and word, of the Deity, are used, as "pass words;" the profane and farcical representation of "the burning bush," the ark of God, the pot of manna, and the rod of Aaron; we think can amount to nothing less than blasphemy. In short, all the ceremonies and appendages of the masonic institution, from the first to the forty-third degree, we consider directly calculated, and most artfully contrived, to lead on, step by step, into *blank Atheism*. We fear not to appeal to any unprejudiced minds who will examine these degrees, as they have been disclosed by Bernard and others; and to affirm, without the least apprehension of being contradicted, that the whole system is directly calculated to overturn every religion, and every civil government on earth. This object is fully disclosed by the "Knight Adept of the Eagle or Sun." After explaining masonic symbols, in the preceding degrees, as secretly, though *really*, levelled against the first principles of every existing religion and government, the "Grand Master, or Thrice Puissant," addresses the candidate in the following words: "Behold, my dear brother, what you must fight against and destroy, before you can come to the knowledge of the true good and sovereign happiness! Behold this monster which you must conquer—a serpent which *we* detest as an idol that is adored by the idiot and vulgar under the name of *religion*."

In looking at the principles of Freemasonry, we are constrained to believe, that *it subverts the administration of justice*. This is the natural tendency of masonic oaths; as will appear from the following extracts. To aid a brother, and keep his secrets, the master mason binds himself explicitly. "Furthermore, do I promise and swear, that I will not give the grand hailing sign of distress, except I am in real distress, or for the benefit of the craft, when at work; and should I ever see that sign given, or the word accompanying it, and the person who gave it appearing to be in distress, I will fly to his relief at the risk of my life, should there be a greater probability of saving his life than of losing my own." "Furthermore, do I promise and swear, that a master mason's secrets, given to me in charge as such, and I knowing them to be such, shall remain as secure and inviolable in my breast as in his own, when communicated to me, murder and treason excepted; and they left to my own election." Now who would expect, that a master mason, feeling himself bound by his masonic oath, would disclose "the truth, the whole truth, and nothing but the truth," when called to testify against a brother in a court of justice, especially when he saw from that brother "the grand hailing sign of distress?" But, let us hear the Royal Arch mason. "Furthermore, do I promise and swear, that I will aid and assist a companion Royal Arch mason, when engaged in any difficulty; and espouse his cause so far as to extricate him from the same, if in my power, whether he be right or wrong. Furthermore, do I promise and swear, that a companion Royal Arch mason's secrets, given me in charge as such, and I knowing them to be such, shall remain as secure and inviolable in my breast as in his own, murder and treason *not excepted;*" or, as it is administered in some Chapters, "*in all cases without exception.*" We now ask any citizen, who is not a mason, if, engaged in litigation with one of the fraternity, he is willing his cause should be submitted to a jury, bound under no less penalty, than to have each his "skull smote off," that they will aid and assist their "companion, when engaged in *any difficulty*, and espouse his cause, so far as to extricate him from the same, *whether he be right or wrong?*" If the jurors have any regard to the masonic oath, will they not feel bound to render a verdict in favor of their brother or companion, whether just or unjust? This is no more than a fair and literal expression of the Royal Arch obligation; and we have the testimony of men, who have been familiar with masonic usages, and whose integrity has long been establish- in view of the public, that the cause of justice has been thwarted repeatedly through the influence of masonic oaths.

Freemasonry tends to defeat the design of the civil law,

and to paralize the arm of justice in the punishment of crime.

Freemasons are not only sworn to keep their brother's secrets, and to defend and espouse his cause, whether right or wrong, but to warn him of approaching danger, and, if possible, effect his escape. The force of such obligations, regarded by the brotherhood, must afford a broad covering for the blackest crimes, and lay the foundation for many a villain to elude the stroke of justice. In demonstration of this fact, we appeal to the MORGAN conspiracy. The success and facility, with which many, engaged in that barbarous transaction, have insulted and set at defiance the majesty of the civil law, afford melancholy proof, that masonic obligations are but too well observed. It affords an affecting illustration of those unhallowed words, to keep a companion's secrets, in all cases whatsoever, and to espouse his cause, and grant him aid "in *any difficulty* so far as to extricate him from the same, whether he be right or wrong." It cannot be denied, nor ought to be concealed, that whole lodges, chapters and encampments, and even the Grand Lodge and Grand Chapter of one of the States, have been prompt to relieve their criminal brethren and companions in distress; and have not hesitated to bestow of their funds, to thwart the exertions, and paralize the effects of the civil power. Even those Freemasons, who have been convicted of the foulest crimes against the laws of their country, have had their prisons turned to palaces, their hearts cheered with every desirable luxury, and are still owned by the fraternity, as trusty companions and worthy brothers. It is indeed, mockery, and adding insult to injury, for any to pretend, in the face of these "stubborn facts," that Freemasons do not mean to shield one another from the arm of the civil law.

It is an alarming consideration *that the public press has been so much under the control of masonic influence.* A free press may be considered the very bulwark of our civil and religious liberties. Who are our sentinels and watchmen, but those who manage the public press? But our editors, with a few honorable exceptions, relative to this subject, have been, as it appears to us, unreasonably reserved. Bating a few, who have been continually chanting the praises of Freemasonry, and pouring forth abuse and Billingsgate on all who dare oppose; and here and there a champion for the truth, who had the temerity, in opposition to masonic threats and masonic corruption, to sound the alarm, and tell *aloud* the tale of wo, which had yet scarce been *whispered* to the western zephyr; almost the whole corps seemed to be mute with astonishment. Masonic bribery had almost effectually poisoned all our streams of public information. No one could know the truth; no one could tell what to believe. Were it not for the anti-masonic presses, which have sprung up, almost simultaneously, like here and there a star to "glitter upon the mantle of night;" our political horizon would still have been left in worse than Egyptian darkness. But from the demonstration we have had of masonic control over the public press, a free people have reason to be jealous, and take the alarm. If the fountains of intelligence must either be stopped, or corrupted, by a powerful, secret combination, we may as well barter away our birthright for a mess of pottage, or sell our liberties at auction, like the Roman empire, despoiled of its strength, opulence and glory.

We cannot but learn, with serious apprehensions for our dearest rights, *the artful and insidious measures, with which Freemasons have been thrust into offices of power and trust.* In looking at these offices, in places where, perhaps, one eighth of the freeholders are masons, we shall find more than seven eighths of the offices in possession of the brotherhood. Where, fellow citizens, will you find a public key, of any considerable importance, that is not in the hands of a mason? Where will you find an important public office, of any considerable lucrative encouragement, that is not filled by a mason? We are sure, that the disparity in official appointments, as divided between Freemasons and other classes of our fellow citizens, is so great, that it could not have been the result of accident. Whoever will examine this part of the subject, will find that facts speak for themselves, and that their testimony is irresistible.

Now, although we would not deny to Freemasons, as *men*, in common with others, any right, prerogative or perquisite, of civil community, to which talents and integrity may justly entitle them; yet we are constrained to consider any secret or clandestine measures, which they take to thrust their own members into office, as altogether a usurpation; and such an one as is directly calculated to subvert the very first principles of our confederate republic.

We do not feel ourselves at liberty to conclude this document, without urging our fellow citizens to reflect upon the awful *imprecations* of Freemasonry. These are so numerous, that we could not give a full view of their horrid and blasphemous import, without transcribing a very considerable part of every masonic "obligation." We will select, as an example only the following, from one of the Knight's degrees. In receiving his libation from a *human skull*, the candidate swears, "May this libation appear as a witness against me, both here and hereafter,—and as the sins of the world were laid upon the head of the Saviour, so may all the sins committed by the person whose skull this was, be heaped upon my head, in addition to my own, should I ever knowingly or wilfully violate or transgress any obligation that I have heretofore taken, take at this time, or shall, at any future period, take in relation to any degree of masonry, or order of knighthood." Upon such imprecations as these, let every citizen make his own comment.

We also feel it our duty, though with great reluctance, to advert to the *malignant and persecuting spirit*, inculcated in some of the first principles of Freemasonry, and which has been too faithfully carried into effect against all those, who have had the temerity to transgress her secret and mysterious laws. Take, as an example, an extract from an obligation administered to the Thrice Illustrious Knight of the Red Cross. "You further swear, that should you know another to violate any essential point of this obligation, you will use your most decided endeavors, by the blessing of God, to bring such person to the strictest and most condign punishment, agreeably to the rules and usages of our most ancient fraternity; and this by pointing him out to the world as an unworthy vagabond; by opposing his interest, by deranging his business, by transferring his character after him wherever he may go, and exposing him to the contempt of the whole fraternity and the world, but of our illustrious order more especially, during his whole natural life." Here too, let our fellow citizens judge, whether such a spirit as this, enforced by a *sanguinary law*, becomes a "handmaid of religion," or of an institution professing to inculcate the first principles of "charity," "universal philanthropy," and sound "morality." As it respects ourselves, we are fully satisfied, that such obligations as the above will account for the scandal and reproach, which, without discrimination, have been heaped upon all those who have burst the bonds of the masonic institution, and borne testimony against its secret principles of iniquity.

There are several other topics, relative to this subject, which we think deserve the serious consideration of our fellow citizens; but this protracted address must come to a close, and leave much unsaid, which we could wish to have discussed. We cannot, however, sum up what we have already suggested, and what we might still desire to lay before the citizens of this Commonwealth, in more appropriate language, than that of the Le Roy Convention, in their anti-masonic declaration of independence.

"That it (the masonic institution) is opposed to the genius and design of this government, the spirit and precepts of our holy religion, and the welfare of society generally, will appear from the following considerations:

"It exercises jurisdiction over the persons and lives of citizens of the republic.

"It arrogates to itself the right of punishing its members for offences unknown to the laws of this or any other nation.

"It requires the concealment of crime, and protects the guilty from punishment.

"It encourages the commission of crime, by affording to the guilty facilities of escape.

"It affords opportunities for the corrupt and designing to form plans against government, and the lives and characters of individuals.

"It assumes titles and dignities incompatible with a republican form of government, and enjoins an obedience to them derogatory to republican principles.

"It destroys all principles of equality, by bestowing

favors on its own members, to the exclusion of others equally meritorious and deserving.

"It creates odious aristocracies, by its obligations to support the interests of its members, in preference to others of equal qualifications.

"It blasphemes the name, and attempts a personification of the great Jehovah.

"It prostitutes the sacred scriptures to unholy purposes, to subserve its own secular and trifling concerns.

"It weakens the sanctions of morality and religion, by the multiplication of profane oaths, and an immoral familiarity with religious forms and ceremonies.

"It destroys a veneration for religion and religious ordinances, by the profane use of religious forms.

"It substitutes the self-righteousness and ceremonies of masonry for the vital religion and ordinances of the gospel.

"It promotes habits of idleness and intemperance, by its members neglecting their business to attend its meetings and drink its libations.

"It accumulates funds at the expense of indigent persons, and to the distress of their families, too often to be dissipated in rioting and pleasure, and its senseless ceremonies and exhibitions.

"It contracts the sympathies of the human heart for all the unfortunate, by confining its charities to its own members; and promotes the interests of a few at the expense of the many.

"An institution thus fraught with so many and great evils, is dangerous to our government and the safety of our citizens, and is unfit to exist among a free people: We, therefore, believing it a duty we owe to God, our country, and to posterity, resolve to expose its mystery, wickedness and tendency, to public view—and we exhort all citizens, who have a love of country and a veneration for its laws, a spirit of our holy religion, and a regard for the welfare of mankind, to aid us in the cause which we have espoused."

All of which is respectfully submitted.

MOSES THACHER, *Per Order.*

RESOLUTIONS

Adopted by the Massachusetts Anti-masonic Convention.

Resolved, That all Societies should be open and amenable to the public, and that the existence of any Association whose objects, principles and measures are secret and concealed, is hostile to the spirit of our free institutions.

Resolved, That the disclosures of Freemasonry made by Wm. Morgan, by the Le Roy Convention, and by Elder Bernard and others, show the system to be selfish, revengeful and impious, and its oaths to be dangerous to our private rights and our public interests.

Resolved, That there is evidence before this Convention that *Royal Arch* Freemasons, impelled by a sense of their masonic obligations, have robbed their country of the services of a free citizen, that the institution retains within its bosom the men who have done this violence, and that the grand lodge of New York has contributed of its funds to pay the expenses of the same, and that chapters and subordinate lodges have also appropriated liberally of their goods to support the perpetrators of *kidnapping* and *alleged murder*.

Resolved, That the system is one and indivisible, whether consisting of three degrees or fifty; that it is erected on the same foundation, constructed in the same form, inhabited by the same spirit, and governed by the same laws; that the acts of exalted Freemasons, and of lodges and chapters in one State, are the responsible acts of the whole system in the United States, and that it is proper to make Freemasonry answer for the conduct of its constituted authorities wherever they are situated.

Resolved, That in view of the premises we respectfully request the grand fraternities of Freemasons in the State of Massachusetts, to *disfellowship* the grand lodge, the grand chapter, and the grand encampment of the State of New York, which hold in their masonic embrace the perpetrators of the violence upon William Morgan, and either to deny the truth of the above named disclosures, or to renounce the system, and the oaths of Freemasonry, which have been palmed upon the honest Freemasons of the present generation as the favorite work of the wise king Solomon, and of their tutelar, St. John.

Resolved, That the Anti-masonic State Cómmittee be directed to furnish each one of the grand officers of the grand lodge, and the grand chapter, and the grand encampment, and the grand council of the Freemasons in this State with a copy of these Resolutions, particularly urging this our earnest request, and that when this Convention adjourns, it be to some day convenient to receive their answer, in the hope that the wisdom of their reply will relieve the public mind of any anxiety respecting the institution of Speculative Freemasonry.

Resolved, That in the opinion of this Convention the oaths imposed by Freemasonry are in a very high degree profane, and entirely destitute of any moral obligation, or legal binding force.

Resolved, That *there is evidence* of an intimate connexion between the higher orders of Freemasonry and French Illuminism.

APPENDIX.

Renunciations of Freemasons.

Extract from the Renunciation of the Rev. David Bernard, of Warsaw, Genesee Co. N. Y.

It is with much reluctance I appear before the public in defence of that which is dearer to me than life. Though I value my good name thus highly, I should not attempt a refutation of the foul charges which have been with much pains circulated against me, and appear in the public journals in vindication of my character, were it not for the duty I owe to my family and friends, and above all, to the Church of the living God, of which I have the honor (though unworthy) to be a member and minister. And it is not because I was unable to make every thing appear "clear as the sun," as respects the course I have pursued in forever leaving and renouncing Freemasonry, that I have not done it before. But it is because my brethren and friends advised me to hold still, and because I determined to show my enemies, that all their slander, and hellish machinations, could not overthrow me, though I remained silent: And thanks be to the name of my Master, I have been enabled to pursue such a course as has received the approbation and fellowship of the churches, the answer of a good conscience, and the approving smiles of my God.

It may not be amiss here to observe, that I have taken ten degrees in Speculative Freemasonry, and was the *first Royal Arch Mason*, with the exception of Wm. Morgan, that ever denounced the institution as corrupt, to my knowledge. This is one reason, no doubt, why the fraternity have been so inveterate against me.

Now to the point, respecting my leaving the institution. Five weeks before the abduction of Morgan, I heard that he was writing masoury. My informant was a Baptist minister of high standing, and a high mason. He declared to me, that a greater piece of depravity he had never heard of; and furthermore, said *repeatedly*, that "he was willing to be one to put Morgan out of the way." He said that "God looked upon the institution with such complacency, he would never bring the perpetrators to light," and *attempted to justify* the deed from the scriptures. He also informed me, that there had been a meeting of the masons at Batavia and Stafford. The above expressions I highly disapproved of at the time, and told him that if Morgan had done wrong, we should not. The above I feel willing to be qualified to, if called upon in any proper manner. From what I learned from the above gentleman, and others, I had no doubt some measures would be taken to stop the printing of masonry, but did not believe the masons would be so abominably wicked and daring as to put Morgan to death.

When I was at the east, 250 miles from Batavia, I heard masons of high standing converse upon the subject of his abduction, which was several weeks before he was taken off. On my way home, I saw Elder John G. Stearns, and he presented me one of his books on masonry, just published. When I reached home I read the work and could find no fault in it. I showed the book to a mason, who immediately purchased it. I learned also, that Morgan was taken off and probably put to death. I began conversing with the masons upon the subject, and they almost universally justified it. I then began not only to give the subject due reflection, and investigation; but to express my abhorrence and utter detestation of the foul and most awful deed. I began also to converse freely on the principles of the institution with masons, and others. About this time a special meeting of the lodge was called in Covington, which I attended, and after the meeting was duly opened and the subject of the abduction brought up, I arose and decidedly disapprobated it, and advised the lodge to do the same. But instead of attending to my advice, they began to question me about what I had said of masonry, and relative to my bringing Stearn's book into town; all of which to the worthy body, appeared criminal. During this meeting, if I may judge, I saw what I call a manifest approbation of the Morgan outrage, in most of the members, and it was a full meeting. At this meeting there were a number of Reverend gentlemen, one of whom said, as nearly as I can recollect: "Cities have their laws, Churches have their laws, masons have their laws, and here is the proper place to try a mason. If Morgan has had his throat cut from ear to ear, and his body buried in the rough sands of the sea, where the tide ebbs and flows once in 24 hours, he cannot complain of not having justice done him." Here he closed, and it was echoed with an Amen! Amen! One of the members of the church in Covington, said about this time at a private house, that the worst death inflicted on Morgan, would have been no more than just.

The next regular meeting of the lodge I attended; being requested by the Master, at the above named special meeting, and here a scene passed which I shall never forget. If ever a poor mortal was abused, I was. Dr. Daniel White was one of the foremost, in treating me shamefully. Here I did not know what to do; I rather thought there would be warm work, I therefore kept perfectly cool, as I can abundantly prove, and nothing passed my lips but what I am willing should be repeated a thousand times. I then and there declared some of my then principal objections to Freemasonry. They were not removed. I finally told them to take their own course, such were my views, and if they chose they could expel me. It has been said that I begged them not to do it, but this is false, and I can prove it. I told them I did not ask them to expel me, but they could take their own course. I finally left them, hoping and praying that they would forever disown me, as I did them.

When I left the Church in Covington, they gave me a good letter of recommendation. I also received letters from the 2d Le Roy, 1st York, 1st Middlebury, 2d Elba and Warsaw churches, all of which justified and approved the course I have taken; and I hope I may ever conduct so as to merit their confidence and that of the public. I have ever been ready, and am still, to meet my accusers or any body else, before the churches with which I am connected. I preach to the first church in Middlebury and the church in Warsaw. I hold my standing in the second church in Le Roy, where I united last winter. My reason for uniting with that church is, it was the first in the country that came out from Freemasonry, and as I could not conscientiously walk with those who practised it, I became one of them. I wish to injure no man. I trust I am a friend to all men. But I am a decided enemy to Freemasonry; and it is because, from a thorough investigation of its principles before and since I left it, I fully believe that it is not only the most abominable but also the most dangerous institution that ever was imposed upon man; it is anti-republican and anti-christian. It is somewhat imposing, owing to its borrowed garments, but this renders it more dangerous, for like the wily serpent, it lures but to destroy. Man never invented, hell never devised, wicked men and devils never palmed upon the public a more *foolish, corrupt, awful, soul destroying and Heaven daring institution, than Speculative Freemasonry! It may truly be said to be* HELL'S MASTER PIECE.

Having thoroughly investigated its ceremonies, its oaths, and its principles, as in the light of eternity, I feel fully warranted in making these statements. The condition on which the oaths are taken, and their evil tendency, being opposed to the glory of God and the best interests of man, render them far from being binding.

I solemnly renounce all fealty to masonry, and do most earnestly beseech my brethren in Christ Jesus, of every name, to come out and bear unequivocal testimony against it. Think, O think, dear Christians, that hundreds and thousands of precious and immortal souls will be lost forever, unless they return and repent, but that the name of the precious Jesus is rejected, your Saviour, your precious and adorable Saviour taken away—the cause of your bleeding Redeemer injured—the hands of the wicked strengthened, and the Almighty God dishonored! And O, let me entreat you in the mercy and bowels of Jesus Christ, to reflect that you have to answer for the blood of those who shall find also, when it shall be forever too late, that masonry is not a Saviour! And while I entreat you, let me warn the wicked. O wicked man, thou shalt surely die—your house is built on the sand—the winds, rains, and floods of Jehovah's wrath will soon beat upon your naked soul in one eternal storm! Though you may expect to mount up as the eagle on your boasted god, you will find that the Almighty will dash you to pieces like a potter's vessel. Be warned then, be wise and flee from masonry—flee from the wrath to come—flee to the gushing side of Jesus, whose blood you are ever trampling under your feet. He can save you, for he is merciful—he can save you, for he is Almighty. Farewell, dear sinner; if you choose, you can still slander me, still calumniate my character. Recollect when I pray to my Lord I always remember you; though you hate me, I love you; though you blast my reputation, though you kill my body, you cannot kill my soul. This is secure from all your machinations, and will in the blood of Christ triumph forever.

Farewell, dear sinners: But we shall meet again, when the last trump shall sound we shall meet. At the retribution of the great day, we shall meet and hear our final doom, we shall receive our everlasting reward—masonry then, and its adherents will eternally perish, while Christ and his people will reign forever.

DAVID BERNARD.

Renunciation of Rev. Joshua Bradley, Principal of Rock Spring Seminary, Illinois.

In a letter to a friend in New-York.

I was brought into existence and educated in a region where masonry was cherished and respected, and where I never heard any cogent arguments offered against it; I therefore was early inclined to think it an institution worthy of my attention. After I left college in 1799, I became acquainted with many masons, who were amiable, benevolent, influential in society and government; also, some ministers whom I highly esteemed, were members and zealously engaged in recommending its morality, virtues and utility to mankind. All I read, heard, or saw of the progress of this denomination, had a tendency to incline me to join them. In 1814, I visited Newport, R. I., where I was first settled in the ministry. An opportunity was then presented to accomplish my wishes and gratify my curiosity. There I took all the degrees that I ever considered important to myself and others. Some terms in the obligations and the titles of their officers, I never liked, but these were so explained by those who presided, that I finally passed onward, as all had done who had gone this way before me, without much difficulty.

I then considered, and have ever since, that the Knighthood has no affinity to masonry. I never had a thought that masonry was religion; for God in his infinite mercy had brought me by his Holy Spirit to believe in Christ, at the age of about 17 years. That pure religion which I then experienced, has been replete with every thing that I or a world needs in time or eternity. But masonry is a human, and cunningly formed system of deception. Is it not rightly named, "Speculative Freemasonry?" Millions have been drawn within its veil, and led away captive by its false pretensions and exhibitions of morality, charity and brotherly love. And many may still rejoice for a season in their delusions, despise reproof, and perish without remedy.

While I lived in New England, I saw nothing very alarming in the transactions of masons; but in 1817 I settled in Albany, N. Y., where I formed an extensive acquaintance with the fraternity from all parts of that State, and began to take an active part in their lodges and chapters, till May, 1826. During this period I tried in all laudable ways to enlighten and turn the attention of thousands, to found academies and educate in all the useful arts, the children of poor masons and their orphans—to expel unworthy members, to lay out their large and accumulating funds for the benefit of those to whom they were obligated, and to save themselves from fraud and every species of deception. I was well aware from documents obtained, and from oral information, that the craft were in imminent danger of overwhelming themselves in a sea of difficulties, which would rise and sweep through that State, if not over the Union—bearing on its waves the iniquities of many of the order that might be seen and known by every individual of discernment. I was no prophet, neither the son of a prophet, nor did I need a messenger from the skies to inform me of the future destiny of the fraternity in New-York, or any other part of the globe, when I knew from history and the revelation from heaven, that the destruction of every society slumbered not, which would foster within its embraces, members, who would spend their funds in riotous courses and every scene of abomination. Many have done this in every country where masonry has been permitted to erect her edifice, and entice to her dark recesses all whom she may devour. Should any consider me advancing upon ground doubtful, and altogether beyond the regions of possibility, I would only ask masons to open their archives and read for themselves. What occasioned the existence of the Lodge of Reconciliation in England? Was it not to bring into *union* the terrible parties of masons who arrayed themselves against each other, and were trampling upon every particle of reason, and setting at naught every thing worthy of our existence? Who robbed No. 31 of their jewels, implements, charter and every book? Their Deputy Grand Master. What did that lodge write to their Grand Master, who is the king of Great Britain? How did he treat that lodge? English masons know, and some of us in this country have read the letters that were written upon those base transactions. But I will put a few questions that can easily be answered by masons in the State of New-York.—What treasurer of T. Chapter in Albany, squandered $1450 away in a manner too injurious to himself to be described by me? How many hundreds did the same individual receive from country brethren, for charters, which he did not return, nor refund their money? What treasurer of the Grand Chapter put all his property out of his hands, and kept back $5000, which he had received while in office? Who were the representatives of about thirty lodges in and about the city of New-York, who tried all possible arts of deception upon the representatives from the country in Tammany Hall, till midnight, and then seized all the funds, clothing, papers and implements, and retired to St. John's Hall, and there elected officers, contrary to the laws of the Grand Lodge and all usages among masons, or any class of mankind under the influence of reason? About $20,000 were held by them, and about three hundred country lodges treated contemptuously. Who received from June, 1824, to June, 1825, more than $900 for charters, and kept the whole from the treasurer? These fraudulent transactions were practised upon the fraternity from 1818 to 1825, and none of the violators of their solemn obligations could we get expelled: And as to inflicting any other penalty upon them, never entered my mind, or was ever hinted by any one with whom I associated; neither do I believe that any good man could be so blinded as to consider the fraternity possessing power to destroy a member who had violated their laws. When a certain master mason a few years since, published all the lectures in a very singular way, that was supposed by him and some others impossible to be read without his key; but finally the whole was found out by some who were not masons; what was the penalty inflicted upon him in 1826? Nothing but expulsion from the Grand Chapter of New-York.

I cannot admit that Washington, Franklin, De Witt Clinton, and many other virtuous and discerning statesmen in America, and more than two hundred learned and pious ministers of the gospel, ever believed that the obligations imposed on them at their initiation and advancement in the order, either made them guilty of blasphemy or laid them under any necessity of removing any violater from his family, country, or inflicting any corporeal punishment upon him. Therefore, I have not received my conviction from the expositions that anti-masons have given upon the oaths or obligations taken by masons. My conviction commenced from my preparations to answer some recent anti-masonic writers. Ever since the excitement began, I felt a strong inclination to defend the system.

The indescribable wickedness of some masons in the Morgan affair, had waked up a host of new, learned and scrutinizing enemies, who were penetrating every region around them, and seizing every weapon to destroy the whole fabric. In surveying the vast field of their occupancy, I found only two positions of strength and importance, viz. 1st, that secret societies ought not to exist; 2d, that obligations taken by their members are not binding. Could these two be fairly removed, every other might, and masonry again rise and gain a triumph. In 1827 I was solicited to deliver an address in St. Louis on the 24th June; I accepted, and then briefly exhibited my sentiments on masonry, to a large congregation, in which were a number of the order from different parts of the Union, of respectable standing and holding offices of great responsibility in our national government. This discourse was approved and published. Some of my remarks against anti-masonic performances and exertions, put forth against this mystic society, I now detest. For some months I stood prepared to meet their advance upon the fraternity, spreading over the vast valley of the Mississippi. I almost came to a determination to send some of my views to be published in your region; but my distance from the seat of opposition, and my knowledge of men in the order of greater ability and erudition than myself, who resided in the midst of the contest, prevented me. I fondly hoped that some would enter the field and come off triumphant. None have yet appeared sufficiently clothed in truth, to overthrow the two positions above mentioned, and I am now fully persuaded that they are founded in righteousness and cannot be demolished. That lively confidence, which once appeared to glow among masons, now withers and must finally vanish away.

The commotions in the east have awakened me to consider anxiously what I must do as an individual. I have tried to persuade myself to hold a neutral position for some months past, on account of the afflicting hand of Providence upon my wife, that must soon lodge her in the grave, if not removed, and my present residence in a city where masonry is respected and moves onward without any annoyance. Neutrality, in this day of prevalent divisions, is unpleasant and unreasonable, in my estimation. Therefore, I am willing it should be known with whom I can associate, for the happiness of mankind, and the glory of God—"*Magna est veritas, et prevalebit.*"

Should my friends in your vicinity deem this communication of any importance to the public, for the promotion of anti-masonry, it is at their service. My next will be an address to professors of religion who are still in the fraternity, and others whom I may have grieved with my former publications on masonry, and my zeal and labors among them.

JOSHUA BRADLEY.

May 9, 1829.

Renunciation of Rev. Mr. Mann, of Suffield, Con.

THE following renunciation will be read with interest and pleasure throughout the country. The author of it is extensively known in Connecticut, Rhode Island, Massachusetts, and New Hampshire. No man's character stands fairer than his does, as a man, a gentleman, a Christian, and a Christian minister.—*A. M. Intelligencer.*

MR. EDITOR,—The subject of Freemasonry, affecting as it does the reputation of individuals, the welfare of the churches, and the peace of the community, is a subject of great importance. Every movement in regard to it, whether on the part of its friends or of its enemies, should be made with due consideration. In deciding on the merits of an institution which has a mixture of good and evil in its composition, and against which popular opinion has arrayed itself, and that too, with uncommon energy, we are liable to misjudge. Realizing the truth of this, I have endeavored for some time past to examine seriously and candidly the nature and tendency of Freemasonry. The result of this examination, I now communicate under a sense of the duty I owe to my friends, to my country, and to the church of the Redeemer.

I became a member of this institution in my native town, and was raised to the degree of Master mason within a year after completing my course of education at College; and some time previous to my settlement in the ministry I was advanced to the degree of Mark

Master mason. Subsequently to this, in compliance with the wishes of particular friends, I proceeded to the Royal Arch degree. My attendance on the meetings of the Fraternity have been discontinued for the few last years, and always have been limited principally to public or special occasions. The reason of this has been that I have not been fully satisfied with the institution, and have feared that all was not right concerning it.

It is not my design in this communication to rail against an institution with which I have long been connected, nor to divulge its secrets, nor to criminate any of its members. Many of them I esteem and love as good citizens, and good Christians. Nor am I sensible that by doing this, I am actuated by any selfish motives. I am aware that by taking this step, I shall wound the feelings of some, and, perhaps, excite the ill will and severe reproaches of others. The latter I shall endeavor to forgive, and by the former I shall hope to be forgiven.

Having examined with some degree of attention the nature of Freemasonry, and having considered the extraordinary occurrences which have recently marked its history and furnished to the world a fearful comment on its principles; I can no longer, with a clear conscience, retain any connexion with the institution, and do hereby declare my secession from it. The reasons which influence me to this step, are the same which have been announced by others who have taken the same course. I have long feared that Freemasonry had a strong tendency to Deism. Even in the prescribed forms of prayer, we rarely find any recognition of the Saviour. It is not an answer to this objection to say, that this institution existed before the manifestation of Christ in human nature. It is as vain to challenge for masonry a great antiquity, as it is impious to claim for it an equality in point of excellence, with Christianity itself. It does not admit of a doubt that its origin is to be placed in modern times. Although portions of the gospel are interwoven with its forms, I conceive that masonry presents false grounds of hope; leads men to depend on their own defective righteousness;—to expect the favor of God without the interposition of a Redeemer, and even without repentance; and thus has a most injurious influence on their eternal interests. Under the most favorable circumstances, which, in any place, have attended masonry, it has occasioned a great waste of time and money, which might and ought to have been employed for better purposes. And furthermore, it interferes materially with domestic religious duties.

Without declaring the institution a downright imposition in all its parts, I confess, that I was greatly disappointed at every step of advancement through its degrees, as to the benefit to be derived from it. I doubt not, that many a man has felt ashamed and conscience-smitten when he has appeared to be satisfied with a thing of such inanity. The moral precepts which are to be found among its instructions, may be much better learned from the gospel itself. As to the union which it is said to form among men, it may be observed, that the religion of Jesus effects the most important and lasting union among good men which can be formed on earth; and, as to bad men, to bind them together by solemn oaths in secret societies to stand by, and defend, and promote each other, must be regarded as a dangerous procedure, both in relation to church and state.

The recent disclosure of facts made to the legislature of New York, and in numerous other ways, has shown clearly that, in regard to our political interests, the institution of masonry is to be greatly dreaded. It is a powerful engine, which may be wielded with tremendous and destructive force against the liberties of our beloved country.

But, Sir, permit me to add an objection, which, a little while ago, I could not have supposed would ever exist against an institution which professes to be founded in pure morality and benevolence. It is stained with the blood of the innocent. It has perpetrated murder in the most outrageous and horrid manner. It has trampled thus on the laws of God and man. It has set at defiance all authority, and even every principle of humanity. The evidence is overwhelming, that these shocking barbarities, at which the inquisition itself might blush, have been committed by masons; and they have been justified by masons, as being in accordance with the obligations of the institution; and the wretched perpetrators have been screened from justice and protected by masons! Sir, I can no longer regard such an institution as a moral one, much less as a religious one. If this is a practical exposition of its laws, it ought not to be tolerated by any friend of our species.

I feel, that I cannot free my garments from the blood of the murdered, if I countenance or uphold an institution which has committed such deeds. Does not the blood of the martyr of Batavia cry to heaven for the vengeance of Him who hath said, Vengeance is mine, I will repay? Do not the cries of the widow and the orphan ascend to the ear of Him who styles himself, the Judge of the fatherless and the widow? Against whom is this cry uttered? Not merely against those whose hands have laid hold on violence; but, against those, also, who continue to sustain a society which is guilty of such atrocities.

It does not satisfy my conscience to say as many of my brethren do, that we disapproved of the violent measures which have been pursued. The question I have to ask is this;—were the proceedings against Morgan in accordance with masonry or not? If they were, how can any of the fraternity be free from the implication of murder, in a moral sense, who continue to uphold and favor such an institution? Under such circumstances, is not the maintenance of masonry a virtual justification of the whole procedure?

If the members of Congress were to make laws, encouraging piracy and murder, would not they, and all who should approve of such enactments, and maintain them, be implicated in all the crimes which should be committed in consequence of them?

Will it be said at this late day, that perhaps Morgan is not dead? Then let him be produced. Let us see him;—let us embrace him; let us give him back to the bosom of his broken-hearted wife and his mourning children. Let us restore him to our country, and thus wipe away the foul stigma which has been brought upon it by the outrage committed against its laws, and the setting at defiance of its justice.

Does it not become professing Christians and ministers of the meek and benevolent Redeemer to consider whether they can consistently retain their connexion with the institution? With all the light which is now poured upon this subject, does it not admit of the clearest proof, that its obligations and practices are irreconcilable with the gospel! Are we not taught such precepts as these;—Avoid the very appearance of evil. Thou shalt do no murder. Be ye not called Master, for one is your master in heaven. Thou shalt not take the name of the Lord thy God in vain. The wisdom which is from above is first *pure*, then *peaceable*, gentle and easy to be entreated, full of mercy and good fruits, without *partiality* and without *hypocrisy*. By the deeds of the law shall no flesh be justified. By *grace* are ye saved, *through faith*, and that not of yourselves, it is the gift of God. No man can come unto the Father but by Jesus Christ.—Let masonry be *thoroughly* tried by the word of God, and by its actual effects on morals and religion; and, then, let the decision on its merits be given in view of the transactions of that day, when God shall bring every *secret thing* into judgment whether it be good or whether it be evil.

JOEL MANN.

Suffield, Oct. 9, 1829.

Renunciation of John R. Mulford.

In making the following statement of my views and disclosures on the subject of Speculative Freemasonry, I am not conscious of being governed by any motives except a desire to discharge my duty as a member of civil society, and of the church of Jesus Christ, and also to promote the cause of truth and justice in our social relations; but above all, the cause of a pure and undefiled religion, as it is taught in the living oracles of God, without the corrupt mixtures of human invention.

I joined Whippany lodge, in this county, about thirteen years ago, and took the first three degrees of masonry, and continued to visit the lodge about five years—then I silently withdrew, and have since had no fellowship with masonry.

My reasons for thus forsaking the lodge, and why I feel it my duty publicly, and forever to renounce the order of Freemasonry, are as follows, viz:

That the principles of masonry inculcate neither religion, morality, truth, nor justice, but the contrary of all these, which I have both experienced and witnessed. While I continued a lodge-going member, a mason told me he did not believe there was any better religion than masonry. This alarmed me; and I began to look at the institution with a more jealous eye. Since that time, I have seen and felt its pernicious influence in many ways, some of which I will mention.

I have seen a grand jury selected by a masonic sheriff, with an express view to prevent an indictment against a brother mason, and was told by the foreman of that jury, that had it not been the case of a brother that was coming before them, *he* should not have been there. I have also seen a mason brought up to be tried on an indictment, and observed him make the masonic signal of distress, and another sign to the jury, which latter sign of the hand drawn across the throat, two of the jurors answered ; and these same jurors when out, refused to convict on a clear case of guilt. I have also seen masonic signs exchanged between the bar and bench. I have also seen its influence in the choice of public officers, having heard it mentioned in the lodge that such a brother was to be run for assembly man, by which I understood that we (the brethren) were to support him, and he was run and elected. I have seen three editions of Morgan's Illustrations of Masonry ; and to guard the public against deception in so important a matter, I feel it my duty to state that the first one is a true and genuine exposition of masonry as I was taught it in the lodge ; whereas, the two last have been altered ; the one in many particulars, and the other in pass words and in changing the signs, no doubt to deceive the people. For these reasons, and many more that I could name, I consider masonry as a corrupt and awfully wicked system, and unfit for the society of Christians or honest men ; and considering the pretensions it makes of republicanism, charity, the handmaid of religion, &c. I view it as one of the greatest impositions ever practised upon mankind, that of Mahomet not excepted. I am perfectly satisfied from what I have seen, that had the masons the reins of power in their hands, or in the hands of men whom they could, as they say, "MANAGE," we should soon be reduced to a state of "hewers of wood and drawers of water," they our "Grand Masters, Most Worshipful's," &c. and we *the people their* SLAVES. I would here forewarn all persons, especially the youth, from entering the lodge to find the secrets of masonry, or any thing good; they will only find a scene of folly and wickedness, and purchase this at the expense of both money and credit.

Of this latter class, I have known individuals to enter the lodge with correct morals and steady habits; and in a few years become dissipated and worthless members of society. Such is its corrupt and corrupting influence.

If such persons wish to know the true secrets of masonry, and will take the trouble to call on me, I will communicate to them as far as I have gone in this "mystery of iniquity," "without money and without price."

As a member, therefore, of the church of Christ, and of civil society, I do hereby publicly, "solemnly, and sincerely," renounce Freemasonry forever, and can, and will hold myself no longer bound by its horrible and bloody oaths.

JOHN R. MULFORD.

Genungtown, Chatham Township, Morris Co. N. J. July 31, 1828.

Renunciation of Benjamin W. Weeden.

From the Vermont Luminary.

Mr. Editor,—Permit me, through the medium of your useful paper, to state to the world, that I hereby renounce all connexion with the institution of Speculative Freemasonry. Believing it to be an institution fraught with wickedness, and dangerous to the liberty of our country.

I would further state, that the book called Morgan's Illustrations of Masonry, and the disclosures of the Le Roy Convention, as far as the seventh degree of masonry, are as near correct as any mason could write them.

BENJAMIN W. WEEDEN,
Once a Royal Arch Mason.

Hartland, Vt. March 18, 1829.

Renunciation of Rev. Levi Chase, of Fall River, Mass.

I have belonged to the institution of Freemasonry since the year 1815. Having been at first infatuated with its formal parade of sanctity and alluring show, I proceeded from step to step until I had taken the three first degrees, under the false impression that its preposterous claim to divine origin was well founded. But the conduct in the lodge to which I belonged, convinced me that its ceremonies were but solemn mockery and contemptible trifling—which induced me to desert the cause, and for seven years I did not attend a lodge. I was then informed by members of the fraternity, that there was not that light in the lower degrees which was naturally expected; but in the higher degrees my expectations would be fully realized. Placing entire confidence in their persuasive words, I then united with Freemasons in Warren, R. I. where I took the degree of *Mark Master*, together with the honorary degrees of *Past Master* and *Most Excellent Master*,—and I do now say and affirm, that the secrets and oaths of the first three degrees, as published by Capt. William Morgan, in his "Illustrations of Masonry," are true,—and I believe that his life has been taken by masons for thus developing their secrets; and as this outrage upon humanity as well as law, flowed necessarily from the obligations and principles of the institution, every genuine mason must approve of it and use his influence to screen the perpetrators from offended justice. I have likewise examined the degrees of Mark Master, Past Master, and Most Excellent Master, as published to the world by a Convention of seceding masons held at Le Roy, Genesee county, N. Y. and find them to be correct—the same as were conferred on me. I now offer the following reasons for seceding from masons:

1st. I consider the institution of Freemasonry, by claiming to be divinely instituted, places itself in direct hostility to the Church of Christ, inasmuch as the name of the Lord and Saviour Jesus Christ is not named in the first six degrees;—and the apostle Paul says, "that at the name of Jesus every knee should bow, of things in heaven, and things in earth, and things under the earth; and that every tongue should confess that Jesus Christ is Lord, to the glory of God the Father."

2d. That the institution of Freemasonry, in requiring members at their admission to the several degrees to take an oath, requires them to swear profanely; and all who take these oaths are guilty of profane swearing, inasmuch as the masonic fraternity have no right whatever to administer an oath, according to the laws of God or man, to a candidate at his admission to the different degrees of masonry.

The question has been asked by masons, who wish to asperse the characters of those who have renounced masonry, "Why did not they renounce it before?" For one, I will give them the reason why I did not. The masonic oaths locked my tongue in silence—death, in all its horrid shapes and frightful forms, stared me in the face—I considered the oaths binding. But the scene has changed—a new era has commenced—the masonic spell is broken—the mystic tie is dissolved, and many who have long groaned under the pressure of masonic oaths and anathemas, have emerged from their prison. Yes, dear Christian brethren, the fatal blow that took the life of Capt. William Morgan, has rent the masonic veil from top to bottom, and now, I believe that God, in His providence, is opening the way for an entire separation between His church and the masonic institution.

I have not written the above on account of any ill will against the masonic fraternity, but from pure motives, with a desire it might be to the declarative glory of God and the good of mankind.

LEVI CHASE.

Fall River, Jan. 23, 1829.

Letter addressed to the Editor of the Free Press, Boston, by John Whittlesey, of New-Salem, Conn.

Mr. Editor,—Sir, The philanthropic spirit which impels you forward, in the sacred cause in which you are engaged, carries its own reward with it, viz. that of an approving *conscience*. The astonishing spread of light, (emanating from God, through the medium of the *free presses* of our country,) among the inhabitants of Massachusetts and the adjoining States, and the effect produced thereby, sounds an alarm among the brothers of the craft not to be misunderstood; and although they, in their agitation, may cry out with as much vehemence as the men of Ephesus did at the preaching of Paul, when they thought their craft in danger, and raise as great an outcry against every editor of a free press, and honest seceding masons, as was done against the good apostle, be assured that the same power that rescued him is now exerted for their deliverance, and the downfall of this modern goddess Diana, whom all the craft worship. Yes, Mr. Editor, the hand of God is visible in all this, and ere long the mighty edifice, *professedly* erected by GOD himself, and patronized by the holy St. John, will crumble to the dust, and in the language of the Revelator, "*The voice of harpers, and musicians, and of pipes, and trumpets, shall be heard no more at all in thee, and no craftsman of whatsoever craft he be, shall be found any more in thee, and the light of a candle shall shine no more at all in thee, for by thy* SORCERIES *were all nations deceived*,"—for in thee is found the BLOOD of MORGAN—and although its votaries may cast dust on their heads in their phrenzy, and weep and wail, and cry, alas! alas! at the downfall of their pretended ancient and honorable institution, it will appear in all its naked deformity; dismantled of its tinselled trappings; and instead of "*Holiness to the Lord*" being written on the breast plate, MYSTERY, BABYLON, will be visible; and I would, in the language of inspiration, call upon all good men, and especially all ministers of the gospel, and say, "come out of her my people that ye be not partakers of her plagues." Such men can have no excuse for adhering to the "order" at the present time; it is too late to pretend that all the secrets and ceremonies of masonry are not before the world, as disclosed by William Morgan, and the Le Roy Convention. No good man can consistently deny, but that they are essentially correct, and if so, the oath makes life the forfeit for the *least* transgression, when nothing is more clear than that no man has a right thus to barter away the life given to him of GOD; we are to preserve our own lives, and those of others. The candidate before receiving his oath is assured, that it shall not infringe on his civil or religious liberty: but how manifest it is that such an oath does infringe on both; hence it is not binding, nor will it answer for Christians, and especially for Christian ministers, barely to omit attending the lodges, while they remain silent on this interesting subject, and lend their names to the fraternity as members in regular standing, without a renunciation; this is the very ground which masons and Satan would have them take, and while they pretend to be neutral, they secretly support the masonic cause. But, if the institution be good, why refuse to talk about it, or to attend the lodges? If wicked, why not renounce it? Are they afraid of suffering and of having the displeasure of the fraternity let loose upon them?—of having their *character traduced*, their *business deranged*, &c. Well, he that will seek to save his life, may be sure to lose it, agreeable to scripture—all who will live godly in Christ Jesus may expect to suffer persecution—and, I think, Mr. Editor, the time is not far distant, when this mighty evil, this foe to God and man, will be removed from the church, and she will come up from the wilderness leaning on her beloved; and a virtuous people will drive this would-be tyrant from this soil of liberty. May your efforts, my dear sir, for the good of mankind, be blest; and your truly valuable paper long continue with an extensive patronage, when those opposed to liberty shall be lost in forgetfulness.

I remain, dear sir,

Yours very respectfully,

JOHN WHITTLESEY.

Renunciation of Gen. Henry Sewall, communicated in a letter to a Clergyman of his acquaintance in New-Hampshire.*

AUGUSTA, ME. JAN. 7, 1830.

REV. AND DEAR SIR,—In compliance with your reasonable request, by letter of the 11th ult. I transmit you a sketch of my former career in *masonry*, with my " present views of its moral and religious character, and legitimate bearing on civil and religious institutions," together with my abdication of the *order*. Its disposal is confided to the exercise of your discretion.

Yours in the bonds of Christian affection, H. S.

I was initiated an *entered apprentice* to the masonic rites in October, 1777, at Albany, soon after the capture of Burgoyne, being then an officer in the American army. I was induced to this measure by the belief that I should fare better in case I should be made a prisoner, and by the advice and recommendation of a number of masonic comrades in arms, who assured me that it was a valuable and scientific institution. That part of the army to which I belonged being speedily ordered to join Gen. Washington in the neighborhood of Philadelphia, I of course passed the winter at Valley Forge, and the following summer with the main army then concentrated in the State of New York, and which in the succeeding autumn hovered round West Point for winter quarters in the Highlands, awaiting the movements of the enemy until the opening of the campaign in 1779. During all this period the fluctuating state of the army afforded me no leisure or facilities for making any advances in masonry. In August, 1779, after *carrying the hod* nearly two years, I was passed to the degree of *fellow craft* at West Point in a lodge which I understood then existed in the Connecticut line of the army. In September following I was raised in the same lodge to the *sublime degree*, as it is pompously called, of *master mason*. None of the mystic ceremonies unveiled in the previous degrees afforded me much satisfaction,† but

* The gentleman to whom he communicated his renunciation writes as follows :—" Gen. H. Sewall was an early companion of Washington, and continued with the army until the war was closed. He has been much in public life, and is known extensively. He is a man of superior talents, a consistent Christian and deacon in the church. And he is now ready to leave the beloved country for which he fought, and as we trust, to enter into the joy of his Lord. His views of speculative masonry have not been formed under the excitement of the moment; but appear to have been produced by the Spirit of God, when operating powerfully upon his mind, to have been strengthened by long observation, and confirmed by recent disclosures. Such a man's views ought to have weight; and they will have weight, where prejudice does not triumph over reason. The testimony of such a man must be conclusive; and those, that will not believe it, would not be persuaded though one rose from the dead.

† It is worth notice, that although the *first* degree is professedly *founded* on facts gleaned from the building of Solomon's temple; the *second* degree derives its *pass-word* from a fact which occurred in the days of the Judges [ch. xii. 6.] more than 100 years before. Perhaps the Craft may attempt to reconcile this anachronism by telling us that Jephthah was a *mason*.

those pertaining to this *sublime* degree, and particularly the stale, inconsistent tradition of the murder of master Hiram Abiff and its attendant peculiarities, were too fabulous to obtain my credence. Indeed the personation of Hiram in the circumstances of his burial, and the fictitious search for his grave and for the murderers, actually had the appearance of *solemn farce*. And on the next day after my *sublime elevation*, I told my brethren that I had been disappointed. I did not find that scientific intelligence which they had encouraged me to anticipate. They were somewhat alarmed at my remarks, and endeavored to quiet me by assurances that I should be more reconciled by attending the meetings and lectures of the lodge. By their persuasions, admonitions and promises, they quieted me so far that I accepted an appointment of Secretary in the Washington Travelling Lodge, which was constituted in the army about this time, and continued my connexion with it until the peace took place in 1783. The frequent meetings of the lodge which I attended during this period, were merely convivial, serving no other purpose than to mitigate in some degree the privations, and beguile the cares and fatigues of the soldier's life. I had seen among the hieroglyphics of the lodge, the figure of the 47th problem in Euclid, but I never heard it referred to; nor did I hear it taught in any lesson or lecture, that "*the sum of the squares of the legs* of this triangle *was equal to the square of the hypotenuse*;" or indeed the solution of any other problem whatever. The third degree of masonry was at that time considered its ne plus ultra. Of the higher degrees I have no knowledge except from the late printed disclosures, the authenticity of which I have no reason to doubt. Among them every degree, like the dark "*chambers of imagery*" revealed to Ezekiel, contains "*greater and greater abominations*"!

On retiring from the army I settled on the Kennebec, which was then a new country, and of course I was out of the sphere of masonry, and for a time thought little more of the subject. It was not long however, before my mind was powerfully drawn to the subject of religion; and by a studious and prayerful examination of the "more sure word of prophecy," that true "light which shines in a dark place," I trust I was led by the influence of this perfect rule of faith and practice, during the year 1784, to view speculative masonry in a shape still more deformed. I now considered it widely variant from the principles and radically hostile to the nature of the gospel. Its charity appeared to be *selfishness*, because restricted to its own members. Its religion *Deism*, because entirely devoid of the gospel. Its bold assumption of the holy Bible, unnatural and preposterous. Its application of selected texts, irreverent and profane. Its terms of acceptance with God, a due performance of masonic duties. Its heaven, a celestial grand lodge of worthy masons! Its history appeared fabulous—its claims to antiquity unsustainable—its titles fulsome—its rites barbarous and absurd—its oaths extra-judicial, unlawfully imposed and blindly taken—repugnant to the prior and paramount obligations resting on all members of the civil compact, but especially as subjects of the divine government; and the penal sanctions annexed, horrid and impious! These my sober views of masonry have been strengthened by an extended course of observation, matured by hoary age, and satisfactorily illustrated by the remarkable developements of the day. From the time last mentioned, a period of nearly half a century, I have scrupulously avoided all connexion and withheld all fellowship with that institution, and have actually withdrawn from all lodge meetings, though frequently and pressingly invited to attend. And in accordance with my avowed belief, as above expressed, I now publicly and deliberately declare myself *free from all masonic obligations, which I verily believe never had or could have any binding force.* I consider all *secret societies* in a free government, of dangerous tendency, their very structure endowing them with a capacity for doing more evil than good. But the vail which covered the mystic rites of masonry is lifted. The grand secrets are out; and all the brotherhood, if united, would find it a difficult task to put them in again. Speculative masonry must become extinct; and I care not how soon. It has never been of any real benefit to civil society. It secures nothing to benevolent objects, or any other good purpose, which Christian obligations do not secure from higher motives. Religion needs not for its support, "*the staff of this bruised reed,*" which will only *pierce its hand.*

HENRY SEWALL.

Renunciation of Col. John Hoar.

COLONEL HOAR, author of the following renunciation, is well known to be a gentleman of good report, and he stands fair before the public. He long ago expressed to some of his friends the trouble and trials Freemasonry had brought upon his mind. Uniting with Freemasons he considers one of the greatest errors of his life. The institution he considers a high-handed piece of wickedness and abomination before Heaven, affording no peace, safety or security to those who labor to support it. He has no desire to hurt the feelings of any of his masonic brethren; he would rather honor and respect them, but the institution which they labor to support he believes to be a useless, worthless, wicked thing, (it is so to them,) a device of wicked men, inconsistent with the Christian religion, and of immoral and irreligious tendency.—*Free Press.*

TO THE PUBLIC.

The time is come when a strict inquiry into the principles and practices of Freemasonry is instituted, and many of the brotherhood who heretofore thought but little of either, are beginning to examine the subject in the light of Divine Truth, and the more they examine the more are they dissatisfied with the institution.

This in a good measure is the case with myself; and I feel a sacred obligation resting upon me as accountable to that Being, who sways the sceptre of Universal Dominion, and whose omniscient eye penetrates the abodes of darkness, and takes cognizance of the most hidden transactions, to renounce my standing in the *masonic fraternity*. My eyes have been opened to see the labyrinth of folly and guilt into which the institution is decoying men. My better judgment has been shocked, and my feelings greatly excited while hearing men of abilities, men on whom nature had lavished her richest gifts, express a belief that *masonry* would carry them to HEAVEN.

To assist in riveting still closer the chains of a most awful delusion, by encouraging and supporting the institution, or to remain silent as the grave on the subject, will, I am persuaded, call down the displeasure of Heaven upon me; the blood of souls will be required at my hand. Therefore I consider it an imperious duty to withdraw immediately and entirely from the institution, and to exhort all my Christian brethren who belong to the fraternity, to examine the subject candidly and prayerfully, and if they find they are wronging their fellow men by encouraging them in delusion, and their own souls by feeding on husks; if they find they are wounding the feelings of their Christian brethren by their walk and conversation, to come out from masonry, without delay, and be separate. What concord hath Christ with Belial? What communion hath light with darkness, and what part hath he that believeth, with an infidel?

To masons at large I would say, if you draw from the fountain of masonry your greatest hope and consolation, it will certainly fail you at the giving up of the ghost. Therefore flee to the ark of safety and take refuge in the blood of the everlasting covenant.

JOHN HOAR,
Member of the Church in Monson.

Extract from the Renunciation of Col. H. C. Witherill, of Hartford.

Masons say in defence of their institution, that it is a good one, but like all others, it has been disgraced by bad members, and that if *all would live up to their obligations* it would be an honorable and useful institution. *But nothing can be more erroneous than this assertion. Community has been saved from the worst of evils*, FROM THE VERY FACT, *that masons do not at all times live up to their obligations; if they should, the institution would be* STILL MORE DANGEROUS *than it actually is*—a volume could not contain all the evils which it would produce;—our prisons would be liable at all times to be beset by mobs, and the guilty felon would be set at liberty—prisoners at the bar would have a right to look to Jurors for relief—pirates on the high seas would claim their life and liberty; and the midnight robber and murderer would fly to masonry as to to the horns of an altar for protection.

Renunciation of Lieutenant Governor Leland.

From the Anti-Masonic Christian Herald.

The Rev. Aaron Leland, late Lt. Governor of Vermont, and formerly Deputy Grand Master of the Grand Lodge of that State, recently renounced masonry before the Baptist Holland Purchase Association, New York.

In a report of the committee on the subject, of which he was a member, he remarked, that he had been led by a vain curiosity to unite with the lodge, and had been led on from step to step to the Royal Arch degree—had been master of a lodge for five years—had been Deputy Grand Master of the Grand Lodge of the State of Vermont, and had left the institution about nine or ten years ago. He stated that the first objection which presented itself to his mind, was the practice of *praying for the soul of a brother mason after he had been dead two, three, and sometimes four days*—that he persisted in the practice for a short season to the injury of his conscience—that it was a Romish custom, and he never would preach at the burial of a mason when masonic forms and customs were attended to—that he never would preach to a lodge of masons as *such*, and that he was ashamed that he had ever participated in the principles and practices of the institution.

Important Renunciations.

We the undersigned, having formerly associated with Freemasons, deem it our duty, without intending to increase excitement, or to wound the feelings of our masonic brethren, publicly to declare, that the system of Freemasonry is, in our judgment, of a tendency on the whole pernicious to the moral habits, and dangerous to the civil and religious institutions of our country.

LEONARD BLEECKER, *New York.*
LEWIS TAPPAN, "
Rev. MATTHEW L. R. PERRINE, D. D.
Auburn Theological Seminary.
Rev. JOEL PARKER, *Rochester, N. Y.*
Rev. CHAUNCEY EDDY, *Penn Yann, N. Y.*
HENRY BRADLEY, Esq. "
LEANDER REDDY, "
SAMUEL BUCKINGHAM, "
THOMAS MARBLE, *Arcadia, N. Y.*
WILLIAM WINDFIELD, "
FRANCIS BATES, "
Rev. JARED REID, *Reading, Mass.*
Rev. LYMAN CASE, *Coventry, Vt.*

Renunciation of Rev. Henry G. Ludlow, Pastor of Spring street Presbyterian Church, New York.

To the Editor of the Anti-masonic Beacon.

Mr. Editor,—You may add my name to those of Mr. Bleecker, and others, which appeared in your paper of the 24th January. My reasons for subscribing this formula, are—

1. A full conviction of its truth.

2. As we ought to love our neighbors as ourselves, we ought not to be silent, when by speaking we may prevent their injury. I can hardly think that any candid and intelligent master mason can seriously assert that masonry should be kept up. For my own part I have ever been disgusted with its nonsensical ceremonies, and ashamed of myself for submitting to them. Besides this, it is throwing away money—and time, which is more valuable than money. As speaking may prevent such a sacrifice, I think it my duty to speak.

3. I do not wish my name used to promote the interests of an institution, the character of which I think justly described in the formula. I have not entered a lodge these eight years to my knowledge.

Yours, &c.

H. G. LUDLOW.

January 31, 1829.

Renunciation of Erastus Bates.

From the Free Press.

Mr. Editor,—Understanding you are ready to publish any thing you may judge proper to expose and destroy the great and dangerous evil of Speculative Freemasonry, I beg you would help me to unburden my conscience, which has for a long time goaded me on the subject, and destroyed my comfort and peace of mind. I am unaccustomed to write for the public eye; but I hope to tell my story in a way that you can understand me.

I am a professed, and, I hope, a real follower of the Lord Jesus Christ. I have a good and regular standing in his church, and so far as I know, am kindly regarded by my Christian brethren. But in an evil and *unguarded hour*, and *through a vain curiosity, and the flattering persuasions of masons, who* HIGHLY EXTOLLED THE INSTITUTION, *and held up to my view the prospect of* GREAT ADVANTAGES to be derived from it, I was induced to offer myself as a candidate for admission to the *Olive Branch* lodge in *Sutton*, where, about four years ago, I was initiated as an entered apprentice, passed to the degree of a fellow craft, and soon after raised to what is *foolishly* called 'the sublime degree of a master mason.' Upon my first entering a lodge-room I was sorely disappointed: instead of finding something worthy the dignity of a rational and immortal being, I found myself degraded and debased in the extreme, and reduced to a condition, which it seems no person would choose to be in. I was *stripped of my common apparel, blindfolded*, and with a *rope*, masonically called a cable-tow, about my neck, was led about the room, as a blind animal, to be gazed and laughed at by all present. This I was told was what all the ancient and honorable before me had submitted to, and was necessary to enter the sublime temple of masonry, erected by Solomon, and dedicated to the holy order of St. John. Thought I to myself, if Solomon and John had any thing to do with such business, their character for wisdom and goodness must greatly *suffer!* But what was the most impious and abominable part of the whole transaction, I consented to take an oath or obligation, with the holy name of God annexed, and that before I knew any thing what it contained; which, in its plain, common-sense meaning, deprived me of my freedom and made me the *slave of the whole fraternity*, and *bound me to commit any crime, however heinous, if only commanded by a brother or superior.* I was, indeed, previously told by the most worshipful master that the oath would contain nothing which should interfere with my religion or politics. But in this I was most grossly deceived; for no sooner had I time for reflection than I perceived that it interfered with both, and bound me under the most horrid penalty of having my *throat cut from ear to ear* and *my tongue torn out by the roots*, to violate all my obligations to my God and my country, if it were the will of a brother or a lodge I should do so, and even to conceal the crimes of a brother mason, whatever they might be. I may not exactly remember *all* the parts and points of the obligation imposed upon me, but I do distinctly remember that I was sworn to the most profound secrecy respecting masonry—that I would conform to all the by-laws of the lodge without knowing what those laws were—that I would obey all signs, summonses and tokens, handed, sent, or *thrown* to me by a brother mason, or by a lodge—that I would keep a brother's secrets when given to me as such, as closely in my breast as in his own, murder and treason excepted, and these left to my own discretion—that I would go on a brother's errand, when required, *barefoot and bareheaded*, if within the length of my cable-tow—that I would apprise him of all approaching danger, if in my power, and relieve him if possible of all his distresses, upon seeing the grand hailing sign, or hearing the word—that I would not *violate the chastity of a brother mason's female relations*, KNOWING them to be such, &c. &c. A greater mass of absurdity and wickedness I never heard put together. Yet being then very ignorant of the nature and obligation of oaths, I felt myself bound to keep them, though they were galling, and a snare to my conscience. At length it pleased God to open my eyes to see their abominable nature, and to set me free from this iron yoke of bondage—this worse than Egyptian slavery. And I now bless his name, that he has enabled me to break those wicked bonds asunder, and to breathe the pure air of civil and religious freedom. I now *consider those horrid oaths of no force neither in honor, morality, nor religion*, and that they had infinitely better be *broken* than *kept.* They are required of no law of God or man, and of course it can be no man's duty to take them. They are unlawfully administered and taken. They are deceptive in their nature, and awfully dangerous to the community; and if observed in their true letter and spirit, without any equivocation or evasion of mind, they expose a person to the commission and concealment of the most *abominable crimes, perjury,* REBELLION, and even MURDER, when *required* by a *brother.* If regarded as binding, they must of necessity clash with every civil and religious obligation, and destroy truth and confidence among men. I rejoice exceedingly that I am delivered from among them. They have been an iron yoke upon my conscience and conduct, and I pray God to pardon my rashness and folly in ever submitting to take them upon me. The sin lies in taking such oaths, and not in breaking them; and I am persuaded that no rational man would *ever take them upon him, if he knew beforehand what they were,* and to what they would lead him.

It is not my wish to injure the feelings of any of my former brethren by any thing I have said or done, nor do I think I have given them any just occasion of offence. It is not masons but *masonry* to which I am opposed, and while I highly respect many of the fraternity as honorable and good men, and with charitable feelings would leave them all, it is the deceitful and dangerous *system of masonry I abhor,* and *hereby* FOREVER RENOUNCE. In doing this I expect to meet the reproaches and slanders of my former brethren, it being in full accordance with their obligations: and had I not been restrained by *fear of personal injury,* I should have renounced my connexion with them long ago. If masonic oaths are binding on the conscience, I am fully convinced, that every seceder has good reason to fear for his safety. I do not wonder at the rising spirit of the community against this dark and dangerous institution; their dearest rights and interests are in jeopardy: but I do wonder, and am truly astonished why Christian brethren, and especially *Christian ministers* do not open their eyes to the light which now shines into the caverns of that secret abomination, and renounce all connexion and fellowship with it; and while I would adopt the language of the good old patriarch, and say, 'O my soul, come not thou into their secret; unto their assembly, mine honor, be not thou united!' I would affectionately *warn all my uninitiated Christian brethren, and all* YOUNG MEN, as they value the favor of God, and peace in their own minds, to keep themselves aloof from all masonic lodges, and not enter into those midnight assemblies, where nothing but darkness reigns; but avoid them, pass not by them, turn from them and pass away. '*Blessed is the man that walketh not in the counsel of the ungodly, nor standeth in the way of sinners, nor sitteth in the seat of the scornful.*'

ERASTUS BATES.

Millbury, Mass. Dec. 1829.

Renunciations at the Connecticut State Convention.

In the discharge of what we conceive to be a pressing duty, we shall not attempt to offer any speculations respecting the origin or early design of the institution of Freemasonry, of which we have long been members. Nor would we indulge in any animadversions against the order to wound the feelings of any man. But we have a duty to perform respecting it, which we cannot neglect. For, in it, we do now most sincerely believe, the safety and future weal of our country are deeply concerned. By doing this duty we may incur, and perhaps we ought, all things considered, to expect to incur, the displeasure and reproach of some, and we may also wound the feelings of others. If we do, the fault, we are confident, will not be ours. We are prepared most seriously and honestly to say that, from what we know of the principles, ceremonies, and obligations of masonry, or in other words, its mysteries, we believe it calculated to do no good, and capable of doing great mischief. There is nothing in it to interest men of sense, when such men look at it, without bias, just as it is.

As a *secret society*, we think it should no longer be sustained in this republic, but should be discountenanced by every man who is a friend to equal rights, and an impartial administration of justice, as well as to sound morals and pure religion. We therefore, with a sincere wish to promote the best interests of our country, and of mankind generally, do in this public manner, make these our declarations respecting the masonic institution, affirming that the grand *secrets* of the order are no longer *secrets*, and withdrawing ourselves forever from all connexion and fellowship with it.

JASPER BIDWELL,	3	degrees.	*Canton.*
ELISHA SUGDEN,	3	do.	*Canton.*
NORMAN BIDWELL,	3	do.	*Canton.*
WM. H. HALLOCK,	3	do.	*Canton.*
RUFUS TULLER,	2	do.	*Canton.*
WILLIAM TAYLOR,	3	do.	*Barkhamsted.*
CALVIN BARBER,	4	do.	*Simsbury.*

Renunciation of Jesse Smith.

To all Freemen, and especially those whom Christ hath made Free.

Some years since I joined Speculative Freemasonry, and have taken four degrees. The abduction of Capt. William Morgan induced me to attempt an investigation of the oaths and ceremonies and compare them with the word of God—and in obedience to his command, I do believe the whole to be a *device of Satan—conceived, born, and nursed in darkness*—and in obedience to God's command, I do hereby separate myself and renounce all connexion with said institution, and beseech the followers of the blessed Lamb, to come out of her, that they receive not of her plagues.

JESSE SMITH,

A seceding Mark Master Mason.

Addison, County of Addison, State of Vt. Feb. 2, 1829.

The Spirit of Masonry.

Extract from a Sermon preached at Sherburne, N. Y. by Rev. David Kendall.

It is easy to see that the spirit of the masonic institution is such, and its plans so extensive, that the kingdom of Prince Immanuel, and the kingdom of prince Hiram Abiff cannot be erected and stand together on the earth. Each of these claim the whole earth for a possession. The King of Zion says, " the meek shall inherit the earth, and delight themselves in the abundance of peace; and the wicked shall be cut off. Those mine enemies that would not that I should rule over them, bring hither, and slay them before me." But prince Abiff, on the contrary, claims the whole earth for his " worthy and well qualified " subjects; and requires them to *avenge* his death on all enemies, traitors and cowans, when *the time is fulfilled.*

Neither can the religion of both these High Priests stand together on the earth, any more than their kingly reign. For what is *light* to the one, is *darkness* to the other; what is duty in one, is crime in the other; what is holy truth to the one, is falsehood and lies to the other; what is sanctum sanctorum to the one, is abomination and desolation to the other: inasmuch as whichever of these shall attain to its meridian glory and splendor, it will throw the other into the total darkness of midnight. And whichever of these shall rise and spread to the extent of its intended sublime and sovereign dominion, it will crush the other and grind it to powder, and scatter it like chaff driven before the winds, that no place may be found for it any more forever.

Our subject shows, that *now it is high time* for all, and for every one, to choose decidedly whom they will serve. If the Lord is God, serve him; but if Baal be God, then serve him.

The two—Prince Immanuel and prince Abiff, or Christianity and Masonry—we have found, on scripture trial, to be so totally different, and their claims and requirements so entirely opposite the one to the other, that it is impossible to be a true and faithful servant to both. Either you must love the one and hate the other; or cleave to one and despise the other. For what concord hath Christ with Belial, or what fellowship hath light with darkness, or what agreement hath the temple of God with idols! Nay, ye cannot serve God and Mammon.

As for myself, I have already made up my choice, and now declare, publicly and solemnly, for Prince Immanuel and his cause: and renounce all allegiance and fellowship with prince Hiram Abiff and the masonic institution. Once indeed, by fair words and smooth speeches, I was caught in his snare, and led cable-towed and blindfold in his path of *freedom*, till I had got a triple yoke of bondage upon my neck. This proving too heavy to bear, I retraced my steps silently, before any alarm was given or any cry of bondage, or of immolated victims, had sounded in our borders.

And now as a warning to others to flee out of Babylon, and escape for their lives to the mountain of Zion, I publish my full conviction, that there can be no fellowship between the kingdom of Christ and the kingdom of masonry.—Consequently that no one can be a worthy and well qualified subject of both these kingdoms at the same time. Let every one therefore be fully persuaded in his own mind which he will serve. And when he has made up his choice for either, let him renounce all connexion and fellowship with the other; because it is impossible in this case for any man to serve two masters. From the best authority we learn that the mixed system of *iron* and *clay* shall be ground to powder, when the mighty mystical image of the beast is broken in pieces, and swept away with the besom of destruction.

Extract from the Renunciation of Artemas Kennedy, of Milton, Mass.

I am impelled on examination, to acknowledge that Freemasonry, in its nature and tendency, is hostile not only to our religion, but to the civil institutions of our country—to the regular and equitable administrations of justice, and to the general diffusion of social happiness.

I solemnly declare the oaths, obligations and principles of masonry, to the tenth degree, to be all faithfully and truly delineated by Morgan and the Le Roy Convention, on which account I now consider myself as breaking no masonic obligation, and only assenting to a truth already told and openly published to the world by a thousand witnesses. My greatest astonishment, at present, is, that so many of the order expose their veracity to such strong suspicion, in denying the truth of those late disclosures, and the probable murder of Morgan. His murder is in such strict accordance with masonic principles, that I have been lately told by a member of Christ's church, in this county, *that he hoped Morgan was murdered, and that if he was, he was rightly served.* Not being able to subscribe to, or approve of such principles myself, I have suffered lately, injury and persecution, and have been threatened this day, by a Royal Arch mason, from a great distance, and whom I never before saw, *that he would be one of four to despatch me.* Thus convinced and thus instigated, I feel it a conscientious duty, to disown all future connexion with such society and such principles. The call to this duty is so loud, that it breaks the slumbers of the night; it visits me at the table; it arrests the progress of my daily employment; and will, if not duly regarded, pursue me to the dark recesses of my tomb! I obey the call, break the bond, and *declare myself free of masonic thraldom*, and in so doing, I feel nobler freedom, I behold a more serene and purer light, than ever the *mystic order* presented to my unblinded eyes.

ARTEMAS KENNEDY.

MASONIC OBLIGATIONS UNLAWFUL,

As proved in a Court of Justice on Empannelling the Jury at the Trial of Elihu Mather for a Conspiracy to Kidnap William Morgan, at the Orleans County Court, Nov. 11, 1829.

His Honor Judge Gardiner presiding.

Wednesday, Nov. 11, 1829.—The Hon. John C. Spencer, Special Counsel for the people, called on the trial of ELIHU MATHER, who stood indicted for a conspiracy to kidnap WILLIAM MORGAN.

Gen. V. Mathews, Wm. H. Adams, Esq. and Daniel D. Barnard, Esq. were counsel for the defendant.

Mr. Spencer was assisted by J. B. Coles, Esq. in behalf of the people.

Upon calling the jurors, some conversation took place between the respective counsel upon the *manner* of ascertaining whether the jurors were unbiassed. The counsel for the defendant proposed to put questions to jurors as they were drawn, and if the answers were not satisfactory, then reserve their right to challenge. To this Mr. Spencer objected, and offered to refer the examination of the jurors to the court. Judge Gardiner remarked, that questions would probably arise of considerable importance, and suggested the propriety of pursuing the legal course, which was adopted.

The clerk then proceeded to draw the jury. *William Loomis* and *Simeon Gilding*, were drawn from the panel of petit jurors, and being found acceptable to both parties, were appointed Triers, by the court.

Jonathan French was challenged by the defendant's counsel, and upon being sworn, said he had formed no opinion upon the question at issue. He had, he said, no bias against the defendant. Triers decided that Mr. F. was impartial, and he was sworn as a juror.

Amos Cliff was drawn and challenged by the defendant's counsel. Upon being sworn, said he *had* formed an opinion. He was rejected.

John Follett was challenged by defendant's counsel. Upon being sworn, he said he did not know that he had formed or expressed an opinion. Had heard something about the Morgan business, but had read very little upon the subject. Had no bias or prejudice. The challenge was withdrawn.

Charles Kelly challenged by the defendant's counsel, and sworn. Has not heard much said about Mather, and has formed no opinion against him. Thinks he has not said that the whole fraternity were guilty of the murder of Morgan. The challenge was waived.

Samuel Church was challenged. Seymour Murdock was sworn as a witness. He said he had heard Church say that Mather ought to be punished for the Morgan business. He said that those who drove the carriage ought to be punished. He had heard Mr. Church say this several times. Mr. C. was then sworn. He said he had often said that the *guilty* ought to be punished, but don't recollect of having named Mather. The triers, after a short consultation, rejected Mr. Church.

Chauncey Hood was challenged by the defendant's counsel. Elbridge Farewell testified that he had heard Mr. Hood say, that Elihu Mather had a hand in it. Hood was rejected.

Epaphras Pennel challenged. Zimri Perrigo testified, that he had heard Pennel say that he thought Mather was concerned in carrying off Morgan. Mr. P. sworn; testified that he had no recollection of saying that Mather was *positively* guilty. Had said that if the circumstances related about M. were true, he must be guilty. Had not made up a positive opinion. Was rejected.

Luther St. John challenged and sworn. Had formed a *qualified* opinion. If reports were *true*, he considered Mather guilty—if not true, not guilty. His opinion would be governed entirely by the testimony. Had no bias or prejudice against the accused. Had heard and read much about the abduction of Morgan.

Mr. Spencer contended that Mr. St. John was, in the eye of the law, a competent juror. It would be impossible, he said, to find, in the county of Orleans, an intelligent man who did not believe Mather guilty, if the circumstances alleged against him should be proved to be true. Mr. Adams insisted that Mr. St. John, having formed a qualified opinion, could not be impartial, and therefore urged his rejection. The triers, after a short consultation, decided that Mr. St. John "*is indifferent.*"

D. Reed challenged and sworn. Thinks he has expressed an opinion that Mather was concerned in the Morgan business. Rejected.

Wm. Bullard, upon being drawn, said he had formed an opinion, and was excused.

Robert Anderson, next drawn. Mr. Spencer challenged this juror on the ground that he was a member of the society of Freemasons, and of the degree of Royal Arch. Gen. Mathews demanded that the cause of challenge should be reduced to writing, which having been done, Gen. Mathews and Mr. Barnard denied that the cause stated was a legal ground of challenge. Mr. Spencer then produced his authorities. It was laid down in Archbold, among other causes for principal challenge, that where a juror "*belonged to the same Society or Corporation*" with a party, he was an incompetent juror. The court remarked that the term society, in the sense which it was used by Archbold, had reference to societies recognized by law. Mr. Spencer said he was prepared to prove that the Grand Royal Arch Chapter, of which the juror and defendant were members, was made a body corporate by an act of our State legislature. After hearing the arguments of counsel, the court overruled the challenge for principal cause. Mr. Spencer then challenged the juror "*to the favor.*"

Mr. Spencer here stated that the juror, Judge Anderson, was an important witness in behalf of the people, and ought not to act in the capacity of juror and witness. The defendant's counsel urged that Mr. Anderson's being a witness, did not disqualify him as a juror, and that they could not consent to excuse him for that cause.

The same triers were again sworn, and Mr. Spencer called

Dr. Joseph K. Brown. Witness is a Royal Arch mason. Knows Robert Anderson and Elihu Mather as masons of the same degree. He and they are members of the Gaines chapter. Freemasons are not all of the Royal Arch degree. Lodges are below, and encampments are above the chapter. Witness has met with Anderson and Mather in the Gaines chapter. The avowed objects of Freemasonry are to favor morality and benevolence. Their *charity* is confined to their own members. Witness does not recollect a quarter of the Royal Arch obligation, about helping a companion out of difficulty. The words are—" *That I will aid and assist a Companion Royal Arch mason, wherever I shall see him engaged in* ANY DIFFICULTY, *so far as to extricate him from the same, whether* RIGHT OR WRONG." There is a sign by which a mason can communicate his distress to a brother mason. This is a secret sign in the master's degree. This sign *binds* a mason to go to the relief of a brother. Thinks this obligation is IMPERATIVE, if the person to whom the sign is given has the power to extend the relief.

Cross-examined by defendant's counsel.—Was first initiated at Ridgeway, in 1820. Was made a Royal Arch mason at Gaines, in 1827. The obligation which he then took, was administered verbally. Recollects the striking parts of it, and that part which he had related, in particular. There was *no qualification* or explanation of the obligation, at the time it was administered. A part of the oath related to keeping the secrets. The candidate swears that he would sooner have his head smote off than reveal any part of the obligation. He was requested to attend afterwards, and receive instructions and learn the lectures. Masons told him that they would instruct him, if he attended the meetings of the chapter. He attended once, but no explanation of the oath was then given. They met in the lodge room, but the chapter was not opened. They sat round the stove, and rehearsed their obligations. He had never heard the nature of the Royal Arch obligation before he took it. There was *nothing* in the Royal Arch obligation *which bound him to respect and obey the* LAWS OF THE COUNTRY. Don't recollect that the candidate swears to support the laws of the country, in *any* masonic obligation which he had taken.

[To a question from the defendant's counsel, whether there was any thing in the masonic obligations which *justified* him in VIOLATING the laws of the country, the witness replied that there was one part of the obligation which MIGHT bear that construction, and which he could repeat, if required to do so. The counsel, however, waived the question, and the answer was not given.]

Daniel Pratt.—Witness was a neighbor of Mather and Anderson. He considered them good friends; more intimate with each other than they were with some, but not more than they were with other of their neighbors.

Archibald L. Daniels.—Witness lives two miles and a half from where Capt. Mather lived. He considered Mather and Judge Anderson good friends—perhaps they were more intimate than they were with their neighbors generally.

Here Mr. Spencer rested, and *Robert Anderson* HIMSELF was now called by the defendant's counsel, and sworn.

Witness says there is a clause in the Royal Arch obligation, which, without being qualified, is of the same import as testified to by Dr. Brown. With the qualification, that clause means that when a Royal Arch mason sees a companion engaged in a quarrel, he is bound to get him away. This is the only obligation of such a nature, that witness ever took. The obligation requires me, when I see a companion engaged in a quarrel, to give him a particular sign to come away. I think this qualification forms a part of the obligation. There is nothing in any obligation of masonry which requires me to give a verdict contrary to law. All the charges and lectures in masonry enjoin respect and obedience to the laws. Witness *thinks* that some of the obligations require him to support and obey the laws and constitution of the country. Witness was in the chapter when Dr. Brown was made a Royal Arch mason, and is confident that the oath administered to him was qualified in the manner before stated. Dr. Brown was the only person raised to the Royal Arch, in Gaines, since the abduction of Morgan. Witness thinks there is no bias on his mind—his intimacy with Capt. Mather commenced about politics. They were old bucktails together.

Cross-examined by Mr. Spencer.—Witness *has* said in the fore part of the excitement, that Morgan was not carried off. He thought, *at first*, that it was a trick of Miller and Morgan, to speculate. Has said considerable about the Morgan business. May have said that Morgan was not in the carriage which Mather drove. Had formed an opinion, at first, that Mather did not know Morgan was in the carriage. Has been pretty warm, frequently, upon this subject, and has participated in the feelings of the masons. The clause quoted by Dr. Brown, may be substantially correct, with the qualification in the oath. Thinks the oath contains the words "*dispute or quarrel.*" It is possible this qualification is in the *charge* which follows immediately *after* the oath, but he thinks it is in the oath itself. Is not *sure* that the *obligation* requires obedience to the laws, but the lectures do. The obligations require members to support the constitution of the State chapter, and the by-laws of the chapter to which he belongs. Has not paid much attention to masonry for two or three years, and is not very bright. There is an obligation about obeying regular signs and summons, but witness does not recollect the language of it. He has taken seven different obligations.

By defendant's counsel.—Witness now thinks that Morgan *was* carried off.

Mr. Spencer.—Thinks that if Mather knew that Morgan was in the carriage, he must be guilty. Has not made up an opinion whether Mather did or did not know that Morgan was in the carriage.

Isaac W. Averil.—Witness was a member of Gaines Royal Arch chapter. The Royal Arch oath requires us to "EXTRICATE *a companion out of any quarrel or difficulty, whether he is* RIGHT or WRONG." Masons swear to obey regular signs and summons, when sent, handed, or thrown. This is in the master's degree. Witness has forgotten most of the obligations.

Cross-examined by defendant's counsel.—The qualification about helping a companion out of a quarrel, is not in the oath, but is repeated immediately after it. The explanation given to witness, was, that if he saw a companion engaged in any quarrel in the street, or elsewhere, he was to go and extricate him without inquiring whether he was right or wrong. Never understood that his obligations required him to assist a companion out of the hands of the law.

Milton W. Hopkins.—Witness has been a Freemason—recollects the obligations. One part of the oath in the master's degree, is, "I furthermore promise and swear, that I will obey *all* regular signs and summons, given, handed, sent, or thrown from a brother master mason, or a regular constituted lodge of the same." There is *no qualification* to this. There is another obligation in these words—"*I furthermore promise and swear, that I will fly to the relief of a brother master mason whenever I shall see the grand hailing sign of distress given, or hear the words annexed thereto, if there is a greater probability of saving his life, than of losing my own.*" In another obligation, masons swear to apprise their brethren "*of all approaching danger as far as is in my power.*"

There is no qualification or explanation to the oath relative to the sign of distress, or that about apprising a brother of approaching danger. These oaths are *not* explained to mean any thing different from what their tenor imports. The charges and lectures, witness thinks, are calculated to disguise the real character and tendency of the oaths. Witness has only taken three regular degrees in masonry. He has taken what was called the Secret Monitor's degree, in addition. Witness has seen these obligations imposed in many instances, and in different lodges—has heard them given by the Grand Visitor. The hailing sign may be given by words or by motions.

Cross-examined by defendant's counsel.—Witness was made a mason in Jefferson county, in 1817—he seceded in 1826. He had studied masonry a good deal—when Morgan's book was first published, he could have rehearsed two-thirds of it. Candidates take the oath naked and blindfolded—the charge is not given until they get their clothes on and can see—the charge inculcates virtue and benevolence. Witness thinks the obligations of masonry DO require the concealment of crime. The obligation to which he refers, is this—"*Furthermore do I promise and swear, that a master mason's secrets, given to me in charge as such, and I knowing them to be such, shall remain as secure and inviolable in my breast as in his own,* MURDER and TREASON *excepted*—and that left at my own *discretion.*"

Witness knows that this obligation is administered in the lodge in this town, (Barre,) and is quite sure he has seen it administered in the Gaines lodge. Candidates, just before the oath is administered, are told by the master, that there is nothing in masonry to affect their religion or their politics. Witness has himself administered these obligations.

Dr. O. Nichoson—Says he is a mason—was admitted as such in the Gaines lodge—that the testimony given by Mr. Hopkins respecting the obligations of masonry is correct, so far as he can recollect—recollects no qualifications in the oaths—that the charges are separate and distinct therefrom. Did not suppose when he took the obligations, that they required him to secrete crime; but latterly, on a further examination of the oaths, that by a literal reading, they did require it.

The counsel for the defendant, Col. Barnard, occupied about three hours in an able and ingenious argument, in favor of admitting Mr. Anderson as a juror. He contended, to exclude him, on the ground of his belonging to the society of Freemasons, would be a violation of his rights as a fellow citizen, and establishing a precedent terribly alarming in its consequences. He asked whether Gen. Washington, whom he said was a mason, and a Royal Arch mason, at the day of his death, or Hamilton, or Gen. Jackson, who were all Freemasons, were ever rejected as jurors because they belonged to that society, embracing most of the great men of our nation? Would you reject these men, appealing to the triers, were they now in the place of Mr. Anderson? He said he had lately had occasion to visit the eastern part of the State, and that he found the most respectable portion of the community there, treated the anti-masonic excitement at the west with contempt: that this excitement did not extend to remote parts of our country; and that although the state of feeling among those opposed to Freemasonry here, might call for such a step as the one now pending, yet, if it were taken, it would, it must lead to the most fearful consequences. And to conclude, he said he did not envy that man, the degree nor amount of contempt that must fall upon him, who should be the means of rejecting a man from sitting on a jury, on the ground of his being a Freemason.

In reply to Col. Barnard, the Special Counsel most clearly showed by the law and the testimony, that Mr. Anderson ought to be rejected from sitting on this jury, not because he was a Freemason, but because Robert Anderson and Elihu Mather were both Freemasons, and that the former was bound to the latter in such strong ties as necessarily to produce a bias in his feelings towards him, which would render him in the eye of the law, an incompetent juror. He contended, that he ought to be rejected not only on the ground of the bias, which belonging to the same society of the defendant, must create, but because it had been proved that he was bound by oath upon oath, sufficiently awful to make one's hair stand on end, to protect and fly to his relief, whether right or wrong.

In answering Col. Barnard's allusion to Washington, Hamilton, and Gen. Jackson, he very pertinently asked the triers whether they would shrink from duty, even if Gen. Jackson were now presented for their decision, instead of Mr. Anderson? And has it come to this, he said, that we must be told that the excitement created by the abduction of a free citizen—the depriving our country of a patriot—a wife of a husband, and children of a father, is looked upon with contempt, and that those engaged in vindicating our laws must be sneered at, must be libelled, villified, and slandered by masons,—men wrapped up in mystery and bound with oaths the most horrible? No doubt, he said, the opposite counsel was told these things, and also, that there never was any such man in existence as William Morgan; that the excitement is all a speculation, got up for political purposes, for demagogues to ride into office on. But shall this deter us, he asked, from doing our duty, from avenging crime? God forbid! Our fathers purchased our liberties at too dear a rate thus to act. He utterly denied that Gen. Washington was ever a Royal Arch mason, and he said that he had not attended a lodge for twenty years previous to his death, and that he virtually renounced the institution in his farewell address to his countrymen. Mr. S. contended, that the exigencies of the times never rendered it necessary to object to any man from sitting on the jury, on account of his being a mason, till now. And even now, it was when a brother mason was to be tried. But Mr. S. said, that as to the amount of contempt which the opposite counsel supposed must be visited upon those who should decide that a mason was incompetent to sit as a juror in *such* a case, he would cheerfully share whatever it might be, with the triers, as he considered it a duty, from the performance of which nothing ought to deter them.

After the counsel had closed their arguments, the Court charged the triers in a clear, able, and pertinent manner. He urged the importance of the question they were to decide, and gave it as his opinion, that if they were satisfied that Anderson *had taken such oaths as testified* to by Dr. Brown, and *acknowledged* by himself to have taken as a Royal Arch mason, they WOULD REJECT him; but if they were satisfied that he was under no improper bias in favor of the defendant, then they would not reject him. The triers decided that Robert Anderson *was* NOT IMPARTIAL.

John Dolly was called and challenged to the favor of the Special Counsel, on the same ground as Mr. Anderson.

Dr. J. K. Brown—Testified that Dolly was a mason; that he had set with him in the Gaines lodge.

John Dolly sworn—Says he is a *Royal Arch* mason.

Brown again called—Says, that in the Royal Arch obligation there is one point which says, "I furthermore promise and swear, that I WILL ESPOUSE THE CAUSE of a companion Royal Arch mason whenever I see him engaged *in any quarrel* or DIFFICULTY, so far as to extricate him from the same, whether he be *right* or WRONG. That he had recognised Royal Arch masons in other counties by the same means as he was taught in the Gaines chapter to use to make himself known as such; that if he should ask the said John Dolly the question there taught to be asked, and he should give the answer there taught to be given, to recognise a companion Royal Arch mason, they would know each other as such. Says there are signs in the lower degrees whereby masons can make known to each other that they are in distress or difficulty. By an express point in said obligation, they are never to be committed to writing. The sign of distress in the Master's degree, is never to be given by a mason of that degree, except in cases of real distress, and that, in such case, the brother who sees it is OBLIGED to fly to his relief. This sign is never to be given except in the body of a lodge, or *in some bye, secure place*, for the benefit of the craft. Says a man may be led, by considering his obligation sacred, to PROTECT CRIME.

John Dolly again called—On being questioned by the Special Counsel, said he had met the defendant as a master mason in Gaines lodge; that he had sat in said lodge with Dr. Nichoson.

Dr. O. Nichoson called—Took the obligation of a master mason in the Gaines lodge; had met with Dolly there. Says that it is a fundamental principle of the masonic institution, that no man can enter a lodge without having gone through certain forms and ceremonies, and that among them are certain obligations taken, a part of one of which says, "I furthermore promise and swear, that I WILL OBEY all regular signs and summonses handed, sent, or thrown to me from a brother mason, or from a regularly constituted lodge of the same." Says there is a sign in one of said obligations, called the grand hailing sign of distress, consisting of words and signs, which is imparted to all members of the lodge of which he is a member, which, in pursuance to the fundamental principle above named, this sign came among the ceremonies—that the obligations BIND the mason *to appraise his brother of approaching danger;* also to keep his secrets as inviolably in his breast as in his own, when communicated to him as such, murder and treason excepted; and that left to his own free will and accord. Says he has frequently met in a lodge with Dolly; thinks that he was in the lodge when he was made a mason; does not recollect any obligation in Freemasonry to *obey the laws of his country;* has heard them often repeated; does not recollect any explanation having been given after taking the oaths. One strong feature in the charges given, he thinks, after the first degree, is the injunction of secrecy—to be a good and *loyal* subject. Says the candidate is told before he takes the first obligation, that it is not to affect his religion or politics; that all masons have gone that way before him; that there are lectures given as explanatory of certain signs and tokens.

In answer to questions by defendant's counsel, said he had testified according to his recollections, as he became acquainted with the obligations and ceremonies in the lodge.

In answer to the Special Counsel, he said the lodge must be satisfied that the applicant from another lodge is a Freemason, before he can be admitted—that he makes himself known by certain signs and tokens, and by answering certain interrogatories; and these signs, tokens, and words are required to be the same as those delivered to him, and that they were satisfactory evidence to the lodge that he who gave them was a Freemason, and that *without* being a Freemason, and *taking* the oath, he *could not* thus gain admittance to the lodge in Gaines.

Dr. Brown again called—Says the association of masons is an intimate and friendly association; that they address each other by the epithets *companion* and *brother;* that they have a common fund arising from initiation fees, in which he judged they have a COMMON and MUTUAL INTEREST. Says that certain passages of scripture are recited during the taking of the 7th degree. Says that when the entered apprentice is brought to light, he is presented with the Holy Bible, square and compass, when the master tells him that the Bible is given him as a rule of his faith and practice; the square to square his actions, and the compass to keep him within due bounds with all men, especially the brotherhood. Says it is not required to know the religious sentiments of the candidate; that the question to be asked and the answer to be given, whereby one Royal Arch mason may know another, is, "*Are you a Royal Arch mason?*"—"I AM THAT I AM!" Thinks the Gaines Chapter recognises a higher tribunal, called the Grand Lodge of the State. That one principal object of the funds of this lodge is to relieve brethren in distress; that *so long as a mason continues a member of the institution,* he is considered a WORTHY *member.**

* This is an important disclosure. It shows that "WORTHY" among masons, does not mean an excellent *moral character,* but simply, that the mason retains his connexion with the lodge; consequently those only who *secede* are considered out of the pale of masonic protection; and not entitled to masonic good offices; whilst those that REMAIN, be their moral character ever so infamous, are considered "WORTHY," and masons are sworn to sustain and protect them even in their iniquities.

Dolly cross ex.—Said that at an election in Gaines, he was asked by one Sprague, without any reference to any thing else, " Dont you think that Mather ought to be punished ?" that he answered in the negative, and was going to add, that he once told him that he had nothing to do with the Morgan affair, and that he had no proof to the contrary then, but he supposed Sprague to he intoxicated and did not say further than to give the above answer. Now thought that Mather might be guilty or not, had formed no decided opinion. What Gates told him had but little impression upon his mind, as he was determined not to hear or inquire any thing about it: that the conversation with Sprague was *after* he was summoned as a juror.

Wm. W. Ruggles, sworn—Is a member of Gaines Lodge, has been an officer therein ; says there is a charge that follows the entered apprentice's OBLIGATION ; the *charge*, as he has given it in the Gaines Lodge was, " You now take your place in the lodge as an entered apprentice mason, your duty is to obey the laws of the government under which you live." The Bible is given to him as a guide to his faith and practice. Gave the following points in the obligations both as he received them and had given them to others. " Furthermore do I promise and swear that I will keep the secrets of a brother master mason, whenever given to me in charge, and I receiving it as such, as inviolable in my breast as it would be in his own, *murder* and *treason* excepted." Says there is nothing given, during the ceremony, explanatory of the obligations. " Furthermore do I promise and swear, that I will not give the grand hailing sign of distress, unless I am in real distress, or my life is in imminent danger, or in the body of a just and legally constituted lodge, or in a bye and secure place, for the benefit of the institution. Furthermore do I promise and swear, whenever I see the grand hailing sign of distress, or hear the words accompanying the same, *I will fly to his relief*, if there is greater probability of saving his life than losing my own." Says examples are given in illustration of these two points ; for instance, if one mason sees another exposed to accident, or two were fighting together, he must fly to their relief; when those signs are given they must be obeyed. Says the master gives the illustrations in his own language, as he may think proper at the time ; that there is nothing said in the Gaines Lodge about signs given by an unworthy brother. The cable tow means a certain distance: three miles. Says he is a member of Gaines chapter ; that the Royal Arch obligation is, " *Furthermore do I promise and swear, that I will espouse the cause of a* WORTHY *companion Royal Arch mason, whenever I shall see him engaged in any quarrel or difficulty, so far as to extricate him from the same, whether he be right or* WRONG." Says there is an explanation given of this part of the obligation before the candidate is removed from the place where taken, which is the suppression of bad conduct.

Cross examined—Does not recollect that obedience to the law is inculcated at all in the chapter, or in any except the first degree. Says he was exalted in 1828 ; if there are any laws on the subject, they are in writing; knows it has by-laws ; knows of no limitation how the funds of the chapter are to be applied ; the lodge is the legal owner of its funds ; are for an express purpose ; has been Warden and Master of Gaines lodge ; was there received as a mason ; made himself known as such by language and signs peculiar to masons, whereby they know whether a man is a mason or not, without understanding which, he cannot make himself known to the Gaines lodge as a mason, and that the same rules and regulations extend to the chapter as far as his knowledge extends.

The testimony being closed in this case, Mr. Adams, one of the counsel for defendant, addressed the triers in an argument of more than four hours, in which he urged that it must be shown by the juror himself, that he had a strong bias in his mind, in favor of defendant. Said that he could show as conclusively that there was blasphemy in the articles and creed of the Episcopal church as in the masonic obligations, taking both unexplained. He contended that there was nothing wrong in the the obligation to keep the secrets of a master mason, murder and treason excepted—that any gentleman was in duty bound to keep secrets committed in confidence: that this obligation did not require a mason to conceal crime. Declared that he was not the friend nor the apologist of the thing called masonry. He did not believe that an institution which has embraced the greatest men of the age was instituted for the purposes of crime—said it was asking too much to suppose that such men as Washington, La Fayette, &c. were blackhearted hypocrites—could not believe that men belonging to this asosciation were bound to protect crime: but this, he said, the opposite counsel must make out in order to reject Mr. Dolly from sitting on the jury.

The special counsel, in addressing the triers, said that Elihu Mather stood indicted for carrying off William Morgan, and that John Dolly, it had been proven, belonged to the same society with him, and that he stood challenged for favor, as biassed in his favor, and that he could not stand indifferent towards him, as required to be by law. He produced authorities to show that the most distant relative could not be permitted to sit on a jury, because the laws suspect his mind is prejudiced; that men's minds, who are constantly at the same table, would be prejudiced in favor of each other, so as to struggle against testimony. He contended that in consequence of his being admitted into the lodge at Gaines, that it was evidence to that lodge, that he had taken the obligations there administered. As to the word *worthy* in the obligation, he contended that it meant nothing, as it had been proven that a mason was considered *worthy* while a member of the institution. He alluded to the case that had been so often cited to show the value of the institution, where the lives of individuals had been preserved in war. He said the interposition of the sign of distress, where two men were contending for their respective governments, whereby the arm of the one was stayed from doing what his country demanded at his hands, might prove highly injurious to that government, and was a base sacrifice of its interests to the most selfish purposes. He said the sign of distress was the most dangerous trait in the institution, as, taken in connexion with the obligations, all masons were bound to obey it. He alluded to Mr. Dolly's stating that he had withdrawn from the institution; that he did not intend to have any thing more to do with it, except he should be summoned, as showing the binding nature of the obligations. The *exception of murder and treason* in the master's obligation, he said, proved conclusively that every other crime is meant to be concealed. As to obeying the laws, so much insisted on by the opposite counsel, when they were to conceal every crime but murder and treason, he could not see how it could be done. It is enough to know, he said, that the person on whom these obligations rest, has to struggle between his duty to his country and those which he feels they impose upon him to his brethren. He said that in rejecting a member of the Presbyterian church from the jury in a case between a brother and a stranger, there would be no treason when proven that he was bound to prefer that brother to a stranger, but that the law would sanction it; and he was not to be charged with attacking religion by challenging such a man, as having an improper bias on his mind in favor of his brother; neither was he to be told in this case, by challenging Mr. Dolly on account of his being a Freemason, that he was doing violence to any man's privileges as a free citizen. If, said Mr. Spencer, the example of Washington in his *youth*, must be quoted to prove that masonry is right, let us not be denied the example of this great and good man in his riper years to despise it—and to which he referred when he said—"*beware of secret societies.*"

The court stated its views of the law as applicable to the present case.

The triers decided that Mr. Dolly *was not impartial.*

Grinnel Davis was called and rejected.

Samuel Clark was called and rejected.

Jonathan Whitney, was called and admitted.

Three others were called and rejected. The panel having been gone through with, the Sheriff was ordered to summon five talismen.

A. L. Owen was called and empanelled.

Rufus Ingersoll, Carlos C. Ashley, Thomas Roberts, and Alderman Butts, were next sworn, and the panel completed.

www.ingramcontent.com/pod-product-compliance
Lightning Source LLC
LaVergne TN
LVHW010219110826
845151LV00004B/1145
9781425527013